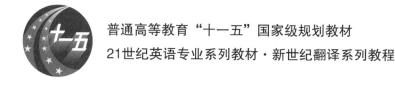
普通高等教育"十一五"国家级规划教材
21世纪英语专业系列教材·新世纪翻译系列教程

U0569123

Developing Interpreting Competency
Liaison and Escort Interpreting
(Second Edition)

口译进阶教程
联络陪同（第二版）

梅德明 ◎主　编

万宏瑜 ◎副主编

华汀汀 ◎参编者

北京大学出版社
PEKING UNIVERSITY PRESS

图书在版编目 (CIP) 数据

口译进阶教程. 联络陪同 / 梅德明主编. —2 版. —北京：北京大学出版社，2023.6
21 世纪英语专业系列教材. 新世纪翻译系列教程
ISBN 978-7-301-34056-1

Ⅰ. ①口… Ⅱ. ①梅… Ⅲ. ①英语—口译—高等学校—教材 Ⅳ. ① H315.9

中国国家版本馆 CIP 数据核字 (2023) 第 097216 号

书 名	口译进阶教程：联络陪同（第二版）
	KOUYI JINJIE JIAOCHENG：LIANLUO PEITONG（DI-ER BAN）
著作责任者	梅德明　主编
责 任 编 辑	郝妮娜
标 准 书 号	ISBN 978-7-301-34056-1
出 版 发 行	北京大学出版社
地　　　址	北京市海淀区成府路 205 号　100871
网　　　址	http://www.pup.cn　新浪微博：@ 北京大学出版社
编辑部邮箱	pupwaiwen@pup.cn
总编室邮箱	zpup@pup.cn
电　　　话	邮购部 010-62752015　发行部 010-62750672　编辑部 010-62759634
印 刷 者	北京飞达印刷有限责任公司
经 销 者	新华书店
	787 毫米 ×1092 毫米　16 开本　17.25 印张　503 千字
	2008 年 10 月第 1 版
	2023 年 6 月第 2 版　2024 年 8 月第 2 次印刷
定　　　价	56.00 元

总　序

    北京大学出版社自 2005 年以来已出版"语言学与应用语言学知识系列读本"多种,为了配合第十一个五年规划,现又策划陆续出版"21 世纪英语专业系列教材"。这个重大举措势必受到英语专业广大教师和学生的欢迎。

    作为英语教师,最让人揪心的莫过于听人说英语不是一个专业,只是一个工具。说这些话的领导和教师的用心是好的,为英语专业的毕业生将来找工作着想,因此要为英语专业的学生多多开设诸如新闻、法律、国际商务、经济、旅游等其他专业的课程。但事与愿违,英语专业的教师们很快发现,学生投入英语学习的时间少了,掌握英语专业课程知识甚微,即使对四个技能的掌握也并不比大学英语学生高明多少,而那个所谓的第二专业在有关专家的眼中只是学到些皮毛而已。

    英语专业的路在何方? 有没有其他路可走? 这是需要我们英语专业教师思索的问题。中央领导关于创新是一个民族的灵魂和要培养创新人才等的指示精神,让我们在层层迷雾中找到了航向。显然,培养学生具有自主学习能力和创造性思维能力是我们更为重要的战略目标,使英语专业的人才更能适应 21 世纪的需要,迎接 21 世纪的挑战。

    如今,北京大学出版社外语部的领导和编辑同志们,也从教材出版的视角探索英语专业的教材问题,从而为贯彻英语专业教学大纲做些有益的工作,为教师们开设大纲中所规定的必修、选修课程提供各种教材。"21 世纪英语专业系列教材"是普通高等教育"十一五"国家级规划教材和国家"十一五"重点出版规划项目"面向新世纪的立体化网络化英语学科建设丛书"的重要组成部分。这套系列教材要体现新世纪英语教学的自主化、协作化、模块化和超文本化,结合外语教材的具体情况,既要解决语言、教学内容、教学方法和教育技术的时代化,也要坚持弘扬以爱国主义为核心的民族精神。因此,今天北京大学出版社在大力提倡专业英语教学改革的基础上,编辑出版各种英语专业技能、英语专业知识和相关专业知识课程的教材,以培养具有创新性思维和实际工作能力的学生,充分体现了时代精神。

北京大学出版社的远见卓识，也反映了英语专业广大师生的心愿。由北京大学等全国几十所院校具体组织力量，积极编写相关教材。这就是说，这套教材是由一些高等院校有水平有经验的一线教师们制订编写大纲，反复讨论，特别是考虑到在不同层次、不同背景学校之间取得平衡，避免了先前的教材或偏难或偏易的弊病。与此同时，一批知名专家教授参与策划和教材审定工作，保证了教材质量。

当然，这套系列教材出版只是初步实现了出版社和编者们的预期目标。为了获得更大效果，希望使用本系列教材的教师和同学不吝指教，及时将意见反馈给我们，使教材更加完善。

航道已经开通，我们有决心乘风破浪，奋勇前进！

胡壮麟

北京大学蓝旗营

编者的话

　　《口译进阶教程》自出版发行以来,作为我国出版社推出的第一套含一至四册的口译课程专业教材,受到广泛欢迎。《口译进阶教程》以我国高等院校英语专业和翻译专业的学生为主要教学对象,按循序渐进、拾阶而上的专业教学原则而编写,是我国口译教学工作者精心打造的第一套进阶式系统性教材。

　　我们秉持"经典性与时代性相结合、典型性与广泛性相结合、专业性和通用性相结合、真实性和参阅性相结合、语言结构与交际功能相结合、专业知识与口译技能相结合"的口译教材编写原则,以及"博采众长、精道为重、趋实避虚、剪裁致用、隐括情理、凝练字句"的编写风格,调整和更新了第一版的部分内容。

　　本教程第二版旨在满足我国高校翻译专业本科教学和相关专业翻译教学的需求。本教材根据口译工作的时代要求和职业特点而取材,根据口译教学的目的和学习规律而编写,精取传统口译教材之长,博采现行口译教材之优。根据口译工作双向传递信息的基本要求,《口译进阶教程》将英译汉和汉译英两种口译形式的教学活动贯穿于整个教学过程,以搭建口译平台、组织口译活动为教学手段,以讲解口译知识、传授口译技巧为教学内容,以培养口译能力、提高口译水平为教学目的。

　　本教程含四册:第一册为《口译进阶教程:联络陪同》,教授涉外接待和陪同工作所需的口译知识和技能;第二册为《口译进阶教程:通用交传》,教授通用性较强的交传知识和技能;第三册为《口译进阶教程:专业交传》,教授专业性较强的交传知识和技能;第四册为《口译进阶教程:会议同传》,教授有关一般会议的同传基础知识和技能。

　　我们主张本教程以翻译专业二年级和三年级学生为主要教学对象,每学期用一册。至于一年级和四年级的口译教学,我们建议一年级的教学以强化学生的语言能力为主要目的,四年级的教学应在进一步提高学生口译综合能力的同时,加大口译实习的比重。本教程可以用作口译教学的主干教材,但是教师应该根据具体的教学对象和教学实际,积极补充教学内容,尤其是要补充一些符合当时国内外形势以及当地社会文化建设和经济建设所需的材料。

对于本教程可能存在的纰缪或疏漏之处，编者在此祈盼使用者不吝赐教。

梅德明

上海外国语大学

2022 年 9 月 10 日

目　录

第1单元　迎来送往 Meeting and Seeing Off ·············· 1
　　口译技能:口译的性质、过程及特点 ·············· 10
　　参考译文 ·············· 13

第2单元　日程安排 Scheduling ·············· 17
　　口译技能:口译的形式 ·············· 25
　　参考译文 ·············· 28

第3单元　休闲购物 Shopping ·············· 33
　　口译技能:译员须具备的素质 ·············· 41
　　参考译文 ·············· 44

第4单元　校园生活 Campus Life ·············· 49
　　口译技能:译前准备 ·············· 57
　　参考译文 ·············· 60

第5单元　人物访谈 Interviews ·············· 65
　　口译技能:外事礼仪 ·············· 74
　　参考译文 ·············· 77

第6单元　会展活动 Exhibitions ·············· 81
　　口译技能:译员的角色 ·············· 89
　　参考译文 ·············· 92

第7单元　商贸展销 Trade Shows ·············· 97
　　口译技能:文化差异的应对和处理 ·············· 105
　　参考译文 ·············· 108

第8单元　商务谈判 Business Negotiation ·············· 113
　　口译技能:记忆理解(1) ·············· 121
　　参考译文 ·············· 124

第 9 单元　旅游观光 Sightseeing ·· 129
　　口译技能：记忆理解（2） ·· 137
　　参考译文 ·· 140

第 10 单元　医疗服务 Medical Service ·· 145
　　口译技能：公共演讲技能（1） ·· 152
　　参考译文 ·· 156

第 11 单元　饮食文化 Catering Culture ·· 161
　　口译技能：公共演讲技能（2） ·· 169
　　参考译文 ·· 172

第 12 单元　体育健身 Sports ··· 177
　　口译技能：跨文化意识（1） ·· 186
　　参考译文 ·· 190

第 13 单元　风俗节日 Festivals ·· 195
　　口译技能：跨文化意识（2） ·· 204
　　参考译文 ·· 208

第 14 单元　文化风情 National Cultures ·· 213
　　口译技能：称谓的口译 ·· 222
　　参考译文 ·· 227

第 15 单元　艺术风潮 Art and Fashion ·· 233
　　口译技能：中国菜名的口译 ·· 242
　　参考译文 ·· 247

第 16 单元　生态环境 Ecology and Environment ························ 251
　　口译技能：学习资源 ·· 259
　　参考译文 ·· 262

第

一

单元

迎来送往

Unit

1

Meeting and Seeing Off

背景知识
Background Information

With China's entry into the WTO and the Olympic Games held in Beijing, the relationship between China and Western countries in politics, economy, and culture is getting increasingly closer. It is no doubt that etiquette will play an important role in this process. Every nation has its own etiquette standard which is created with the spirit of the nation. Generally, when we communicate with members of our own culture, we have internalized the etiquette that governs the behavior within the context, and we are able to communicate without giving much thought to those rules. But when we are engaged in intercultural communication, we must be aware of how our culture influences the communication context; otherwise, we may encounter a variety of surprises.

In this unit, settings where meeting and seeing-off events occur are to be dealt with, in which it is important that the greeting protocol of the host culture and the guest culture is observed. Americans tend to be informal and friendly. Both men and women shake hands on occasions of meeting and leaving. A small kiss on the cheek or a hug is appropriate between men and women who have known each other for a long time. First names generally are used with the exception of senior persons or formal settings. However, these greeting behaviors typical to North Americans are uncommon in many cultures. China offers a contrasting example. Chinese greetings are formal and use titles and last names. First names are used only among close friends. Business cards are in standard Chinese and are routinely exchanged. Therefore, a general knowledge of meeting and seeing-off etiquette is helpful because there are many occasions on which we are likely to encounter people from cultures different from our own.

对话口译

Dialogue A

 Vocabulary Work

Study the following words and phrases and translate them into the target language.

排球领队	排球协会副主席	pick up the luggage	俯瞰
a house with an open view	教练	酒店大堂	设宴
sightseeing	metropolitan	have a special liking for...	

 Text Interpreting

Listen to the following dialogue and interpret it into the target language.

A：请问,您是澳大利亚排球队领队汉森先生吗?

B：Yes.

A：我是中国排球协会副主席王川,很高兴认识您,欢迎到中国来。

B：Nice to meet you, too. Thank you for coming to meet us.

A：不客气。旅途好吗?

B：It was pleasant all the way. By the way, where do we pick up the luggage?

A：这边请。取完行李之后,我们将开车送你们去友谊宾馆。宾馆位于海边,俯瞰大海。离机场开车只要 20 分钟。你们一定会喜欢的。

B：That's wonderful. I love living in a house with an open view. Do we have anything planned for this evening?

A：有,今天晚上 8 点钟在旅馆召开领队及教练的会议。这样安排可以吗?

B：It's Ok for me.

A：那么我们 7 点 50 酒店大堂见。

B：That'll be fine. Thank you so much.

A：不用谢。明天晚上 7 点还将设宴为您洗尘呢!对了,在此期间,你们是否想去参观一些地方?我很乐意带你们去逛逛。

B：Well, it depends! If anything comes out good and satisfactory, I'd leave a day for sightseeing. I have always wanted to see the Museum of Modern Art and the Metropolitan

Center for Performing Art. You see, I have a special liking for arts.

A：没问题。观光的事由我来安排。

B：Thanks very much.

对话口译

Dialogue B

  *Vocabulary Work*

Study the following words and phrases and translate them into the target language.

球技精湛,球风正派	奥运会	相互了解	公平竞争
西半球	participate	前所未有	打包
货车	一路平安		

  Text Interpreting

Listen to the following dialogue and interpret it into the target language.

A：欢迎来北京,库克先生。我是中粮集团海外部主任张帆。

B：Nice to meet you, Director Zhang. I'm very excited to visit your company and of course, to tour around Beijing and the whole country.

A：您专门从加拿大赶来,我很高兴。我们为您来此参加工作,成为我部门的一员感到骄傲和荣幸。我真诚地希望您的来访会是有价值、有意义的。

B：It is indeed my pleasure and privilege to have received your gracious invitation and work with a distinguished group of people like Director Zhang. I had been looking forward to this visit for years. I had a dream that someday I would visit China and work in the beautiful city of Beijing for a while. I'm very grateful that you have made my dream come true.

A：您对这次来京短期工作有如此高的寄托,真令人高兴。我们会尽力使您在京期间过得愉快。考虑到您的方便和舒适,您可以居住在公司的外宾专用别墅。从别墅骑自行车十分钟左右就可到我海外部的办公楼。您一定会喜欢的。

B：That's wonderful. I believe my wife will like here, too.

A：我希望您的家人能早日与您在此团聚。我公司会支付包括国际机票在内所需的一切费用。

B：Thank you so much for your concern. My wife teaches at a primary school and the best time for her and our daughter to come over is when school breaks in the summer. Two more months. We simply can't wait to see each other here in Beijing.

A：真遗憾,您还要等那么久。

B：You are very nice, Mr. Zhang, really.

A：长途飞行后您一定很累了。今晚有招待晚宴,您需要休息一下。晚上六点我派车来接您。

B：Very good.

A：我得走了,我们晚上再见。

B：Bye now.

篇章口译(英译汉)

Passage A (E-C)

 词汇预习 *Vocabulary Work*

Study the following words and phrases and translate them into Chinese.

recession	slowdown
ministerial declaration	trade negotiation
give a strong impetus to...	trade exchanges
give a stimulus to...	mutual understanding

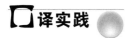 *Text Interpreting*

Listen to the English passage and interpret it into Chinese at the end of each segment.

Ladies and Gentlemen，

Your responsibility today is great. The Eleventh WTO Ministerial Conference coincides with a difficult period where several countries have seen their economies undergoing recession and slowdown. // You will be the focus of attention until a ministerial declaration satisfactory to all parties is issued; a declaration launching a fresh round of trade negotiations that reinforces confidence in the Organization, gives a strong impetus to trade exchanges，and at the same time gives a stimulus to the world economy. //

The world is looking forward to a new round that would give prominence to development, consolidate the principles of justice and equity in the multilateral trade system, and open wide the market for the commodities of less developed countries and contribute to the flourishing of their economies. //

A successful meeting will demonstrate that all nations, rich and poor alike, are working together for a better and more just world. // It will show that cooperation and mutual understanding are the way to solve our problems. //

Passage B (C-E)

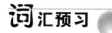 *Vocabulary Work*

Study the following words and phrases and translate them into English.

平等互利	合作伙伴关系	开拓性	双边关系
多边关系	频繁交往	衷心的	东道主

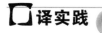  *Text Interpreting*

Listen to the Chinese passage and interpret it into English at the end of each segment.

今天我们聚会在一起，在平等互利的基础上，就广阔领域里建立合作伙伴关系交换我们彼此的看法。// 这是一次具有历史意义的开拓性会议，它反映了我们希望进行交流与合作、增进相互理解和信任的共同愿望。// 我深信这次会议将对我们的双边关系和多边关系产生积极的影响。// 并且深信，两国高层领导人之间的频繁交往，不仅有助于我们两国之间关系的改善，而且还有助于亚太地区乃至整个世界的和平与稳定。// 我愿借此机会，向会议的东道主表示衷心的感谢。最后，让我们为会议的成功，干杯！//

口译讲评

Notes on the Text

Dialogue A

1. 请问,您是澳大利亚排球队领队汉森先生吗? 这句话中的领队,应注意根据内涵翻译。中西方领队的含义不同,西方受体育私有化的影响,参加重要国际赛事的带队者,多为队伍的出资者,因而译作 manager。中国参加大型体育项目的队伍的领队,多为带队者的含义,则直译为 group leader。

2. 我是中国排球协会副主席王川。译为:I'm Wang Chuan, Vice-President of the China Volleyball Association. 若译为 I'm Vice-President of the China Volleyball Association, Wang Chuan. 虽然符合了汉语的语序,却不符合英语中同位语的习惯,因而要将 Vice-President of the China Volleyball Association 放到 Wang Chuan 的后面。此外,汉语中表示副职的头衔常以"副"字表示,英语词 vice, associate, assistant, deputy 等有相同的作用。例如:
副总统/大学副校长 vice president
副教授 associate professor
副总经理 assistant/deputy general manager
副市长 deputy mayor
学术头衔系列除了有"正""副"级别外,还有"助理"级,英语中常用 assistant 一词。例如:
助理工程师 assistant engineer,助理编辑 assistant editor。

3. 宾馆位于海边,俯瞰大海。译为:It is located by the beach, overlooking the sea. 这两个分句可以用现在分词作伴随状语连接,合并成一个状语句,更符合英语的语言习惯。

4. 明天晚上 7 点还将设宴为您洗尘呢! 译为:We will host a reception dinner in your honor at 7:00 tomorrow evening. 这里的"洗尘"不是洗去尘土的意思,而是设宴款待之意。因而译为 host a reception dinner in your honor,或者 give a welcome dinner。

Dialogue B

1. 您专门从加拿大赶来,我很高兴。译为:I'm very happy that you have come all the way from Canada. come all the way 表示"专程造访;远道而来;大老远跑来",加拿大距离中国路途遥远,所以这么译是比较准确而地道的。

2. 我们会尽力使您在京期间过得愉快。译为:We will make an all-out effort to make your stay pleasant. make an all-out effort 表示"尽力"。all-out 意为"竭尽全力的,全面;彻底的",根据不同的搭配有不同的理解。例如:

an all-out attack 全面进攻

an all-out effort 全力以赴

an all-out reform 彻底的改革

3. 考虑到您的方便和舒适，您可以居住在公司的外宾专用别墅。译为：For your convenience and comfort, we accommodate you in one of the company's villas for overseas visitors. 这里的"考虑到"我们用介词 for 引导短语 for one's convenience and comfort，表示"考虑到某人的方便和舒适"，非常符合英文的表达习惯，也很简洁。也可以用词组 for the convenience of 表示"为……的方便起见"。

您可以居住在……，我们译为：we accommodate you in ...，这比 you can live in ... 更准确，因为这是我们作为东道主的安排。例如：

The delegates were accommodated in university hostels. 代表们被安排在大学宿舍住宿。

4. 从别墅骑自行车十分钟左右就可到我海外部的办公楼。译为：It's about ten minutes' bicycle ride from the office building of the Overseas Department. 乘坐某种交通工具花多少时间通常可以有类似的表示，例如：

步行十分钟 ten minutes' walk

乘公交车十分钟 ten minutes' bus ride

乘飞机两小时 two hours' flight

Passage A

1. Your responsibility today is great. 今天我们肩负着重要的使命。该句的翻译采用了重组法。在翻译时，为了使译文流畅和更符合译出语的习惯，在弄清原语的意义和结构的基础上，彻底摆脱原文语序和句子形式，对句子进行重新组合。如：Decision must be made very rapidly; physical endurance is tested as much as perception because an enormous amount of time must be spent making certain that the key figures act on the basis of the same information and purpose. 必须花大量时间确保关键人物均根据同一情报和目的行事，而这一切对身体的耐力和思维能力都是一大考验。因此，一旦考虑成熟，决策者就应迅速做出决策。

2. The world is looking forward to a new round that would give prominence to development, consolidate the principles of justice and equity in the multilateral trade system, and open wide the market for the commodities of less developed countries and contribute to the flourishing of their economies. 世界期待新一轮贸易谈判。这轮谈判突出强调发展，加强了多边贸易体系中公平和平等的原则，为经济欠发达国家所生产的商品开放市场，从而促进他们的经济繁荣。该句采用断句法，根据译出语的思维方式、语言习惯和表达方式，译文对原句进行拆分或组合，将一个句子拆成好几个句子，同时还可给译员留出一定停顿的时间。

3. open wide the market for the commodities of less developed countries. 为经济欠发达国家所生产的商品开放市场。该句采用增译法，商品前增加了"所生产"。翻译时根据汉语的思维方式、语言习惯和表达方式，译文中需增添一些原文中没有的词、短语或句子，以便更准确地表达出原文包含的意义。如：What about having dinner with us next

Saturday? 下周六和我们一起吃晚饭,你觉得怎么样?(增加主语和谓语)

4. A successful meeting will demonstrate that all nations, rich and poor alike, are working together for a better and more just world. 一次成功举行的会议将会展示,所有的国家,无论是贫穷还是富有,正在为建立一个更加美好和公正的世界携手努力。该句翻译将 rich and poor alike,译为"无论是贫穷还是富有",将形容词 alike 转译为"无论……还是……",更符合汉语的表达习惯。

Passage B

1. 这是一次具有历史意义的开拓性会议。该句中"这是一次……会议",可套用句型 This meeting is one of...,而非 This is a ... meeting。这样翻译更符合英语的语言结构。同时,"开拓性会议"不可译为 pioneering meeting,因为"开拓性"修饰的不是会议,而是与会者的努力,因而译作:This meeting is one of pioneering endeavor and historic significance.

2. 我深信这次会议将对我们的双边关系和多边关系产生积极的影响。并且深信,两国高层领导人之间的频繁交往,不仅有助于我们两国之间关系的改善,而且还有助于亚太地区乃至整个世界的和平与稳定。这两句话都包含了"深信",不妨按照英语的习惯,合并成一句话,中间用 and besides 进行连接。因而译为:I am deeply convinced that this meeting will exert a positive impact on our bilateral and multilateral relations and besides,that a frequent exchange of visits between the top government officials of the two countries is beneficial not only to the improvement of our relations,but also to the peace and stability of the Asian-Pacific region and the world as a whole.

3. 最后,让我们为会议的成功,干杯!"为……干杯"可使用以下句型翻译:

To..., Gan Bei!

Now,I should like to propose a toast to...

Please allow me to propose a toast to...

May I ask you to join me in a toast to...?

With the wine of the host,I request you all to raise your glasses and drink to...

相关词语 *Relevant Words and Expressions*

主持会议 chair a meeting	致意 send regards(to)
合作愉快 fruitful cooperation	接风晚宴 reception dinner
提供住宿 accommodate	飞行愉快 pleasant flight
有收获的 rewarding	热情款待 hospitality
欢迎辞 welcome speech	代表 on behalf of
回顾 in retrospect	卓越 excellence
前列 leading position	期盼与祝福 full expectation and blessings
宽广的 inclusive	包容的 indiscriminate

重要人物 dignitary　　　　　　　　里程碑 milestone
获得 acquisition　　　　　　　　　雄心勃勃的 ambitious
致力于 committed（to）

 译技能　　*Interpreting Skills*

口译的性质、过程及特点

　　口译作为交际的一种形式早已存在于人类历史。它是随着各民族相互交流的需要而产生并发展起来的。口译这个术语的英文表达为 interpretation，而它也经常被称为 oral translation。严格意义上来讲，翻译（translation）包括笔译（written translation）和口译（oral translation）。由此可见，口译是翻译的一种形式。

　　口译的工作性质是指译员将原语或译出语（source language）所表达的内容即时、准确地用目的语或译入语（target language）口头表达出来。就其过程而言，即听力理解—转化—产出。但是，实践证明口译不能被简单地看作是纯语言的行为。它应属于更为广泛的交际领域的一部分。也就是说，口译的目的在于意义的传送，即译员应表达话语所含的信息意义而非将表达意义的语言转换成其他的语言。这清楚地表明了口译性质根本是要求译员将语言所传递的意思与语言意义加以区别。塞莱斯科维奇曾指出：原有语言和译文中存在着非字面的概念，这个非字面的概念一旦被抓住之后，便可用任何一种语言加以表达。由于口译是一项交流活动，因此语言在其中只是一种工作手段而非交流的目的。对于译员来说，其目的是要帮助交流的双方通过不同语言的使用来达到理解的目的并确保交流的顺利进行。

　　概括地说，口译是：抓住有意义的语言信息—理解意义—复原意义。对于口译中强调意思的表达，刘易斯·卡罗尔也曾说过：Take care of the sense, the words will take care of themselves.（一旦抓住了意思，译文的表达自然有其自身的语言规律。）如：In the US, there are still some dry towns. 按照字面意思，大部分学生将其译成：在美国，现在还有一些干旱的城镇。但是，这里的 dry 不是指"干旱"而是指"禁酒"。

　　说到口译的特点，我们自然会将其与笔译作比较。虽然口译与笔译同属于一个翻译的范畴，但口译是一种特殊的交际活动，因而有着其显著的特点。前者是动态的，后者则是静态的。

　　口译的工作环境较为特殊：它受时间和空间的限制。译员在工作中必须面对现场的听众。若是同传译员，则必须适应翻译箱狭小的空间。此外，译员作为交流双方的桥梁，其口译的时间有一定的限制。他必须在规定的时间间隔内产出有效的内容。而笔译则不受时间和空间的限制。

　　口译的工作方式比较独特。由于口译的性质是即时表达信息，译员的工作压力大，据研究，口译的速度是笔译的三十倍。由于译员必须当场独立地解决问题，他们无充足的时间对译文加以揣摩以求完美。译员优先考虑的是达意。而笔译员则有充足的时间查阅工具书、参考文献并对译文进行润色以求雅。此外，笔译员还可以通过任何方式向人请教。译员在轻松的环境中执行，完成任务，没有明显的压力。

　　口译的产出与笔译不同。口译的产出是口头表达形式，译员难免会吞吞吐吐，不断自我纠正译出的内容。译员在词语的选择上采取先入为主的方式：即选择首先进入脑海中的词汇。译员所用的句子结构与表达方法相对笔译而言比较简单。由于口译还具有不可预测性，译文有时会前后不协调。此外，译员会受现场紧张气氛的影响，从而导致表达的不流畅。当然，口译时，译员可当场观察到交流双方的即时反应，因而可以随时对自己的译文作补充和解释，灵活性较大。由此可见，口译要求译文达意，产出快而顺。相对而言，笔译的起点和终点均为文字形式，因此笔译员翻译时要特别忠实于原文，对一切内容都需解释清楚，要求译文的完整性较强，准确性高。

 译练习 *Enhancement Practice*

第一项 Project 1

听力复述　Retelling

Listen to the following passages once and then reproduce them in the same language at the end of each segment.

English Passage：

On the morning of August 23，2007，the 30 campers of the 2007 "Embracing China，Feeling Beijing" left for the United States. The Director-General and the Deputy Director-General went to the Capital Airport to see them off. // It is difficult to gather but more difficult to say goodbye. With tears in their eyes，the campers boarded the plane and looked forward to gather together again. Director-General encouraged campers to study hard and conveyed his best wishes to their parents. Finally，he had pictures together with all campers. //

Chinese Passage：

我们公司的总裁和营销经理想同你们继续商讨合资企业之事。他们计划四月下旬出发并在贵国停留一个星期左右。// 请告知我们，这一访问计划对你们是否方便？你们对于这一行程有何建议？如果对访问的时间无异议的话，可否尽快要求你方使馆签发所需签证？//

第二项 Project 2

主题讨论 Discussion

Hold a 5-minute discussion with your partners on the topic "Western Greeting Rituals in Contrast with Chinese Hospitality".

第三项 Project 3
听译练习 Listening and Interpreting
A. Sentence Interpreting
Listen to the sentences and interpret them into Chinese.

1. If all is ready, we'd better start for the hotel.

2. I hear they're announcing my flight over the public address system.

3. I must, on behalf of my company, thank you again for your generous help.

4. I am glad to learn that you, Mr. President, will come to our school next year. I look forward to meeting you again in Beijing.

5. My visit is a symbol of the good faith with which we seek to build up the strength of our friendship, our cultural and academic exchange ties.

B. Sentence Interpreting
Listen to the sentences and interpret them into English.

1. 您知道行李认领处在哪儿吗？

2. 我到了那里后一有机会就去拜访您。

3. 不管怎样，您是远道来到中国，不是吗？我想您一定很累了。

4. 我很高兴向各位介绍我们公司的历史、现状以及今后十年的目标。

5. 我感谢史密斯先生的邀请，使我有机会在这美好的金秋时节来到你们这座古老而又现代化的城市。

C. Dialogue Interpreting
Listen to the dialogue and interpret it into the target language.

A：It was very kind of you to give me a tour of the place. It gave me a good idea of your product range.

B：带我们的客户来参观工厂是我们的荣幸。不知道你总体印象如何？

A：Very impressive, indeed, especially the speed of your NW Model.

B：那是我们新开发的产品，性能很好。两个月前刚投放市场。

A：The machine gives you an edge over your competitors, I guess.

B：当然。就速度而言，目前没有厂家能和我们相比。

A：I see. How do you control the quality?

B：所有产品在整个生产过程中都必须通过五道质量检查关。

A：What's the monthly output?

B：目前每月一千套，但从十月份开始每月一千二百套。

A：What's your usual percentage of rejects?

B：正常情况下为2%左右。

A：That's wonderful. Is that where the finished products come off?

B：是的。

A：Could you give me some brochures for that machine? And the price if possible.

B：好的。这是我们的销售目录和说明书。

A：Thank you. I think we may be able to work together in the future.

参考译文 Reference Version

对话口译 A：

A：Excuse me，are you Mr. Hansen，the manager of the Australian volleyball team?

B：是的。

A：I'm Wang Chuan，Vice-President of the China Volleyball Association. Nice to meet you，and welcome to China.

B：我也很高兴认识您。谢谢您来接我们。

A：It's my pleasure. How was your trip?

B：全程都很愉快。顺便问一句，我们在哪儿取行李？

A：This way，please. After that，we'll drive you to the Friendship Hotel. It is located by the beach，overlooking the sea. It is only 20 minutes' drive from the airport. I am sure you will like it.

B：好极了。我喜欢视野开阔的房子。我们今天晚上有活动安排吗？

A：Yes. We are going to have a meeting for team managers and coaches at eight o'clock this evening in the hotel. Is that all right for you?

B：可以的。

A：Then we'll meet in the lobby at 7:50 this evening.

B：很好，非常感谢。

A：It's my pleasure. We will host a reception dinner in your honor at 7：00 tomorrow evening. By the way，are there any sights you'd like to see while you are here? I'd be glad to show you around.

B：看情况吧。如果一切顺利如愿的话，我很想留出一天时间观光。我一直想看看现代艺术博物馆和都市表演艺术中心。我对艺术特别感兴趣。

A：That's no problem. I'll make some arrangements for this tour around.

B：谢谢！

对话口译 B：

A：Welcome to Beijing，Mr. Cook. I'm Zhang Fan from China Oil & Foodstuffs Corporation. I'm director of the company's Overseas Department.

B：很高兴见到您，张主任。能访问贵公司我很兴奋，当然啰，我还能看看北京和整个中国，真令人兴奋。

A：I'm very happy that you have come all the way from Canada. We are very proud and honored that you will work with us，and be part of our department. I sincerely hope that your visit will be worthwhile and meaningful.

B：受到贵公司的友好邀请,来此与张主任这样杰出的人士一起共事,我深感愉快和荣幸。我曾梦想有朝一日能访问中国,能在美丽的北京工作一段时间。我很高兴您让我梦想成真。

A：I'm very glad that you have so high expectations for this business trip in Beijing. We will make an all-out effort to make your stay pleasant. For your convenience and comfort，we accommodate you in one of the company's villas for overseas visitors. It's about ten minutes' bicycle ride from the office building of the Overseas Department. I'm sure you will like it.

B：好极了。我太太也一定会喜欢这里的。

A：I hope your family will join you soon. Our company will pay for all the expenses，including international flights.

B：非常感谢您的关心。我太太是小学老师,她与我们女儿来这里的最佳时间是暑期。还要等上两个月。我们真的等不及在北京相会了。

A：I'm sorry you have to wait for that long.

B：张先生,您真是个大好人,真的。

A：You must be very tired after a long flight. You'll need a rest for tonight's reception party. I'll send someone to pick you up at six.

B：好的。

A：I'm leaving. See you in the evening.

B：再见。

篇章口译 A：

女士们、先生们：

今天我们肩负着重要的使命。第十一届世贸组织财长会议在许多国家遭遇经济衰退和滑坡的困难时期召开了。// 你们将会成为关注的焦点,直到签署符合多方利益的部长级宣言。本次宣言将发起新一轮贸易谈判,以加强成员国对世贸组织的信心,进一步推动贸易往来,同时刺激世界经济。//

世界期待新一轮贸易谈判。这轮谈判突出强调发展,加强了多边贸易体系中公平和平等的原则,为经济欠发达国家所生产的商品开放市场,从而促进他们的经济繁荣。//

一次成功举行的会议将会展示,所有的国家,无论是贫穷还是富有,正在为建立一个更加美好和公正的世界携手努力。// 也同时说明,合作和互信才是解决问题的途径。//

篇章口译 B：

Today, we meet here to exchange views on cooperative partnership in a wide range of areas on the basis of equality and mutual benefit. // This meeting is one of pioneering endeavor and historic significance，one that reflects our common desire for exchange and cooperation，and for mutual understanding and trust. //I am deeply convinced that this meeting will exert a positive impact on our bilateral and multilateral relations and besides，that a frequent exchange of visits between the top government officials of the two countries is beneficial not only to the improvement of our relations，but also to the peace and stability of the Asian-Pacific region and the world as a whole. // I wish to take this opportunity to express my heart-felt thanks to the host of this meeting. //Finally，please allow me to propose a toast. To the success of the meeting，Gan Bei! //

听译练习：

A：

1. 如果一切都准备好了,我们最好动身去宾馆吧。
2. 我听到扩音喇叭在播我的班机信息了。
3. 我必须代表我的公司再次感谢你们对我慷慨的帮助。
4. 我高兴地得知,校长先生将于明年访问我校,我期待在北京与你再次见面。
5. 我的访问是良好诚意的象征,我们怀着这种良好的诚意,希望能在友谊的基础上建立文化和学术交流关系。

B：

1. Do you know where the baggage claim area is?
2. I promise I'll take the first chance to call on you when I get there.
3. Anyhow，it's a long way to China，isn't it? I think you must be very tired.
4. It is with great pleasure that I shall inform you of the history，the present and objectives of our company in the next decade.
5. I wish to thank Mr. Smith for inviting me to this ancient yet modernized city in this golden fall.

C：

A：谢谢你们陪同我看了整个工厂。这次参观使我对你们的产品范围有了一个很好的了解。

B：It's a pleasure to show our factory to our customers. What's your general impression，may I ask?

A：很好,尤其是你们的 NW 型机器的速度。

B：That's our latest development. A product with high performance. We put it on the market just two months ago.

A：和你们的竞争对手相比,我想这机器可以让你们多占一个优势。

B：Certainly. No one can match us as far as speed is concerned.

A：哦,那你们如何控制质量呢?

B：All products have to go through five checks in the whole manufacturing process.

A：月产量多少?

B：One thousand units per month now. But we'll be making 1,200 units beginning with October.

A：每月不合格率通常是多少?

B：About 2% in normal operations.

A：那太了不起了。成品从那边出来吗?

B：Yes.

A：能给我一些那种机器配套的小册子吗？如有可能，还有价格。

B：Right. Here is our sales catalog and literature.

A：谢谢。我想也许将来我们可以合作。

第
2
单元

日程安排

Unit
2

Scheduling

背景知识
Background Information

Scheduling is the process by which you look at the time available to you, and plan how you will use it to achieve the goals you have identified. By using a schedule properly, you can understand what you can realistically achieve with your time; plan to make the best use of the time available; leave enough time for things you must do; preserve contingency time to handle "the unexpected"; and minimize stress by avoiding over-commitment to yourself and others.

A thought-through schedule allows you to manage your commitments, while still leaving you time to do the things that are important to you. It is therefore your most important weapon for beating work overload.

Before you can schedule efficiently, you need an effective scheduling system. This can be a diary, calendar, paper-based organizer, PDA or a software package like MS Outlook. The best solution depends entirely on your circumstances.

You may go through the following steps in preparing your schedule:

1. Start by identifying the time you want to make available for your work. This will depend on the design of your job and on your personal goals in life.

2. Block in the essential tasks you must carry out to succeed in your job.

3. Schedule in the urgent activities, as well as the essential maintenance tasks that cannot be delegated and cannot be avoided.

4. Block in appropriate contingency time to handle unpredictable interruptions.

5. In the time that remains, schedule the activities that address your priorities and personal goals.

If you have little or no discretionary time left by the time you reach step five, then revisit the assumptions you have made in steps one to four.

对话口译

Dialogue A

 词汇预习 *Vocabulary Work*

Study the following words and phrases and translate them into the target language.

九华山庄	长途飞行	宾馆大厅	居庸关
奇迹	战略要地	terrific	温泉
微量元素	烤鸭		

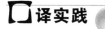 **译实践** *Text Interpreting*

Listen to the following dialogue and interpret it into the target language.

A：女士们，先生们，下午好，我叫张雨，是你们在北京的向导。

B：Very nice to meet you, Miss Zhang. Thank you for coming all the way to meet us at the airport.

A：不客气。欢迎大家参加长城和九华山庄一日游。现在我想花几分钟时间向大家介绍一下明天的行程安排。

B：OK, please. We've been looking forward to this trip for a long time.

A：长途飞行后大家一定都累了，今天晚上好好休息一下，明天早上8点请在宾馆大厅里集合。

B：We can have breakfast at about 7:30 then.

A：对的。我们的旅游车将于8:10左右离开宾馆，到达长城居庸关大概需要1个小时。

B：We've long heard of the Chinese saying "He who does not reach the Great Wall is not a true man!"

A：是的，长城是不同朝代中国人民所创造的一个奇迹，居庸关在2000多年来则素以战略要地而闻名。

B：It must be terrific to go there.

A：没错。我们将在那里停留3小时左右，欣赏长城的美景，然后在12:30左右吃午饭。

B：What are we going to do after lunch?

A：我们会去九华山庄泡两个小时温泉。九华温泉源自1 230米深的地下，富含多种微量元素。

B：That sounds very nice. Hot springs are very beneficial to people's health.

A：是的，放松后，我们将去市中心的全聚德饭店品尝一下著名的烤鸭。

B：Oh, that's wonderful.

A：相信你们会玩得很愉快的。若有什么需要我帮忙的地方，请告诉我。

B：OK. Thanks a lot!

对话口译

Dialogue B

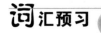 ***Vocabulary Work***

Study the following words and phrases and translate them into the target language.

组委会	致欢迎辞	主题发言人	主题演讲
新加坡国立大学	lunch break	杂技表演	a very tight schedule

 ***Text Interpreting***

Listen to the following dialogue and interpret it into the target language.

A：请问您是马丁先生吧？

B：Yes, I'm Jerry Martin. And you are...?

A：我叫宋颖，是联合国妇女地位委员会第63届会议组委会的成员。

B：I'm so glad to meet you here, Ms. Song.

A：我也很高兴见到您！我向您介绍一下明天大会的日程安排好吗？

B：Yes, of course. I'd like to hear about it very much.

A：8:30至9:30是开幕式，大会主席将致欢迎辞并介绍主题发言人。

B：I guess there will be two or three speeches after the opening ceremony.

A：是的，随后有两场主题演讲。第一场是题为"妇女应该待在家里吗?"的演讲，第二场是题为"妇女当权"的演讲。

B：I've long heard of them, and I'm so looking forward to their speeches.

A：接下来是午餐休息时间，从下午12:30到1:30。

B：What are we going to do after the lunch break?

A：接着就轮到您发言了，马丁先生，时间是下午1:30。

B：OK. Thank you. What is next?

A：您的演讲之后，从下午3：00到5：30有两场讨论会。晚餐后，我们将于7：30去观看一场中国杂技表演。

B：Well，it really is a very tight schedule.

篇章口译（英译汉）

Passage A (E-C)

 Vocabulary Work

Study the following words and phrases and translate them into Chinese.

set way	guideline	category	review
intersperse	retention	procrastination	
rule of thumb		adjust	

 Text Interpreting

Listen to the English passage and interpret it into Chinese at the end of each segment.

There is no set way to make a schedule，and what we provide here are a few guidelines. //

The first step is to find a piece of paper for recording your schedule. For best results，you should first schedule the set parts of your day. // Your classes fit into this category because you should try to attend all of them. Keep in mind the principle that the purpose of attending class is to learn the subject. // Along with your classes，you should try to schedule time before each lecture class to review your notes from the previous class，and after each class to clean up and review the notes from that class. // Besides，be certain to schedule personal essentials，such as eating，sleeping，and exercising. //

Remember that you learn best when you are healthy. The average person needs at least seven hours of sleep a night. // Intersperse your study periods throughout the week，and retention is aided by regular study. Cramming not only builds the bad habit of procrastination，but it is nearly useless for long-term retention. //

A rule of thumb is two hours of study for each hour of class，but this should be adjusted as you discover how much time each class requires. //

篇章口译(汉译英)

Passage B (C-E)

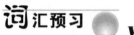 **Vocabulary Work**

Study the following words and phrases and translate them into English.

兵马俑	考古发掘	古城墙	城市防御体系
碑林	大雁塔	石碑	大慈恩寺
佛塔			

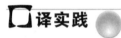 **Text Interpreting**

Listen to the Chinese passage and interpret it into English at the end of each segment.

欢迎各位参加为期两天的西安之行。我叫江澜,很荣幸能为大家作导游。// 现在我想为大家介绍一下在这座美丽城市里的行程安排。//

10分钟以后,我们要去参观中国最好的博物馆之一陕西历史博物馆。// 午饭过后,大家将看到西安最精彩的景点之一,有着2000多年历史的兵马俑。// 这座巨大的宝藏位于西安市以东35公里处,是20世纪最伟大的考古发掘。// 晚饭后,您可以沿着古城墙走一走,这里是中国保存最好、也是最为古老的城市防御体系。// 明天我们会参观两个景点,上午是碑林,下午是大雁塔。// 碑林拥有900年的历史,保存有大量不同时期的石碑。// 大雁塔位于距市中心4公里左右的大慈恩寺内,是我国最著名的佛塔之一。//

希望大家在此地游览愉快!

口译讲评

Notes on the Text

Dialogue A

1. 一日游。可译为 day trip,也可译为 one-day tour 或 day excursion。旅游的类型多种多

样,这里略举几例:包价旅游 package tour;出境游 outbound tourism / travel;度假旅游 vacation tour;观光旅游 sightseeing tour;环球旅行 round-the-world tour; globetrotting;配导游旅游 guided / conducted tour;七日游 one-week visit;自由行 free walker。

2. 不到长城非好汉。这句话除了 He who does not reach the Great Wall is not a true man. 这一译法之外,You are not a hero unless you climb on the Great Wall. 也比较常见。

3. 全聚德饭店。全聚德是"中国驰名商标"之一,中华著名老字号,始建于 1864 年(清同治三年),创始人是杨全仁,以做北京烤鸭闻名。全聚德起始店在北京前门,目前在和平门、王府井以及亚运村等地开有连锁店,在上海也有分店,有到北京"不到万里长城非好汉,不吃全聚德烤鸭真遗憾"的说法。目前,全聚德年营业额有 7 亿多元,每年销售烤鸭 300 余万只,接待宾客 500 多万人次,资产总量达到 6 亿人民币,无形资产有 7 亿多元。

Dialogue B

1. 在英文中称呼他人时,常用的有 Mr. , Miss, Mrs. 和 Ms. 等。其中 Mr. 和 Miss 分别是"先生"和"小姐",Mrs. 是用来称呼已婚女士的,后面加夫姓。而 Ms. 则是由于女权运动,针对 Mr. 演变而来的,不分已婚未婚(如这里的"Ms. Song 宋女士"),且不用加夫姓,现在使用越来越广泛。

2. chairperson 和 chairman。随着 20 世纪 70 年代西方妇女解放运动的蓬勃发展,社会上要求男女平等和消除歧视女性的呼声日益高涨,一些与性别有关的英语词汇从以男性为主的单词变化为中性词(neutral words),如:chairman 变为 chairperson;salesman 变为 salesclerk 等。

3. 发表演讲。在英文中的表达方法通常有 give / make / deliver a speech。

4. schedule. 与 schedule 相关的常见搭配有 a full / heavy / tight schedule 排得很紧的日程表,ahead of schedule 提前,behind (the) schedule 落后于计划/进度,on schedule 按时,准时。

Passage A

1. class. 几个有关 class 的常见搭配:assemble (a) class 上课;dismiss (a) class 下课;attend classes 听课;boycott classes 罢课;an advanced class 高级班;an intermediate class 中级班;a beginners' class 初级班。

2. Keep in mind the principle that... keep in mind 的意思为"记住",如 At this point I cannot undertake to accept your suggestion,but I will keep it in mind. 在这一点上我无法接受你的建议,但我会记住的。

3. The average person needs at least seven hours of sleep a night. 这里的 average 意思为"普通的;平常的",因此可译为"一般人"。其他例子如:an average family 普通家庭,an average performer 演技平平的演员,等等。

4. Intersperse your study periods throughout the week. intersperse 的本义为"散布""散置",此处若译为"将你的学习时间散置在整整一周当中"则不符合中文的表达习惯,不如译成"将学习时间穿插在一周当中"。

Passage B

1. 大家将看到西安最精彩的景点之一。这句也可以译为 you will see one of the most wonderful tourist attractions in Xi'an，但这样的话，就不免显得拖沓冗长，不如 you will see one of Xi'an's highlights 简洁明了。

2. 这座巨大的宝藏位于西安市以东……。表示"位于"这一概念除了参考译文中的 lie 之外，还可用 be located / situated。

3. 兵马俑。位于西安市临潼区东 5 公里的下河村，被誉为"世界第八奇迹"。1974 年当地农民在打井时偶然发现，以后又在附近发现了二号坑和三号坑。第一号兵马俑坑东西长 230 米，南北宽 62 米，深近 5 米，总面积 14 260 平方米。坑内有与真人马大小相同的武士俑和拖战车的陶马六千多件，排成方阵，造型逼真。二号坑有一千多件兵马俑，是以战车、骑兵为主组成的 4 个兵种混编的阵列。三号坑属于指挥位置所在的小坑，有六十多个兵马俑。

4. 碑林。西安碑林创建于公元 1087 年，是收藏我国古代碑石时间最早、数目最大的一座艺术宝库，陈列有从汉到清的各代碑石、墓志共一千多块。这里碑石如林，故名碑林。西安碑林内容丰富，它既是我国古代书法艺术的宝库，又汇集了古代的文献典籍和石刻图案；记述了我国文化发展的部分成就，反映了中外文化交流的史实，因而驰名中外。

5. 大雁塔。全称"慈恩寺大雁塔"，始建于公元 652 年，是尽收佛学经典，由皇家主持建造的寺院，有着显赫的地位和宏大的规模。楼阁式砖塔采用磨砖对缝，砖墙上显示出棱柱，可以明显分出墙壁开间，是中国特有的传统建筑艺术风格。据史书记载，慈恩寺是唐高宗李治为其母文德皇后祈求阴福所造，它北面正对大明宫含元殿，附近环绕曲江池、杏园和乐游园，风景秀丽迷人。大雁塔是慈恩寺的第一任住持方丈玄奘法师自印度归来，带回大量梵文经典和佛像舍利，为了供奉和储藏这些宝物，而亲自设计并指导施工的。

相关词语 *Relevant Words and Expressions*

茶歇时间 tea break

观光 sightseeing

会议登记处 conference registration desk

截止日期 deadline

庆典致辞 celebration remarks

五星级酒店 five-star hotel

召开全体人员大会 convene a plenary meeting

颁奖典礼 awarding ceremony

欢迎/闭幕酒会 welcome/closing reception

开/闭幕式 opening/closing ceremony

开/闭幕词 opening/closing remark / speech / address

自助午餐 buffet lunch

喝咖啡休息时间 coffee break

结束语 closing remarks

就职演说 inaugural address

讨论会 symposium

下榻 stay

口译的形式

　　口译可根据其模式和场合、内容进行不同的划分。按照口译的工作模式,口译可分为:交替传译和同声传译。按照口译的场合及内容,口译可分为:会议口译、耳语传译、视译、联络陪同口译、法庭口译、媒体口译,以及电话口译。

　　交替传译(consecutive interpreting):交传亦称即席口译或连续口译,是比较传统的口译模式,常用于会议、媒体采访等场合。交传时,译员须在有限的间隔时间内将讲话的内容用译入语传递给听众。通俗地讲,译员逐段翻译讲话的信息。交传要求译员有很强的笔记能力。但是,交传的使用会使各种场合活动的时间增加一倍。对听众而言,他们也必须高度集中注意力,因为讲话中不断出现停顿。

　　同声传译(simultaneous interpreting):同声传译是指译员在讲话者发言的同时,通过耳机边听边译。这种口译模式自第二次世界大战以来广泛用于各种国际会议。由于脑力和体力的特殊需求,同声传译一般有两位译员在隔音的翻译箱内轮流翻译,分担任务。就时间而言,同传相比交传而言不占用会议的时间,并且可同时使用多种语言。

　　会议口译(conference interpreting):会议口译用于多语种会议的场合,它包含交传和同传两种口译模式。大会译员根据会议的性质及环境采取不同的口译模式。

　　耳语传译(whispering interpreting):耳语传译是同声传译的一种形式。它需要译员用耳语的方式同步、轻声地将听到的信息传译给身边的一两位听众。耳语传译时译员无须使用同传设备,其服务对象只是少数(一般不超过三人)不懂工作语言的听众。

　　视译(sight interpreting):视译是指读、译相结合的口译方式。译员边看书面材料边将其内容准确、完整地传译给听众。译员有时就直接按照所给的书面材料读译;有时需边听讲话者,边看书面材料,同时在传译。这是一种比较特殊的口译形式,常见于大会口译。

　　联络陪同口译(escort interpreting):联络陪同口译一般指译员陪同个人或团体旅游、参观、参加会议、接受采访等。其口译模式是交传。

　　法庭口译(court interpreting):法庭口译在国外较为常见,尤其在一些移民国家,主要用于法庭和司法机关。在这种口译场合,交传和同传都会被使用。法庭口译要求译员公正、客观地传递信息。因此,国外的译员在法庭口译之前需宣誓。

　　媒体口译(media interpreting):媒体口译这个用语涵盖面甚广,包括记者招待会、公共宣传、采访、电影、录像,以及电视/广播节目的口译。媒体口译场合中交传和同传都会被使用。

　　电话口译(over-the-phone interpreting:OPI):电话口译是指远程口译,交流双方及译员处在不同的地理位置。译员通过电话口译一些涉及医疗、公共服务及司法等方面的个案。这种口译场合一般采用交传。由于译员在电话口译中看不到交流的双方,口译时会带来一定的困难。

口译练习 *Enhancement Practice*

第一项 Project 1
听力复述 Retelling

Listen to the following passages once and then reproduce them in the same language at the end of each segment.

English Passage:

You can lose a great deal of credibility by underestimating the length of time needed to implement a project. If you underestimate time, not only do you miss deadlines, you also put other project workers under unnecessary stress. Projects will become seriously unprofitable, and other tasks cannot be started. // The first step towards making good time estimates is to fully understand the problem to be solved. // You can then prepare a detailed list of tasks that must be achieved. This list should include all the administrative tasks and meetings you need to carry out as well as the work itself. // Finally, allow time for all the expected and unexpected disruptions and delays to work that will inevitably happen. //

Chinese Passage:

旅游是一种积极的休息,旅行的日程安排、行程路线等的制定,需考虑到道路的情况、成员的身体素质、背囊负荷量以及中途停留观光、休息时间等等。// 如水上旅游,在安排日程时,就要考虑到旅游者划桨的熟练程度、船只的结构和形状、航行河流的流速、航道中可能出现的障碍物、气候状况等诸多因素。// 总之,制定日程计划的基本原则是有张有弛,先张后弛,或先弛后张。//

第二项 Project 2
主题讨论 Discussion

Hold a 5-minute discussion with your partners on the topic "How to make schedules".

第三项 Project 3
听译练习 Listening and Interpreting
A. Sentence Interpreting

Listen to the sentences and interpret them into Chinese.

1. The conference room will open at 9 o'clock to allow attendees an opportunity to meet and greet each other.

2. For more information on these activities, please visit our website or contact us and we will mail the information to you.

3. Our start time is set, but the other times are rather fluid and may change on the day of

the event depending on external factors.

4. An essential concept behind project planning is that some activities are dependent on other activities being completed first.

5. By leaving space in your schedule, you give yourself the flexibility to rearrange your schedule to react effectively to issues as they arise.

B. Sentence Interpreting

Listen to the sentences and interpret them into English.

1. 时间表的制定最好定期进行,譬如在每周或者每月刚刚开始时。

2. 以上报价包含酒店接送、英文导游服务、第一景点门票以及午餐费用。

3. 若你想在成都多逗留几日的话,请告知我们,我们可以为您延长宾馆的预定。

4. 第十六届杭州国际茶文化节将于今年 9 月 16 日开幕,21 日闭幕,为期 6 天。

5. 时间表的制定一定要切合实际,时间表不应当是一个无法实现的愿望的列表,而应当是一个帮助你合理安排时间的真正向导。

C. Dialogue Interpreting

Listen to the dialogue and interpret it into the target language.

A:早上好,珍妮,今天好吗?

B:Well, after a very good rest last night, I feel much better now. It was indeed a tough day yesterday!

A:今天是你上海之行的最后一天了,想听听今天的安排吗?

B:All right. I'd love to.

A:这只是一个初步安排,若需要的话,你可以做些改变。

B:OK, thanks a lot!

A:总体安排包括以下内容:上午去拜访一家软件公司,中午品尝地方美食,下午参观上海博物馆,晚上参加浦江游览。

B:What is the name of the software company?

A:萨尼软件公司是上海最大的软件公司之一,我已经和他们约好了时间,我们要在 10 点钟到达那里。

B:Good. Then where are we going to taste the local delicacies?

A:在城隍庙。城隍庙建于明朝,是上海最有名的旅游景点之一。

B:The visit to Shanghai Museum sounds very nice, but I prefer to do some shopping in the afternoon. I want to buy some presents for my friends and relatives.

A:哦,当然可以,那么我就带你去淮海路购物吧。

B:Thanks! I've heard many people talking about the Pujiang cruise and I know the local people honor the Huangpu River as their Mother River.

A:是的,浦江游览是观赏新旧上海的最佳方式之一。此外,你还可以欣赏到上海中心大厦和东方明珠的美姿。

B:Oh, marvelous!

A：我们晚上 9:30 以前即可回到宾馆。我知道你明天的航班非常早,因此今晚最好早点睡觉。

B：Thank you very much for such a thoughtful arrangement for me.

参考译文 Reference Version

对话口译 A：

A：Good afternoon, ladies and gentlemen. I am Zhang Yu, your guide in Beijing.

B：很高兴见到你,张小姐,谢谢你远道到机场来接我们。

A：You are welcome. Welcome to take the day trip to the Great Wall and Jiuhua Spa Resort. Now I'd like to take a few minutes to tell you about your schedule tomorrow.

B：好的,我们期待这次旅行已经很久了。

A：You must feel very tired after such a long flight, so please have a good sleep tonight and we'll meet in the lobby of the hotel at 8 o'clock tomorrow morning.

B：那么我们可以在 7:30 左右吃早饭。

A：That's right. Our tour bus will leave the hotel at about 8:10 and it will take us an hour or so to Juyong Pass of the Great Wall.

B：我们早就听说过中国一句老话,"不到长城非好汉"。

A：Yes, the Great Wall is a marvel created by Chinese people in different dynasties, and Juyong Pass has been well noted for its strategic place for more than 2,000 years.

B：去那里一定非常棒!

A：Absolutely. We will enjoy the splendor of the Great Wall there for about 3 hours, and then have lunch around 12:30.

B：午饭后做什么呢?

A：We will go to Jiuhua Spa Resort for two hours' spa bathing. The Jiuhua hot spring comes from 1,230 meters underground, and is rich in microelements.

B：听上去很不错。温泉对身体健康极为有益。

A：Yes. After relaxation, we will go to Quanjude Restaurant in downtown to taste the famous Beijing roast ducks there.

B：哦,太好了!

A：I'm sure you'll enjoy yourselves. If there's anything I can do to help, please let me know.

B：好的,非常感谢!

对话口译 B：

A：Excuse me, are you Mr. Martin?

B：是的,我是杰瑞·马丁。您是……?

A：My name is Song Ying. I am from the organizing committee of the 63rd session of the

United Nations Commission on Status of Women（CSW 63）.

B：很高兴在这里见到您，宋女士。

A：Very nice to meet you too! May I show you the schedule for tomorrow's conference?

B：当然好，愿闻其详。

A：The opening ceremony is from 8：30 am to 9：30 am at which the chairperson of the conference is going to make a welcome speech and introduce the keynote speakers.

B：我想开幕式之后会有两到三场演讲吧。

A：Yes, there will be two keynote speeches afterwards. The first one is "Is Women's Place at Home?", and the second one is "Women in Power".

B：我久仰他们两位的大名，很期待听到他们的演讲。

A：Then there will be the lunch break from 12：30 pm to 1：30 pm.

B：午餐休息之后做什么呢？

A：It will be your turn to give a speech at 1：30 pm, Mr. Martin.

B：好的，谢谢你！接下来呢？

A：Your speech will be followed by two symposiums from 3：00 pm to 5：30 pm. Then after dinner, we will go to watch a Chinese acrobatic show at 7：30 pm.

B：哦，安排还真够紧凑的。

篇章口译 A：

时间表的制定没有固定方法，我们这里提供的只是几个指导原则。//

第一步是要找记录时间表的纸张。为取得最佳效果，你应该首先安排一天中的固定日程。// 上课就属于这一类，因为你应该尽可能地去上每一堂课。要记住：上课的目的是为了学会这一科目。// 除了上课以外，你还应该尽量安排一些时间，在课前复习一下上次课的笔记，并在课后整理、复习一下当堂的笔记。// 此外，一定要把必须要做的个人事情也安排进来，如吃饭、睡觉和锻炼。//

记住：在身体健康的状态下才能最有效地学习。一般人每晚至少需要 7 个小时的睡眠。// 将学习时间穿插在一周当中，有规律的学习才有助于记忆。填鸭式学习不但会养成拖延的坏习惯，而且对于长久记忆来说几乎毫无用处。//

一条经验法则是，为一节一小时的课，需要学习两个小时，但这也应当根据每节课所需时间的不同而进行调整。//

篇章口译 B：

Welcome to take the 2-day trip in Xi'an. My name is Jiang Lan, and it's my honor to be your tourist guide here. // Now I'd like to show you your schedule in this beautiful city. //

10 minutes later, we will be on our way to visit Shaanxi Historical Museum, one of the best museums in China. // After lunch, you will see one of Xi'an's highlights—the 2,000-year-old terra cotta warriors and horses. // This vast treasure lies 35 kilometers east of Xi'an and is the most significant archeological excavation in the 20th century. // After

dinner, you may feel like a walk along the ancient city wall, the best preserved as well as the oldest city defense system in China. // There are two more tourist attractions awaiting us tomorrow: the Stele Forest in the morning and the Big Wild Goose Pagoda in the afternoon. // The Stele forest has 900 years of history, and holds a large collection of the stone steles in different periods. // Situated in the Da Ci'en Temple, about four kilometers from the urban center, the Big Wild Goose Pagoda is one of the most famous Buddhist pagodas in China. //

I hope you will enjoy your tour here.

听译练习：

A：

1. 会议室将于9点钟开门，以便与会者彼此见面寒暄。

2. 若想了解关于这些活动的更多信息，请访问我们的网站，或与我们联系，我们会将信息邮寄给您。

3. 我们的出发时间已经确定，但其他时间非常灵活，可随当日外部因素的影响而改变。

4. 制订项目计划时需考虑的要点之一是，一些活动的进展取决于另外一些活动是否首先完成。

5. 在日程安排中留出一些余地，这样你就可以灵活地调整日程，以有效应对出现的问题。

B：

1. Scheduling is best done on a regular basis, for example at the start of every week or month.

2. The quotation includes hotel pick-up service, English tour guide service, main entrance tickets and lunch.

3. If you choose to stay in Chengdu for a few more days, please let us know, since we can extend the hotel booking for you.

4. The 16th Hangzhou International Tea Culture Festival will open on September 16 this year and close on September 21, lasting 6 days.

5. You need to be realistic in scheduling, and a schedule shouldn't be an unattainable wish list, but a real guide to help you plan your time well.

C：

A：Good morning, Jenny. How are you today?

B：嗯，昨晚休息得非常不错，现在感觉好多了。昨天可真够累的。

A：Today is the last day of your visit in Shanghai. Would you like to listen to the plan for today?

B：好的，非常乐意。

A：This is only a tentative schedule, and you may make some changes if necessary.

B：好的，非常感谢！

A：The general plan includes visiting a software company in the morning, tasting some local delicacies at lunch, visiting Shanghai Museum in the afternoon, and taking a

Pujiang cruise in the evening.

B：这家软件公司叫什么名字？

A：Sunny Software Company，one of the biggest software companies in Shanghai. I've made an appointment with them and we are supposed to get there at 10:00.

B：很好，接下来我们要在哪里品尝地方美食呢？

A：In the City God Temple of Shanghai. It was built during the Ming Dynasty and is one of the most famous tourist attractions in Shanghai.

B：参观上海博物馆的主意不错，但我下午更想去购物，我想给亲戚朋友们买些礼物回去。

A：Oh，yes，of course. I will take you to Huaihai Road to do some shopping then.

B：谢谢！我听很多人谈论过浦江游览，我知道本地的人们将黄浦江尊称为母亲河。

A：Yes，a Pujiang cruise is one of the best ways to see both old and new Shanghai. In addition，you can also enjoy the beauty of the Shanghai Tower and the Oriental TV Tower.

B：哦，太好了！

A：We will be back to the hotel by 9:30 pm. I know your flight is very early tomorrow morning，so it's better for you to go to bed early tonight.

B：谢谢你为我做的如此精心的安排。

第3单元

休闲购物

Unit 3

Shopping

背景知识
Background Information

The improvement in Chinese living standards is also reflected in people's shopping habits.

In the 1990s, Chinese people still went to free markets and bargained with dealers when buying food stuffs like meat, eggs, vegetables and fruits. The appearance of supermarkets changed the shopping habits of most of urban residents. When supermarkets first emerged in China, the Chinese went there just for curiosity. The comfortable environment, abundant goods, good services and relatively reasonable prices there have lured more and more people.

In addition, goods and services offered by supermarkets have become more comprehensive. From home appliances to needles and threads, from seafood to processed foods, all can be found in supermarkets. Today, people can easily go to a supermarket and find what they need, as supermarkets of different sizes are everywhere in urban areas. CMMS (China Marketing and Media Study) data shows the number of people who shop at supermarkets is climbing by 25 per cent year-on-year.

Aside from supermarkets, more and more people buy daily necessities, durable consumer products, cigarettes, alcohol, and garments in *zhuanmaidian*, a Chinese term meaning a store which sells products under a single brand name, especially a very famous one. Only a few years ago, most Chinese believed that *zhuanmaidian* is a place for the richest people, but now very few people think so. The phenomenon shows that people are paying greater attention to the quality of products, and low prices are no longer the most important factor people consider when deciding where to shop.

Nowadays, people are doing a lot more shopping on the Internet because a lot of retailers have Web sites, and it's cheaper sometimes to go right to their Web sites. And it's fast and convenient. People can get things sent to them almost right away. Consumers now can purchase virtually anything on the Internet. Books, food, electric appliances, and even stocks are available from Web sites. For a growing number of time-starved consumers, shopping from their home computer is proving to be a convenient alternative to driving to the store.

对话口译

Dialogue A

 Vocabulary Work

Study the following words and phrases and translate them into the target language.

cheongsam	面料	演变	体态
优雅大方	缩水	试衣间	discount

  Text Interpreting

Listen to the following dialogue and interpret it into the target language.

A：您好,小姐,想要买点什么?

B：Chinese cheongsam is famous for its elegance and I've been longing for one for a long time.

A：我们有各种面料和式样的旗袍。您喜欢哪种?

B：Well，I don't know much about Chinese cheongsam actually，so will you please introduce some of them to me?

A：当然可以,旗袍从满族古时的一种服装演变而来。它可长可短,可以是长袖的、中袖的、短袖的,甚至是无袖的,以适合不同的场合、天气及个人喜好。

B：Why do Chinese women like to wear the cheongsam then?

A：这主要因为旗袍极好地迎合了女子的体态,线条简洁,优雅大方。

B：Wow，this one looks so beautiful. What is it made of?

A：它是用高质量丝绸制成的。这种丝绸经过一种特殊技术处理,因此不会缩水。您想试穿一下吗?

B：OK. I'd like to try on a size 38.

A：好的,给您。试衣间在那边。

    ……

B：It fits me so well. I like it very much. How much does it cost?

A：590 元。

B：I wonder if you can give me a discount.

A：可以的,在本店购物 500 元以上即可享受 9 折优惠。

B：Ok，I'll take it.

对话口译

Dialogue B

词汇预习 *Vocabulary Work*

Study the following words and phrases and translate them into the target language.

新奇独特	极具特色	merchandise	书画作品
手工艺品	调节的	国营商店	advisable
古董	发票	GST	

译实践 *Text Interpreting*

Listen to the following dialogue and interpret it into the target language.

A：This is the first time I've been in China. Could you give me some hints about going shopping here?

B：当然可以！中国有着各种各样新奇独特、极具特色的商品，你绝不会为带什么东西回去而失望或发愁。

A：I want to buy some gifts for my friends and relatives，so could you tell me some of the special merchandise?

B：可供选择的独特商品有很多，如中国的丝绸、茶叶、书画作品、玉石珍珠及手工艺品等。

A：How are the commodities priced in China then? Are all the prices fixed?

B：在中国，商品的定价通常有三种。第一种是国家制定的固定价格；第二种是国家制定的调节价格；第三种是市场价格。大部分旅游商品都属于第三种——市场价格。

A：Do you mean that I will have to bargain when I buy the tourist merchandise?

B：在国营商店里是不大讨价还价的。但在许多出售纪念品的小摊上最好还还价，因为那里的要价会非常高。

A：Maybe it's advisable that I watch how much the Chinese customers pay before I decide to buy.

B：嗯，这倒是个好主意。

A：Can you recommend me some famous department stores?

B：在几乎所有的中国城市里都有为外国游客提供服务的友谊商店，你不妨到那里去看一看。

A：All right. What are the points for attention if I want to buy some antiques?

B：不要买 1795 年以前的古董,因为这些古董是不允许出口的。同时,要记得保留所有的购物发票,在离境时海关有可能会要求你出示发票。

A：We have to pay a 5% or so GST in Canada. Do I need to pay any tax here in China?

B：不,在中国无须支付商品服务税。

A：Thanks a lot for your information.

B：不客气。

篇章口译(英译汉)

Passage A (E-C)

 Vocabulary Work

Study the following words and phrases and translate them into Chinese.

bargain	plush bath towel	bed linen	take advantage of
shopping mall	discount store	suburban community	house ware
do bargain shopping	Thanksgiving Day		

Text Interpreting

Listen to the English passage and interpret it into Chinese at the end of each segment.

Many tourists visiting the USA on vacation enjoy shopping for bargains. // American whiskey, fashion jeans, children's clothing, plush bath towels and fine bed linens are all popular items for shoppers from other countries. // You can find many bargains in the US if you know where to shop and how to take advantage of the competitive sales. //

There are still some department stores and downtown shopping areas in most US cities, but the big shopping malls and discount stores are usually located out in the suburban communities. // Some of the major outlet centers are located in the countryside miles from the nearest major city, so it is best to have an automobile if you want to do any serious bargain shopping. //

Department stores are large establishments that offer a wide selection of merchandise including fashion clothing, house wares, luggage and jewelry. // They normally offer good quality merchandise, well-known brands and the latest fashions, but not low quality products at bargain prices. // They frequently have seasonal sales with attractive discounts. At such times, you can get high quality or fashion merchandise at bargain prices. // For example, in November, the Thanksgiving Day sale is one of the biggest shopping days of the year. //

篇章口译（汉译英）
Passage B (C-E)

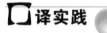  **Vocabulary Work**

Study the following words and phrases and translate them into English.

| 具挑战性 | 百货商店 | 夜市 | 路边小摊 |
| 信用卡 | 计算器 | 瑕疵 | 有效票据 |

Text Interpreting

Listen to the Chinese passage and interpret it into English at the end of each segment.

在中国购物既有趣又颇具挑战性，下面我想就购物给大家提一些建议。//

中国商店的营业时间通常是早上10点至晚上10点。// 也有些大型百货商店或"夜市"会一直营业到晚上11点，甚至更晚。// 在某些商店，营业时间也会因季节而变：夏天长一些而冬天则短一些。//

讨价还价在中国非常常见，尤其是在小商店里或路边的小摊上。// 中国大部分的百货商店都可以接受信用卡，但相对而言，移动支付更多一些。// 你可以带上计算器来帮助汇率转换，若你还的价格被接受了，就应该将东西买下来。//

仔细检查一下所购买的商品，以确保没有任何瑕疵。// 此外，别忘了索要购物发票，因为这是你退换商品所需的有效票据。//

口译讲评

Notes on the Text

Dialogue A

1. 店员用英语询问顾客"想要买点什么"可以有多种问法,除了参考译文中给出的 Can I help you? 之外,还可以说 May I help you? /What can I do for you? /Could I be of service to you? 等。

2. 旗袍是一种内与外和谐统一的典型民族服装,被誉为中华服饰文化的代表。它以流动的旋律、潇洒的画意与浓郁的诗情表现出中华女性贤淑、典雅、温柔、清丽的性情与气质。旗袍的英文 cheongsam 根据粤语中的"长衫"一词音译而来,其他的译法也有 chi-pao, qipao 等。

3. 英语询问价格的常用语有 How much is it? / How much do you charge for it? / What is the price for this one? / How much do I have to pay? / How much does it cost? 等。

4. discount 的意思为折扣,"打折销售"可以说 sell at a discount,"打六折"可以说 40 per cent discount 或者 40 per cent off。

Dialogue B

1. give sb. some hints. 意思是"指点某人······",如 Can you give me some hints on how to do this job? 可译作:"这工作怎么做,你能指点我一下吗?"

2. 新奇独特、极具特色。在口译中,要力求简洁明了,紧紧抓住中心词,因此这两个词只要分别用 unusual 和 characteristic 译出就可以了。

3. How are the commodities priced in China then? Are all the prices fixed? 这两句话中都出现了 price 一词,前句中的 price 用作动词,意为"定价";而后句中则用作名词,即"价格"。

4. bargain. 既可用作动词,也可用作名词。作动词时意为"讨价还价",作名词时意为"便宜货"。

5. GST. goods and services tax 的缩写,是新西兰和加拿大一种应用广泛的增值税,也就是商品服务税。在加拿大购物要缴纳 5％的商品服务税,再加上各省份的省税,总税率在 13％左右。在新西兰购物,零售价格中通常包含有 15％的商品服务税。

Passage A

1. take advantage of. 意思是"利用"。例如:We'd better take advantage of the warm weather by going for a walk this afternoon. 我们最好趁着天气暖和,今天下午出去散散步。除了作为一个中性词组之外,take advantage of 有时也带有贬义含义,表示"利用某

人的处境、弱点等"，如：He often took advantage of her trustful nature. 他经常利用她轻信的本性。

2. outlet. 名品折扣中心。最早诞生于美国，其英文原意是"出口、出路、排出口"的意思，在零售商业中专指由销售名牌过季、下架、断码商品的商店组成的购物中心，在汉语中有时也直接音译为"奥特莱斯"。outlet 吸引顾客有三样法宝：（1）驰名世界的品牌——荟萃世界著名或知名品牌，品牌纯正，质量上乘；（2）难以想象的低价——一般以低至 1—6 折的价格销售，物美价廉，消费者趋之若鹜；（3）方便舒适的氛围——远离市区，交通方便，货场简洁、舒适。

3. ...it is best to have an automobile if you want to do any serious bargain shopping. 该句中的 serious 和"严肃、庄重"毫无关系，而是带有"认真、当真"的含义，因此整句可以译为：你若是真想好好地购买一通便宜商品的话，最好是有一辆汽车。

4. Thanksgiving Day. 美国人的感恩节，定于每年 11 月的第四个星期四。这是美国人民独创的一个古老节日，也是美国人合家欢聚的节日，因此美国人提起感恩节总是倍感亲切。该节日源自 17 世纪英国清教徒于到达美洲的次年（1621 年）为庄稼丰收而感谢上帝并感谢印第安人的真诚帮助而举行的欢庆日。初时感恩节没有固定日期，由各州临时决定，直到美国独立后，感恩节才成为全国性的节日。每逢感恩节这一天，美国举国上下热闹非常，人们按照习俗前往教堂作感恩礼拜，有的城乡市镇还有化装游行、戏剧表演或体育比赛等。分别了一年的亲人们也会从天南海北归来，一家人团团圆圆，品尝美味的感恩节火鸡。

Passage B

1. 营业时间。除了 business hours 以外，opening hours 亦可。

2. 中国大部分的百货商店都可以接受信用卡。Credit cards are acceptable in most Chinese department stores. 这句还可以翻译成 Credit cards can be accepted / used in most...

3. 相对而言。comparatively speaking，同一类型的常用表达法还有"通常而言"（generally speaking）、"从技术角度讲"（technically speaking）、"从科学角度讲"（scientifically speaking），等等。

4. 移动支付更多一些。Mobile payment is more prevalent. 这句当然也可译成 Mobile payment is more common. 但为了避免与上句（Bargaining is very common in China...）重复，此处用了 prevalent 一词。

 相关词语 *Relevant Words and Expressions*

畅销旅游商品 merchantable tourist goods
传统旅游商品 traditional tourist commodities
浮动价格 floating price
最低价格 lowest / floor / bottom price
最高价格 highest / ceiling price
付现金 pay with cash

复制品 reproduction；replica；duplicate

供不应求 supply behind demand

质量保证 guaranteed qualities；quality assurance

质量等级 quality grade

质量证书 certificate of quality；quality certificate

主要旅游商品 staple tourist commodities

专卖旅游商品 monopolized tourist commodities

供过于求 supply exceeds demand

加工工艺 process technology

民间工艺 folk craft

民族服装 national costume

青铜器 bronze ware

唐三彩 trio-colored glazed pottery of the Tang Dynasty

文房四宝（笔、墨、砚、纸）the four stationery treasures of the Chinese study（writing brush，ink stick，inkstone and paper）

  译技能 *Interpreting Skills*

译员须具备的素质

口译是一项复杂的交际活动。译员处于操不同语言的交流双方之间，起着桥梁的作用。因此，为了确保信息准确、快速、有效地传递，译员首先应具备：(1) 出色的双语能力，(2) 广博的知识，(3) 敏捷的反应，(4) 出众的记忆力，(5) 高度的集中力，(6) 清晰的表达，(7) 娴熟的应付技巧，(8) 高度的责任心。

出色的双语能力是指译员有相当强的双语及双语所承载的文化的应用能力，尤其是指译员的听力辨析和理解信息的能力。译员须辨析不同的口音，适应不同的讲话习惯。此外，译员须拥有超大的词汇量，熟悉不同的语域及讲话风格。

广博的知识是指译员应具备百科全书般的知识，也就是说译员应对各个领域的背景知识都略有所知，即现在被广为引用的：know something of everything and know everything of something。译员可以不是专家，但须是通才。这需要译员平时做长期的知识积累，对任何事物都应表示关注。

敏捷的反应是指译员一旦接收到信息后须立刻对其进行分析处理，并准确、快速地将信息用目的语表达给听众。这里的准确与快速是并驾齐驱的。在实际口译场合中，译员口译的时间是有限的，一般不允许占用太多讲话者的时间。当然，这种快速、准确的表达是基于译员平时对语言知识及语言外知识长期有效的积累。

出众的记忆力是指口译员须拥有超强的记忆力。其一指译员应博闻强记，包括词汇、术语及各种知识。其二指译员须将讲话内容通过笔记有效储存在记忆中。当讲话者结束一段讲话时，译员能快速回忆信息并准确产出。

高度的集中力是指译员在实际的工作场合中应高度思想集中。一旦出现疏忽，译员将会丢失信息，立刻影响听众对原语信息的理解，甚至造成误解。这将非常不利于译员的处境。当然，注意力的高度集中可以通过大量的实践得以加强。

清晰的表达是要求译员尽管在很大的工作压力下还能流利、清楚地用目的语表达讲话者的内容。译员应避免因犹豫产生的停顿，不断重复。

娴熟的应付技巧是指译员在实际操作过程中会遇到各种不利因素。因此，作为一名译员，除了必要的各种口译能力外，还须具备各种应付策略。如遇到快速讲话者，若是交传，译员可以适当让讲话者重复关键的内容或用概括的方法；若是同传，译员则可大致概括讲话的内容，而非被动地跟着讲话者。

高度的责任心是指译员须遵循职业道德。他/她接收任务后应通过各种方式积极地做准备工作，口译时忠实地传递信息，不表达任何自己个人的观点。因此作为译员，其立场是中立的。此外，译员还应主动联系主办方或讲话者以充分了解任务的性质和会议的主题并积极配合他们出色地完成任务。

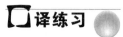 **译练习** *Enhancement Practice*

第一项 Project 1

听力复述 Retelling

Listen to the following passages once and then reproduce them in the same language at the end of each segment.

English Passage：

Wal-Mart Stores, Inc. was founded by American retail legend Sam Walton in Arkansas in 1962. Fifty-eight years later, Wal-Mart serves more than 200 million customers per week. It is now the world's largest private employer and retailer with more than 10,000 stores in 27 countries. // Wal-Mart's business model is based on selling a wide variety of general merchandise and marketing at "always low prices". The company refers to its employees as "associates". All Wal-Mart stores in the US and Canada also have designated "greeters", whose general role is to welcome shoppers at the store entrance, and play a role in loss prevention. //

Chinese Passage：

Mall 全称 Shopping Mall，常常音译为"摩尔"或"销品贸"，意为大型购物中心，属于一种新型的复合型商业业态。// 摩尔特指规模巨大，面积在 10 万平方米以上，集购物、休闲、娱乐、饮食等于一体，包括百货店、大卖场以及众多专业连锁零售店在内的超级商业中心，并同时具有长廊、广场、庭院的特点。而大于 20 万平方米的，则可叫作 Super Mall，即超级摩尔购物中心。//

第二项 Project 2

主题讨论 Discussion

Hold a 5-minute discussion with your partners on the topic "Shopping in China".

第三项 Project 3

听译练习 Listening and Interpreting

A. Sentence Interpreting

Listen to the sentences and interpret them into Chinese.

1. In this cash-rich, time-poor society, shopping online no doubt has become an ideal solution.

2. Almost one-fourth of all personal spending in the United States takes place during the holiday season, so holiday sales are especially important.

3. In Singapore, consumers are generally very price conscious and want value for their money in their purchases of food and other items.

4. The demand for Western-style convenience foods is growing around the world, a likely result of the modernization of food consumption patterns.

5. Mola Center is an excellent international shopping destination with over 280 shops and restaurants, and you'll find everything imaginable here, from beachwear to high fashion, casual dining to fine dining.

B. Sentence Interpreting

Listen to the sentences and interpret them into English.

1. 这条项链的原价是 90 美元,如果你买两条的话,就可以给打八折。

2. 我回家后发现这只瓷花瓶的底部有一条裂缝,你能帮我换一只吗?

3. 在中国的大部分商店里,人们是可以讨价还价的;有时,讨价还价比购物本身更有乐趣。

4. 中国国贸商城位于北京市商业区的中心,在这里可以找到您能想到的任何服装品牌。

5. 手工艺品是理想的纪念品和礼品,如北京的景泰蓝和景德镇的瓷器等都是值得大力推荐的。

C. Dialogue Interpreting

Listen to the dialogue and interpret it into the target language.

A：先生,您要买些什么?

B：I want to buy a present for my wife. I'm going back to Australia next Monday.

A：有什么您特别想要的东西吗?

B：I'd like something distinctively Chinese. What would you recommend?

A：嗯,景泰蓝花瓶怎么样? 它们极具中国特色,色泽艳丽,设计精美,每天都有很多人到这里来购买。

B：Good idea. I'm sure my wife will like it.

A：也许您会喜欢这一个。底色是淡灰色,上面还有中国传统的山水画。

B：Well，I'm afraid this one is a little bit too big. Do you have any medium-sized ones?

A：我们有各种规格的,这个怎么样？

B：This one is very nice. How much do you charge for it?

A：860 元。

B：That's more than I thought of paying. Can you lower it a bit?

A：很抱歉,我们店不还价。价格可能稍贵些,不过质量非常好。

B：All right. I'll take it. By the way，can you pack the vase and send it to Australia by mail for me?

A：没问题,先生,请将您的名字写在这张纸条上。

B：Thank you very much. You are very considerate.

参考译文 *Reference Version*

对话口译 A：

A：Hello! Can I help you，Miss?

B：中国的旗袍以优雅而闻名,我早就想买一件了。

A：We have cheongsam of various materials and patterns. What is your favorite?

B：嗯,我并不是很了解中国旗袍,你能给我介绍一下吗？

A：Sure. The cheongsam is evolved from a kind of ancient clothing of Manchu ethnic minority. It can be long or short，some with full，medium，short or even no sleeves at all—to suit different occasions，weather and individual tastes.

B：那么为什么中国女子喜欢穿旗袍呢？

A：The main reason is that it fits well figures of the Chinese women，has simple lines and looks elegant.

B：哇,这一件真漂亮,这是什么质地的？

A：It is made of exceptionally good-quality silk. The silk has been treated with a special technique，so it will not shrink. Would you like to try it on?

B：好的,我要试一件38 号的。

A：All right. Here you are. The fitting room is over there.

……

B：太合身了,我真喜欢。这件多少钱？

A：It's 590 yuan.

B：可以打些折吗？

A：Yes，you will get 10% off if you spend more than 500 yuan in the store.

B：好的,这件我要了。

对话口译 B：

A：这是我第一次到中国来,你能指点我一下如何在这里购物吗？

B：Sure. China abounds with various unusual and characteristic goods, and you will never feel disappointed or worried about what to bring back.

A：我想给我的亲戚朋友们买些礼物回去,你能告诉我一些比较独特的商品吗?

B：There are various kinds of special merchandise available for your choice, such as Chinese silk, tea, paintings and calligraphy, jade and pearls, and handicrafts.

A：那中国的商品是如何定价的呢? 它们的价格都是固定的吗?

B：In China, commodities are usually priced in three ways. First, fixed prices by the state; second, regulatory prices by the state; and third, market prices. Most of the tourist merchandises fall under the third category of market prices.

A：这就是说,我在购买旅游商品的时候一定要讨价还价是吗?

B：It is unusual to bargain in the state-run shops. But at many souvenir stands, it is a good idea to bargain because of the greatly overpriced goods on offer.

A：也许我在决定购买之前,最好先观察一下中国顾客付多少钱。

B：Yeah, that's really a good idea.

A：你能给我推荐一些有名的百货商店吗?

B：In nearly all Chinese cities, there are friendship stores that are designated to provide services to foreign visitors. You might as well go there and have a look.

A：好的,如果我想买些古董的话,需要注意些什么呢?

B：Don't buy any antiques that dated before 1795, since they are not allowed to leave China. Besides, remember to keep all the purchase receipts. The customs may ask you to produce them when you leave China.

A：在加拿大购物必须支付5%左右的商品服务税,在中国也要支付这样的税金吗?

B：No. There is no GST in China.

A：非常感谢你提供的信息。

B：You are welcome.

篇章口译 A：

许多到美国来度假的游客都喜欢购买一些便宜商品。// 美国威士忌、时尚牛仔裤、儿童服装、长毛绒浴巾及优质床单、枕套等都是广受外国购物者青睐的东西。// 如果你知道该在哪里购物,以及如何利用竞争销售的话,就可以在美国找到很多便宜商品。//

大部分美国城市里仍有一些百货商店及市中心购物区,而大型的购物中心和折扣商店则往往设在城郊社区。// 一些大型的名品折扣中心位于农村地区,距离最近的大城市也有几英里之遥,因此,你若是真想好好地购买一些便宜商品的话,最好是有一辆汽车。//

百货商店是一个提供了诸如流行服装、家居用品、箱包及珠宝首饰等众多商品的大型场所。// 通常它们提供的是优质商品、知名品牌商品以及最新时装,而非廉价劣质货。// 它们常常会举办一些价格诱人的季节性特卖活动,此时,你可以低廉的价格购买到高品质或时尚的商品。// 譬如,11月份的感恩节特卖就是一年中的大型特卖活动之一。//

篇章口译 B：

Shopping in China is both interesting and challenging. Here is some advice for smart shoppers. //

Shops in China are usually open from 10:00 am to 10:00 pm. // Some big department stores or "night markets" may remain open until 11:00 pm, or even later. // In some shops, the business hours may also vary by season: longer hours in summer and shorter hours in winter. //

Bargaining is very common in China, especially in the small shops or on the roadside stands. // Credit cards are acceptable in most Chinese department stores, but comparatively speaking, mobile payment is more prevalent. // You may bring a calculator to help you with conversion rates. You should buy the item if your counter offer is accepted. //

Check your purchase carefully to ensure there are no flaws. // Besides, don't forget to ask for the receipt, since it is the valid voucher if you need to return or change your purchases. //

听译练习：

A:

1. 在这个现金充裕、时间紧张的社会里，网上购物无疑成了一个理想的购物途径。
2. 美国几乎四分之一的个人支出出现在假日季节，因此假日中的销售尤为重要。
3. 在新加坡，消费者们往往十分注重商品的价格，希望自己所购买的食品及其他物品物有所值。
4. 全球对西式方便食品的需求日益增长，这也许是食品消费模式现代化的结果。
5. Mola 购物中心是一个卓越的国际化购物场所，拥有 280 家商店和餐馆，您可以在这里找到能想象到的一切，从泳装到精品时装，从休闲美食到高档餐饮，都能如愿。

B:

1. The regular price of this necklace is $90, and now you can have a twenty percent discount if you buy two.
2. I found a crack on the bottom of this porcelain vase when I got home, so will you change one for me?
3. Bargaining is usually allowed in most of the stores in China, and sometimes it is even more enjoyable than the purchase itself.
4. Located in the heart of downtown Beijing, China World Shopping Mall has every clothing brand imaginable.
5. Handicrafts make ideal souvenirs and gifts. Things like Cloisonné made in Beijing and porcelain made in Jingdezhen are all highly recommended.

C:

A: What can I do for you, sir?
B: 我想给妻子买份礼物，我下周一要回澳大利亚了。

A：Is there something special that you are looking for?

B：我想买些有中国特色的东西,你有什么推荐的吗?

A：Well，how about the Cloisonné vases? They are typically Chinese，brilliant in color and splendid in design. Lots of people come in for them every day.

B：好主意,我妻子肯定会喜欢的。

A：Maybe you would like to have a look at this one. The background is light gray with traditional Chinese landscape painting.

B：嗯,这个恐怕太大了些,你们有中等大小的吗?

A：Yes，we've got different sizes. How do you like this one?

B：这个不错,多少钱?

A：860 yuan.

B：这价钱比我的心理价位要高些。便宜一点儿好吗?

A：I'm sorry we only sell at fixed prices. Maybe it's a little dear，but the quality is very good.

B：好吧,我买了。顺便问一下,你们能帮我把花瓶包好邮寄到澳大利亚吗?

A：No problem，sir. Please write your name and address on this slip.

B：非常感谢,你们的服务很周到。

第

单元

校园生活

Campus Life

背景知识
Background Information

Making a leap from high school to university can be a challenge. To help students make the transition, many universities have planned a lot of pre-university activities for them and their family. It's a chance to welcome students to university community and also an opportunity for students to start orienting themselves to what will soon be their new "home".

The program usually includes information sessions on such topics as financial matters, academic success, adapting to university, safety living, superb sports and entertainment facilities, courses and opportunities available. There will be either short presentations by members of the University Management Group with the opportunity for questions, or a talk fair where representatives of a wide range of university services come to you individually. Students will attend interactive workshops and activities to learn about the current and future plans of the university, and they will also be introduced to the new campus and the community where their campus lies through campus walkabouts, building tours and community tours. During the program upper-year students will be on hand to provide their experiences and thoughts on entering the first year.

The Welcome Day takes place 3 or 4 times per year in some universities with a possibility of earning a half unit of credit. They even organize a special information session designed for all new incoming regular foreign students. Different departments will explain the services they offer and will give general advice on the following topics: registration procedure, legal affairs, social affairs, language courses and facilities. This help foreign students make a smooth transition.

对话口译

Dialogue A

 汇预习 *Vocabulary Work*

Study the following words and phrases and translate them into the target language.

即将入学的	住宿	residence	off-campus
homestay	公用设施	厨具	bed linens
洗漱用品			

 译实践 *Text Interpreting*

Listen to the following dialogue and interpret it into the target language.

A：Hello! McMaster Housing Service Centre. Can I help you?

B：你好! 我是即将入学的新生马琳,我想咨询一下麦克马斯特大学的住宿情况。

A：Hi, Ma Lin! This is Sophia, and I'm glad to introduce a few things. All first-year students will be accommodated in Mary Keyes Residence. After the first year, you can apply for living off-campus or homestay as you like.

B：你好,苏菲。麻烦你详细介绍一下玛丽•凯丝宿舍的住宿条件,好吗?

A：Well, residence rooms have single beds and are situated in suites with four private bedrooms. Each bedroom is equipped with a telephone and an internet connection. Long distance phone cards, cables and network cards can be purchased upon arrival.

B：请问套间内有哪些公用设施?

A：Each suite has a shared kitchen, two washrooms, a sitting room and is equipped with a stove, a refrigerator and a microwave oven.

B：太好了! 对了,没有洗衣机吗? 还有,我需要自己带厨具吗?

A：No, we don't have washing machine in the suite. But coin-operated laundry machines are available within the residence building. Cooking utensils and dishes are not provided, so you'd better bring your own.

B：哦,我明白了。那么被褥和洗漱用品需要自己带吗?

A：No, don't worry about that. We offer bed linens, blankets, towel, face cloth and soap whose cost is included in your accommodation fee. And our house keeping team will change bed sheets and refill the empties every week.

B：真是太好了,你们的服务真周到!

A：Yes. I'm sure you will like the place.

B：我会的。谢谢你,苏菲。

A：You're welcome. Good bye.

B：再见。

对话口译

Dialogue B

 词汇预习 *Vocabulary Work*

Study the following words and phrases and translate them into the target language.

在籍学生	approve	符合条件	loan
国家资助的	deadline	提交申请	学费

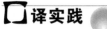 **口译实践** *Text Interpreting*

Listen to the following dialogue and interpret it into the target language.

A：Excuse me, what is work-study?

B：勤工俭学就是给有经济困难的在籍学生提供一些在学校兼职的工作机会。

A：How do I apply for work-study?

B：先填表申请或者到网上申请。可以在我们的网站上进行网上申请。进入"经济资助和奖学金"一栏,通过快捷方式就可以找到"勤工俭学申请表"。这学期的申请是从九月一日开始。

A：Once approved for work-study, am I guaranteed a job?

B：不是这样的。你还必须到"就业服务网"上去申请那里公布的职位。你是否被录用,主要取决于学校用人单位认为你的技能和经验是否适合那个职位。

A：Can a work-study student have more than one job during a term?

B：当然可以。但是你必须首先得到学生经济资助和奖学金办公室的同意。

A：Do I have to apply for student loan programs to be eligible to be considered for work-study?

B：是的。但是,勤工俭学主要是为了资助经济有困难的学生,我们办公室把贷款项目作为衡量经济是否困难的标准之一。

A：I see. Besides work-study, is there any other program that aids students in financial need?

B：有的。如果你是中国公民，你可以申请国家助学项目。发展奖学金一般会资助经济困难、成绩优秀的同学。如果你符合条件，我们强烈建议你申请。

A：How do I apply for them?

B：我们推荐你网上申请。我们将在三到四周内处理你的网上申请。在你提交申请后，请和你们院系的学生工作办公室联系，他们会告诉你申请的结果。

A：What is the deadline for application?

B：10 月 12 日。如果你想用这笔钱付学费的话，请尽快。

篇章口译(英译汉)

Passage A (E-C)

 词汇预习　*Vocabulary Work*

Study the following words and phrases and translate them into Chinese.

student union	council	assign	pass on
training ground	facilitate	peer-led support	helpline
venue	resign		

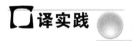 译实践　*Text Interpreting*

Listen to the English passage and interpret it into Chinese at the end of each segment.

　　In the United Kingdom, a students' union is a student organization present in many elementary schools, middle schools, high schools, colleges and universities. // Many students' unions are run by students for students, independent of the educational facility. // The purpose of the organization is to represent students' views within the facility and sometimes on local and national issues. // It is also responsible for providing a variety of services to students. // Students can get involved in its management, through numerous and varied committees, councils and general meetings, or become one of its elected officers. // In certain schools, every class has assigned class representatives who will pass on requests, ideas, or complaints to the union. //

　　Many students' unions are highly politicised bodies, and often serve as a training ground for aspiring politicians. // Some unions, however, are largely nonpolitical, and instead focus on providing on-campus recreation facilities for students. // Most students' unions facilitate student activities like societies, volunteering opportunities, and sports; develop peer-led support through advice centres, helplines, job shops and more; and find social venues to bring their members together. //

In universities in the United Kingdom, all students are automatically members of the students' union unless they resign their membership, and the ultimate purpose of students' unions is to democratically represent the interests of their members. //

篇章口译(汉译英)

Passage B (C-E)

词汇预习 *Vocabulary Work*

Study the following words and phrases and translate them into English.

老龄大学	退休老人	授予	保健
上课	展品	刺绣	插花

口译实践 *Text Interpreting*

Listen to the Chinese passage and interpret it into English at the end of each segment.

清华园老龄大学成立于 2005 年，主要针对退休老人。// 数以千计的老人参加了这里的课程和项目。// 已有 1000 多位学员顺利毕业，被授予证书。// 现在老龄大学共开设 38 个课程，涉及书法、绘画、摄影、计算机技术、中国古典文学、英语、音乐、保健等方面。// 一些学生十多年来一直参加各类课程。// 上课已经成为他们日常生活必需的一部分。// 今年九月，为了庆祝成立 15 周年，一场艺术展在老年活动中心举行。// 老龄大学的学生共创作了 402 件展品参展，包括绘画、毛笔书法、摄影、刺绣和插花等。// 截至去年年底，中国超过 60 岁的老人已达到 2 亿 5400 万，占全国人口的 18.1%，世界老龄人口的 1/4。// 所以为老年人提供充足的设备和完善的服务，帮助他们过上舒适而有意义的生活是非常重要的。//

口译讲评

Notes on the Text

Dialogue A

1. McMaster Housing Service Centre. McMaster 是 McMaster University 的简称。麦克马斯特大学成立于 1887 年,位于加拿大安大略省汉密尔顿市。作为加拿大中型规模的大学,麦大以其独特的创新性和求实理念而成为加拿大最著名的大学之一。Housing Service Centre 是大学内负责学生住宿事务的部门,此处译作"住宿服务中心"。

2. After the first year, you can apply for living off-campus or homestay as you like. 北美的大学多为低年级学生提供校内住宿(live on-campus),高年级学生一般在校外租房子居住(live off-campus),或者寄宿到当地居民的家里(homestay)。

3. 请问套间内有哪些公用设施。"公用设施"此处不可译为 public facilities,因为是同住一个套房里的四个人公用的设施,所以译为 shared facilities 更为贴切。

4. And our house keeping team will change bed sheets and refill the empties every week. refill the empties 此处指 refill the empty containers。这里译作"补充洗漱用品"较为合适。

Dialogue B

1. 勤工俭学就是给有经济困难的在籍学生提供一些在学校兼职的工作机会。"有经济困难的学生"可以译为 students who have financial difficulty,但从委婉的角度来看,译为 students who demonstrate financial need 更为礼貌。

2. 你是否被录用,主要取决于学校用人单位认为你的技能和经验是否适合那个职位。Your hire is then subject to on-campus employers finding your skills and experience acceptable for the position. 这句话的中文句型比较复杂,似乎需要几个从句才能翻译清楚。口译中可以将几处作简单化处理。比如主语用名词短语 your hire,后部用分词短语 finding... acceptable,这些译法不但使句型变得简单,而且更符合英语语言习惯。

3. Do I have to apply for student loan programs to be eligible to be considered for work-study? be eligible to 作符合条件讲,意思是 be qualified for;这里不可使用 be entitled to,意为 have the right to。

4. 我们将在三到四周内处理你的网上申请。可以依序译为 We will deal with your online application in three to four weeks;也可以按照英语法律文书、各种规定中常使用的被动句一样,译为 Your online application will be processed in three to four weeks。

Passage A

1. student union:学生会。这在英美国家中有多种组织形式。中国大学中的学生会比较接近英国的学生会,组织结构如下表:

* President * Vice-President (Services) or Services Officer * Vice-President (Welfare) or Welfare Officer * Vice-President (Education), Education Officer, Academic Affairs Officer or Educational Campaigns Officer * Treasurer (or Finance Officer) * Press and Publicity or Communications Officer * Entertainments, commonly known as Ents Officer	* Athletic Union Officer (or Sports Officer) * Secretary (sometimes Vice-President (General Secretary)) * Equal Opportunities or Liberation Officer * Clubs & Societies or Clubs, Societies and Associations (CSA) Officer * Campaigns Officer * Accommodation Officer

2. Many students' unions are run by students for students... 作者借用了美国前总统林肯的名言 government of the people, by the people, for the people(民有、民治、民享的政府),这里我们从学生会为学生服务的理念来看,可以译为"由学生自己管理,为学生服务"。

3. Most students' unions facilitate student activities like societies, volunteering opportunities, and sports. facilitate 一词在中文中没有对等词语能完全涵盖它的意思,要根据上下文灵活机动地处理它的含义。在 Computer can be used to facilitate study 中,意为"给……带来方便";在本文中可以译为"大多数学生会促进学生活动的开展"。

4. ... develop peer-led support through advice centres, helplines, job shops and more. peer-led support 是指一种由学生自己发起成立的、帮助学生解决困难和为学生提供服务的团体,这里译为"朋辈互助组织"。

Passage B

1. 西方很多老年人对 old 这个词非常忌讳,所以会使用很多委婉语来避免这个词。如在美国社会中,称老年人为 well-preserved men (保养得很好的人),the advanced in age, the mature, the longer living 或 senior citizen。养老院叫作 home for the adults,老人居住的社区称为 adult community。

2. 已有 1000 多位学员顺利毕业,被授予证书。"授予"译为 confer 比较合适,其他的例子如:conferred a medal on the hero 授予英雄一枚勋章;conferred an honorary degree on her 授予她荣誉学位。

3. 老龄大学的学生共创作了 402 件展品参展……。"展品"这里采用了量词活用的方法,译为 pieces。除此之外,还可以译为 items, exhibits 等等。

4. 中国超过 60 岁的老人已达到 2 亿 5400 万。这里"达到某个数量",是英语中常用到的表达,有很多种表达方式,如:reach, amount to, increase to, rise to 等。

相关词语　*Relevant Words and Expressions*

班委会 class council

发刷 hair brush

肥皂粉 soap powder

合唱团 choral group

晒衣夹 clothes-peg，clothes pin

书架 book case

跆拳道社 taekwondo club

文艺委员 entertainment/activity officer；

洗衣皂 laundry soap

学生会 student union/association/
　council/government

学习委员 academic officer；academics

发蜡 hair vaseline

饭盒 lunch box，canteen

挂衣架 coat hanger

热水瓶 thermos bottle

上下床 bunk

梳妆镜 toilet mirror

体育委员 sports officer/athletics

洗衣粉 detergent

宣传委员 publicity officer/communication officer

学生会主席 president of student union

皂片 soap flakes

招新 recruitment

口译技能　*Interpreting Skills*

译前准备

　　联络陪同口译是口译工作的重要组成部分。在日益频繁的国际交往中,大量的工商活动、政治访问、旅游观光等蓬勃展开,其中联络陪同口译扮演着传递信息、沟通联络的重要作用。联络陪同口译人员的任务就是在外事接待、旅游等事务中担任口译工作,在两种语言间提供双向交替传译,并在谈判中充当沟通人员或参加一些公关活动。

　　通常情况下,联络陪同译员在翻译工作开始之前,须明确具体的翻译任务、翻译的基本内容、服务的主要对象,以及工作的具体时间、地点。对于翻译对象的有关背景,如其个人特点,双边关系,我方意图,近期大事,国内外政治与经济发展的新动向、新问题,都应当尽可能地予以熟悉。另外,在口译工作前,也要充分了解被陪同人员的身份、爱好、口音特征等背景信息和日程安排等细节情况。对于有关语言文字翻译方面的主要疑难之处,翻译人员亦应尽量加以掌握。

　　联络陪同口译通常属于非正式场合的口译,比如:公司的外国客户来中国考察,公司派一名员工或者兼职口译员陪客户参观工厂、吃饭、逛街。又如:大学里来了一位访问学者,校方派一名学生全程陪同,协助外宾与本地人士沟通。联络陪同口译的场合涉及生活的方方面面,如宾馆、展会、商店、银行、医院、景区、学校、工厂等等。由于联络陪同口译具有工作范围广、交流题材丰、接待人员多等特点,要顺利完成口译任务,就必须做好充分的译前准备工作。

　　在接到联络陪同口译的任务之后,首先就是明确联络陪同的对象、其来访目的以及口译任务的行程安排表。通常,在口译活动开展之前,安排口译任务的一方会提供这些信息,而口译员也应主动获取关于陪同对象的尽可能详细的背景信息。条件允许的话，译员最好可以得到与陪同对象事先见面交流的机会，其一可以确认口译任务的具体要求，其二可以熟悉陪同对象的口音以及其性格特征，便于口译任务的顺利进行。

联络陪同口译相比正式场合的口译的一个很大区别就是，联络陪同口译员的食和行经常会和陪同对象在一起，其重要的作用就是帮助陪同对象克服在异乡的文化障碍，顺利地完成参访过程。因此，联络陪同口译员有必要在了解所要陪同的对象是哪国人士之后，学习和了解该国家的风俗习惯和文化禁忌。首先要避免自己在无意中冒犯外宾，引起对方的不悦。其次在外宾与本国人士交流中，起到文化桥梁作用，帮助化解因文化差异而导致的交际障碍。

在了解了外宾来访目的和行程安排之后，就可以着手口译内容的准备了，这也是口译成败的关键。口译内容的准备是指口译任务中可能涉及的背景知识或词汇。如口译行程中要陪同外宾参观某个工厂，口译员应该事先询问安排口译任务的一方能否提供与该工厂相关的背景资料，例如工厂所属行业、工厂规模、主要产品等。要是所提供的背景资料有限，口译员就应该利用因特网做准备。口译员事先还应该熟记与该工厂业务有关的行业术语，利用网络的搜索引擎可以查到一些口译当天所需要掌握的概念和词汇。再如口译员有陪同外宾用餐的任务，则口译员事先可以通过查双语字典，了解一些中英文菜名的说法。又如口译员将陪同外宾游览某名胜景点，口译员也应当通过网络或者图书馆来搜集关于该景点的双语介绍。

译练习　*Enhancement Practice*

第一项 Project 1

听力复述 Retelling

Listen to the following passages once and then reproduce them in the same language at the end of each segment.

English Passage：

Trinity College was founded by Henry VIII in 1546 as part of the University of Cambridge. Since then Trinity has flourished and grown, and is now a home to around 900 students. // Trinity exists to give its members a rewarding, richly resourced, and intellectually inspiring place. Princes, spies, poets and prime-ministers have all been taught here, and members of the College go on to a very wide range of professions and careers after taking degrees in all the subjects the University offers. // College life is lively and diverse, with students coming here from all over the world as well as from all kinds of different schools in the United Kingdom. //

Chinese Passage：

北京大学创于 1898 年，初名京师大学堂，是第一所国立综合性大学，也是当时中国的最高教育行政机关。辛亥革命后,于 1912 年改为现名。// 1917 年,著名教育家和民主主义革命家蔡元培出任北京大学校长,他"循思想自由原则、取兼容并包之义",对北京大学进行了思想解放和学术繁荣,北京大学从此日新月异。// 陈独秀、李大钊、毛泽东以及鲁迅、胡适等一批杰出人才都曾在北京大学任职或任教。//

第二项 Project 2
主题讨论 Discussion

Hold a 5-minute discussion with your partners on the topic "Club Activities in University".

第三项 Project 3
听译练习 Listening and Interpreting

A. Sentence Interpreting

Listen to the sentences and interpret them into Chinese.

1. You can take a virtual tour of the campus, exploring its history and architecture.
2. Student government budgets range from as high as $30 million to less than a few thousand dollars.
3. The Students' Union will feature many of its student-run services and there will be a job posting board to give first years a head start to on-campus employment.
4. As an internationally renowned centre for teaching and research, Oxford attracts students and scholars from across the globe.
5. Many departments and services will also have displays and information booths allowing students to see what resources are available to them.

B. Sentence Interpreting

Listen to the sentences and interpret them into English.

1. 现在民族舞社还处于初级阶段,但是我们相信它会成功。
2. 组织者将为学生举办培训,促进团队精神的建立。
3. 社团活动形式多样,包括讲座、展览、调研、实验和海报展。
4. 协会的目的是充分开发成员的创造性,为成员提供实践的机会。
5. 加入新成立的"笑一笑"社团,学生们笑对各种焦虑和烦恼。

C. Dialogue Interpreting

Listen to the dialogue and interpret it into the target language.

A: You look really happy today. Anything special happened?
B: 是啊! 我今天选了一门非常有趣的课程。
A: What kind of interesting class has gotten you this up and about?
B: 是一门 4 学分的应用心理学课程,我可是排队等了好久才选到的课,差一点名额就满了。
A: Is the professor the congenial type, the kind who will allow you guys to breeze through

the course and get four units?

B：你真是太瞧不起我了，听说这个教授可是有名的严呢。

A：Strict in what way? Does he call the roll every period? Or is he fond of giving surprise exams? Or is he strict in grading your papers?

B：应该说他教学很认真。教学材料丰富，考试的题目既有深度又切合实际。那些习惯死背书本的人是过不了关的。

A：Sounds like a lot of fun! Can I sit in?

B：很抱歉，这门课不让人旁听，不过我可以跟你交流上课的内容。

A：That's great! Psychological testing is something I like a lot. Does this class have a lot of psychological testing games?

B：或许有吧。我还没正式上课呢，所以还不是很清楚。

A：Aside from this class, what other classes have you signed up in?

B：还有管理学、营销学、会计学和统计学等。

参考译文 Reference Version

对话口译 A：

A：你好！这里是麦克马斯特大学住宿服务中心。有什么可以帮您的吗？

B：Hello! I am Ma Lin, an incoming student to McMaster University. I would like to know about the accommodation here.

A：你好，马琳！我是苏菲。我很高兴向你介绍这里的情况。所有的一年级新生都被安排在玛丽·凯丝宿舍住宿。一年之后，如果你愿意的话，可以申请校外住宿或家庭寄宿。

B：Hi, Sophia! Would you please introduce the accommodation in Mary Keyes in detail?

A：好的。这里的宿舍每个套房里有四个单人房间。每间卧室都装有一部电话和一个国际互联网接口。你来了之后，购买长途电话卡、连接线和网卡即可使用。

B：What are the shared facilities in each suite?

A：每个套间内有一间公用的厨房，两间卫生间和一间客厅，厨房内配备了一个电炉、一台电冰箱和一个微波炉。

B：Great! By the way, is there any washing machine in the suite? And should I take any kitchen utensil?

A：套房里没有洗衣机，但是宿舍楼里有投币洗衣机。这里不提供厨具和盘子，所以你最好自带。

B：Oh, I see. Do I have to bring my own bed linens and toilet articles?

A：不需要，你不用担心。我们提供床上用品，毯子、浴巾、面巾和肥皂，而且这些东西的费用都包括在住宿费里。我们的客房部每周都更换床单，补充洗漱用品。

B：It's very thoughtful of you!

A：我相信你一定会喜欢这里的！

B：Yes, I will. Thank you, Sophia.

A：不客气，再见。

B：Bye bye.

对话口译 B：

A：请问勤工俭学是指什么？

B：There are several work-study programs providing part-time on-campus employment opportunities for currently registered students who demonstrate financial need.

A：我怎样申请勤工俭学呢？

B：Please fill in this form now or you can apply online. Online applications are available through our website. Access "My Financial Aids & Scholarship" and quick link to "Work Program Application Forms". Applications open since September 1st for the coming term.

A：一旦勤工俭学的申请被批准，我就一定可以得到工作吗？

B：No，there are no guarantees. You must apply for positions posted at the Career Services Website. Your hire is then subject to on-campus employers finding your skills and experience acceptable for the position.

A：在一个学期内，一个学生可以申请一个以上勤工俭学的工作吗？

B：Yes，of course. But you must obtain prior approval from the Office of Student Financial Aid & Scholarship.

A：是不是我一定要先申请学生贷款，才符合勤工俭学的条件？

B：Yes. However，work-study positions are intended to support students who demonstrate financial need. Our office uses loan programs as one standard to determine financial need.

A：我明白了。除了勤工俭学以外，还有其他什么项目是帮助经济困难的同学的吗？

B：Yes，you are eligible to apply for state-funded student aid program if you are a Chinese citizen. And Development Scholarship aims for the top students who have financial problems. We strongly recommend that you apply for them if you are eligible.

A：我怎样申请这些奖学金呢？

B：We recommend that you apply online. Your online application will be processed in 3—4 weeks. After you have submitted your application，please contact student affair office in your department，and they will let you know the result.

A：申请的截止日期是什么时候？

B：October 12th. Please apply as soon as possible if you rely on them to pay your tuition.

篇章口译 A：

在英国，学生会是一种学生组织，许多小学、初中、高中和大学都设有学生会。// 许多学生会由学生自己管理，为学生服务，独立于学校之外。// 它的工作目标是在学校里，有时甚至可以在地方和国家事务上代表学生的观点。// 它也负责给学生提供多种多样的服务。// 学生可以通过众多的各式委员会、事务会和成员大会，或者被选为学生干部的方式

来参与管理。// 在一些学校,每个班级都指派了代表。班级代表将学生的需要、想法或者投诉反映给学生会。//

　　许多学生会是高度政治化的机构,常常是培养有抱负的政治家的基地。// 当然,也有些学生会是完全和政治无关的,他们主要为学生提供校园娱乐设施。// 大多数学生会促进学生活动的开展,例如社团活动、志愿服务和体育活动;通过咨询中心、热线援助、职业介绍等展开朋辈互助活动;寻找成员聚会的地点。//

　　在英国的大学里,除非你放弃资格,所有学生都会自动成为学生会的成员。学生会的最终目标是发扬民主,代表成员的利益。//

篇章口译 B:

Tsinghua's College for Senior Citizens was launched in 2005 for seniors and retirees. // Thousands of people have taken part in its courses and programs. // More than 1000 certifications of different courses have been conferred on the qualified graduates. // The College now provides 38 programs in painting and calligraphy, photography, computer technology, Chinese ancient literature, English language, music, health care, etc. // Some students have been enrolled in various program offerings for more than ten years. // Attending classes regularly has become an integral part of their daily lives. // This year an art exhibition was held in September at the Senior Center to celebrate the 15th anniversary of Tsinghua's College for Senior Citizens. // Students from the College created altogether 402 exhibited pieces, including the paintings, brush calligraphy, photos, embroidery, and ikebana. // The population of over-60-year-old Chinese citizens reached 254 million by the end of last year, accounting for 18.1 percent of all Chinese citizens or one fourth of the world's aged population. // It is of great importance to provide adequate facilities and services for aged citizens and to help them to live comfortable and meaningful lives. //

听译练习:

A:

1. 实际上你可以在校园里走一走,探究它的历史和建筑特色。
2. 学生会的预算从三千万美金到几千美金不等。
3. 学生会以众多学生自我服务项目为特色,学生会的招聘信息板让新生从头了解校园里的工作。
4. 牛津作为国际知名的教学和研究中心,吸引了来自全球各地的学生和学者。
5. 许多院系和服务部门也会设展览台和信息台,让学生了解可以利用的资源。

B:

1. While the folkdance club is still in its infancy, we are confident that it will be a success.
2. The organizers plan to hold training sessions for the students to help build team spirit.
3. The society carries out various activities in the form of lectures, exhibitions, researches, experiments and poster shows.
4. The association aims to tap its members' creativity and provide practical opportunities

for them.

5. Students laugh away their cares and concerns by joining a new club — laughing club.

C：

A：你今天怎么这么高兴？有什么特别的事情吗？

B：Yes，I chose a really interesting class today.

A：是什么有趣的课程，这么深得你心？

B：It's a four-unit Applied Psychology class. I waited in line for so long before I was accepted. I almost didn't get in.

A：是不是这门课程的教授很好说话，可以让你们无忧无虑地混 4 个学分啊？

B：Hey，don't put me down. The professor is a real terror. He's very strict，I heard.

A：怎么个严法？是每堂点名，还是常要随堂考，还是在给分上严格呢？

B：I should say that he is really earnest in teaching his students. He gives his students a lot of course materials；the test questions are very in depth yet practical. Those who are used to memorizing the textbooks for the exams will probably flunk their exams.

A：听起来真的很有趣。我可以旁听吗？

B：I am really sorry. The class is not opened for sit-ins. But tell you what，I can share what we discussed in class with you.

A：那真是太棒了！我很喜欢做心理测验，这门课是不是会有很多心理测验的游戏呢？

B：Maybe. I haven't formally started going to the class，so I'm not clear about that aspect.

A：那除了这门课程之外，你还选了什么有趣的课程？

B：There's management，marketing，accounting，statistics，and so on.

人物访谈

第 **5** 单元

Unit **5**

Interviews

背景知识
Background Information

Verbal communication requires the use of words, vocabulary, numbers and symbols and is organized in sentences. Mastering linguistic skill is not reserved for the selected few but is a skill that each and every one should develop to improve relationships and interactions.

Everyone's brain is forever having thoughts and they are primarily with words. Words spoken, listened to or written affect your life as well as others. They have the power to create emotions and move people to take action. When verbal communication is delivered accurately and clearly, you activate the mind and encourage creativity.

Positive and uplifting spoken or written messages motivate and inspire. Motivation comes from within each individual but you can become the source, and when you are able to affect other people's thinking you can help them improve their lives.

Questioning yourself or others with precise words allow for constructive answers. It makes a difference if you were to ask a "why" or a "how" question. The former gives you a lot of reasons, understandings and explanations, while the later sets your brain thinking for a solution, useful information and a strategy.

By asking questions and wording them specifically, you will invite a positive debate and interaction that will benefit all involved. You will become a better listener and entice others to do the same. Unnecessary arguments are reduced when you are able to express yourself with great command of language skills.

对话口译

Dialogue A

词汇预习 *Vocabulary Work*

Study the following words and phrases and translate them into the target language.

魔术	美国魔术师协会	portions	take the easy way out
从某种程度上说	孤立的	vocal cord	vibrate

口译实践 *Text Interpreting*

Listen to the following dialogue and interpret it into the target language.

An interview with David Copperfield，a world-renowned magician

A：大卫,据我所知,你年龄很小时就开始在家乡表演魔术了。12岁开始职业演出,后来成为美国魔术师协会最年轻的会员。16岁时在纽约大学开设了魔术课程。

B：Right.

A：太不可思议了! 现在你可能是这个星球上最知名的魔术师了。全世界的观众都因你的演出而着迷。

B：Thank you. I feel flattered.

A：那么,这个世界上有没有人知道关于你魔术的所有秘密?

B：No.

A：没有? 一个也没有吗?

B：No.

A：只有你自己才知道一切?

B：Right，that's correct.

A：你怎样确保不让别人知道? 你也是要和别人合作的,不是吗?

B：Yea，but they each, some, um... for some pieces... People have to know portions, but no one person knows everything. Even when we construct the stage, it's constructed with many different people who build individual things. No one person does the entire thing, so it's good.

A：想不想将来把所有秘密都告诉你的孩子?

B：I don't think so. I think it would be better for magic to not tell and have people be motivated to come up with their own way of doing things, invent something new, not take the easy way out. And I think that's what I'm going to do, probably.

A：你的世界是什么样的？你是否认为从某种程度上说，你生活在一个孤立的世界里？

B：No, because I'm sharing it. I'm not isolating. I'm sharing the stories; I'm sharing the wonder with people. So it's not isolated at all, just you know it's just what's behind it.

A：能再解释一下吗？

B：It's like a singer sharing their music. They don't have to know the process to create it. They don't have to see how the vocal cords are vibrating, or how exactly, you know, how difficult it is to play the instrument. All that matters is that you're sharing the result, the beauty of the result, and that's what we do.

对话口译

Dialogue B

词汇预习 *Vocabulary Work*

Study the following words and phrases and translate them into the target language.

唯一的	全球性的	制定……规则	heart
宗旨	服务商	进出口商	议会
批准	a full member	外国同人	

口译实践 *Text Interpreting*

Listen to the following dialogue and interpret it into the target language.

An interview with a Chinese expert on foreign investment in China

A：你好，怀特先生。

B：Hi, Mr. Zhao. I have been thinking about something lately and I'd like to share with you my thoughts.

A：愿洗耳恭听。如能为您效劳，我将很高兴。

B：Currently a growing number of foreign firms have been pouring into China, and some coastal cities are among the best choices of their investment destinations.

A：你说得完全正确。海外人士在中国沿海地区的投资近年来翻了两番。出现这一高涨不

止的投资热有多种缘由。除了中国是世界上经济增长最快的国家这个原因外，中国政府和地方政府很重视对外全面开放。很多海外团体与个人投资者认为在中国直接投资比同中国公司做生意更有利可图。

B：I'm not sure if I understand the logic behind this preference. I'm all ears to your explanation.

A：好的。基本情况是这样的，外国直接在华投资可以在最大程度上发挥有关双方的优势。中国自然资源丰富、消费者市场不断增加、基础设施不断改善，当然喽，我们还有稳定的社会政治环境以及诱人的投资政策。而来自发达国家和地区的外国投资者有充足的资金、先进的技术和管理知识。

B：You are right. I have friends who are interested in direct investment in China. Do you have any idea of the best place in which to invest?

A：我建议你们在海南投资，因为海南的确是投资者的理想场所。海南自由贸易港是目前全球开放水平最高的特殊经济功能区。在这里，境外货物、资金可以自由进出。这是中国实施更深层次对外开放的举措。

B：Great. My next question concerns the forms of investment that are allowed in China.

A：投资方式很多，你可以同中方合资办企业，也可以独资办公司。

B：What you have explained is very enlightening. If we ever decide to invest in China，I'd like you to be our consultant.

A：我深感荣幸。希望能早日为您的投资效劳。

篇章口译（英译汉）

Passage A (E–C)

 Vocabulary Work

Study the following words and phrases and translate them into Chinese.

promote（a book）	philanthropy	civic action	memoir
Hurricane Katrina	matter	CNN	CBS

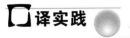 **Text Interpreting**

Listen to the English passage and interpret it into Chinese at the end of each segment.

　　Bill Gates did a Reddit Ask Me Anything session on COVID-19. As usual，Redditors ask a lot of smart questions, and it is a great opportunity to have a fact-based discussion about this pandemic and what people can do to prevent the next one. //

When asked about what worries him the most and what gives him the most hope, he says the current phase has a lot of cases in rich countries. // With the right actions including the testing and social distancing, within several months, the rich countries will have avoided high levels of infection. // He worries a lot about the economic damage but even worse will be how this will affect the developing countries who cannot do the social distancing the same way as rich countries and whose hospital capacity is much lower. //

As for what should be the first step we as a global community take so that we are better prepared for the next pandemic, Bill Gates believes that we need to have the ability to scale up diagnostics, drugs and vaccines very rapidly. // The technologies exist to do this well if the right investments are made. Countries can work together on this. // They created CEPI which did some work on vaccines but that needs to be funded at higher level to have the stand by manufacturing capacity for the world. // No one can predict what the chance of a new virus emerging is. However, we do know it will happen at some point either with a flu or some other respiratory virus. // We prepare for possible wars and fires and now we have to have preparations for epidemics. // The good news is that our biological tools including new ways to make diagnostics, therapeutics and vaccines make it possible to have a strong response system for naturally caused epidemics. //

篇章口译（汉译英）
Passage B (C-E)

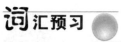 **Vocabulary Work**

Study the following words and phrases and translate them into English.

倾倒	好评如潮	金球奖	家庭生活的变化
涉足	题材	《绿巨人》	特技效果
大块头	动作传感服		

译实践 *Text Interpreting*

Listen to the Chinese passage and interpret it into English at the end of each segment.

欢迎收看"谈话"节目。今天的嘉宾是一位来自中国台湾的电影导演,他的获奖作品倾倒了全世界的电影观众。//

李安是目前在好莱坞工作的最知名的亚洲电影导演之一。// 由他导演的《卧虎藏龙》好评如潮,荣获奥斯卡奖和金球奖最佳外语片奖。//

李安自20世纪90年代开始从事电影导演工作,他的早期作品关注的是中国人家庭生活的变化和代沟问题。// 后来他开始涉足其他各种题材,例如,他拍摄了《理智与情感》这样的英国古典戏剧。// 在其新作《绿巨人》中,李安首次引入了一个用特技效果制作的大块头。// 事实上,他不仅导演了这部电影,有时候他自己就是那个绿巨人。// 他穿上一套动作传感服,而这套服装可以记录他想让巨人表现的方方面面,从愤怒时的样子到恋爱中的表现。//

从李安的创作经历可以看出他拍摄影片的题材非常广泛,但他表示无论如何他的电影都是关于人类情感的。// 为了找出他接拍《绿巨人》和其他影片的原因,我们邀请了李安导演来到演播室。有请李安导演…… //

口译讲评

Notes on the Text

Dialogue A

1. A:没有?一个也没有吗?(No? Not even a single person?) B:No.(对。)翻译否定疑问句和附加疑问句的简略回答时,要注意中英文表达方式的不同。在口译过程中为确保不出现理解和表达错误,必要时可以重复一遍实际情况。如:B:"对,一个也没有。"又譬如,甲问乙:You're not a student,are you?(你不是学生吧?)乙回答:Yes.(不,我是学生。)或者乙回答:No.(是的/对,我不是学生。)

2. Yea,but they each,some,um...,for some pieces.... People have to know portions,but no one person knows everything.原句中出现了停顿、重复和断句的情况,这在真实场景对话中较常见。现场口译时不必将说话人无意间重复的字词或 gap fillers(如:um,er,well,you see 等)逐一译出。这一点与笔译的要求不同。

3. 你的世界是什么样的?你是否认为从某种程度上说,你生活在一个孤立的世界里。"从某种程度上说"是个常见的说法,意思较虚,可视情况翻译为 in some way,to some extent,to a certain extent,in a sense 等。

4. No,because I'm sharing it.由于英语和汉语遣词造句的习惯有所不同,在翻译过程中,有时候需要省略和增补词语。此句可以处理为:"不是的,因为我在和他人分享。"

Dialogue B

1. Currently a growing number of foreign firms have been pouring into China, and some coastal cities are among the best choices of their investment destinations. 译为：现在越来越多的外国公司纷纷涌入中国，而一些沿海城市是人们投资的首选目的地之一。pour into 意为"涌入，蜂拥而至，纷至沓来"。例如：

   Commuters were pouring into the station. 通勤者们纷纷涌入车站。

   Tourists pour into southern cities in the winter. 冬天，旅游者们大量涌入南方城市。

2. 海外人士在中国沿海地区的投资近年来翻了两番。译为：Overseas investment in costal areas of China has quadrupled in recent years. 翻译的时候注意：这里是"翻了两番"，就是成为原来的四倍，所以我们用 quadruple 一词。英语中倍数的表达方式：

   两倍／翻一番 double

   三倍 triple

   四倍／翻两番 quadruple

   近几年来价格已经翻了两番。The price has quadrupled in the last few years.

3. 中国自然资源丰富、消费者市场不断增加、基础设施不断改善，当然喽，我们还有稳定的社会政治环境以及诱人的投资政策。译为：China has abundant natural resources, a growing consumer market, improving infrastructure and of course, a stable social and political environment with attractive investment policies. 这句长句巧妙地用 China has + *adj.* + *n.* 结构，很好地整合了原句的各种信息，结构工整，简洁明了。

4. 海南自由贸易港是目前全球开放水平最高的特殊经济功能区。译为：The Hainan Free Trade Port is a special functional economic area with the highest level of openness in the world.

   2018 年，海南全岛建设自由贸易试验区(a pilot zone for free trade)，两年后，海南开始探索建设中国特色自由贸易港(a free trade port with Chinese characteristics)，这意味着金融、投资、人才流动等更大范围的自由。

Passage A

1. Reddit 是一个社交新闻站点，其口号是"提前于新闻发声，来自互联网的声音"，其用户被称为 redditors，能够浏览并且可以提交因特网上内容的链接或发布自己的原创。

2. He worries a lot about the economic damage but even worse will be how this will affect the developing countries who cannot do the social distancing the same way as rich countries and whose hospital capacity is much lower. 译为：他很担心疫情带来的经济损失，更糟的是，他担心这将影响发展中国家。他们无法像发达国家那样进行隔离，医疗条件也要差得多。这句英语长句在翻译成中文时拆成几句短句，让意思表达更明白，也更符合中文的表达习惯。原文 the developing countries 后面是用了两个关系代词 who 和 whose 分别引导了两个定语从句来修饰先行词 the developing countries。

3. CEPI：Coalition for Epidemic Preparedness Innovation 流行病预防创新联盟

   CEPI was funded by Gates' foundation, Wellcome, Norway, Japan, Germany, and the UK. CEPI 由盖茨基金会、惠康公司，以及挪威、日本、德国和英国等政府共同资助创建。

4. The good news is that our biological tools including new ways to make diagnostics, therapeutics and vaccines make it possible to have a strong response system for naturally caused epidemics. 译为：好消息是，我们的生物工具，包括诊断、治疗和疫苗研发的新方法，让我们有能力建起一个强有力的应对系统，以应对自然引起的流行病种。原句较长，包含一个 that 引导的表语从句，在翻译成中文时拆成几句短句，让行文更简洁流畅。

Passage B

1. 由他导演的《卧虎藏龙》好评如潮，荣获奥斯卡奖和金球奖最佳外语片奖。该句不难，但翻译要符合英语的习惯，可以通过减词和调整语序的方法处理为：His critically acclaimed film *Crouching Tiger Hidden Dragon* captured both the Oscar and Golden Globe Award for best foreign film.

2. 李安自 20 世纪 90 年代开始从事电影导演工作，他的早期作品关注的是中国人家庭生活的变化和代沟问题。"20 世纪 90 年代"译为 the 1990's。现在让我们逆向思维一下，英译汉时应如何处理 the 1990's 呢？港、澳、台地区和海外的华人常直接译成"1990 年代"，但这种说法在中国大陆尚未被接受。目前规范的译法仍是"20 世纪 90 年代"。

3. 在其新作《绿巨人》中，李安首次引入了一个用特技效果制作的大块头。英语中表达"首次""第一次"概念时，常使用副词 ever 来加强语气。参考译为 And in his latest film *The Hulk*, Lee takes on his first ever special effects block buster.

4. 从李安的创作经历可以看出他拍摄影片的题材非常广泛，但他表示无论如何他的电影都是关于人类情感的。翻译"无论如何"时应灵活处理，不一定都译成 whatever 或 no matter what 引导的从句。参考译为：Lee's film resume demonstrates extraordinary range but he says the bottom line is that they all deal with human emotion.

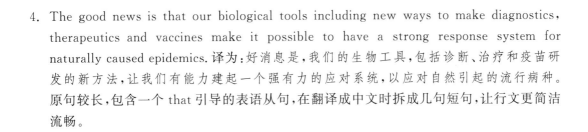

相关词语 *Relevant Words and Expressions*

摆架子 put on airs
闭门羹 be given cold-shoulder
出风头 show off / in the limelight
创意 create new ideas or concepts
非主流 alternative
黄金时段 prime time
嘉宾 distinguished guest / honored guest
模仿秀 imitation show
煽情 arouse one's enthusiasm or fervor
访谈节目 talk show
敬业精神 professional dedication / professional ethics
谋事在人，成事在天 The planning lies with man; the outcome with Heaven. / Man

被采访人 interviewee
采访人 interviewer
创业精神 enterprising spirit/pioneering spirit
多元社会 pluralistic society
好莱坞大片 Hollywood blockbuster
记者招待会 press conference
见面会 meet-and-greet
入境旅游 inbound tourism
社会名流 celebrity
主持人 anchorperson

proposes；God disposes.

替身演员 stunt man/woman；stand-in；double body

天时地利人和 good timing, geographical convenience and good human relations / favorable climatic, geographical and human conditions / favorable objective and subjective factors for success

综艺节目 variety show

访谈式竞选（候选人在电视访谈节目中亮相进行的竞选）talk-show campaign

外事礼仪

联络陪同口译员通常在国家机关、学校、涉外单位、外资企业等企事业单位的各类外事活动中展开工作，综合了商务陪同口译和外事接待的特点。因此，联络陪同口译员不仅需要具备专职翻译的素质，而且需要具备接待人员的素质。

具体而言，口译员要政治上坚定，对外事翻译而言，这是最基本的要求，主要是指口译员要站稳立场，忠于祖国，忠于人民，忠于政府，维护本国、本次口译活动的利益。此外，口译员需要掌握好政策。对于我国党和政府的路线、方针、政策，尤其是我国的外交、外事政策，译员应当深入体会，全面理解。

正因为联络陪同口译具备了外事接待的特征，译员还必须具备一定的礼仪礼宾的知识。在进行外事访问接待、商务访问接待时，如参观工厂、市场考察等，掌握外事活动中基本的行为规范，着装大方，言语得体。因工作经常会在不同地点进行，译员常常需要舟车劳顿，这就要求译员具备充沛的体力和积极的态度，展现出优秀的精神风貌，不卑不亢，有理有节，扮演一名出色的外交人员，令听众感到如沐春风。具体而言，在陪同口译活动中，口译员要少说多听，防止喧宾夺主，与外方人士相处时，一定要谨言慎行，保持适度的距离，既要在生活上主动关心、照顾对方，又要维护自己的国格、人格。在相互介绍、道路行进、上下车船、出入电梯、通过房门、就座离座、提供餐饮、日常安排、业余活动等方面，特别应当遵守相应的礼仪规范。例如就座离座时，口译员应先请被陪同者首先就座或首先离座，以示尊重对方。在进入电梯时，口译员理当稍候被陪同者。具体而言，进入无人驾驶的电梯时，陪同者应当首先进入，并负责开动电梯。进入有人驾驶的电梯时，陪同者则应当最后入内。离开电梯时，陪同者一般应当最后一个离开。不过若是自己堵在门口，首先出去亦不为失礼。

在担任联络陪同口译工作时，译员要特别关注自己的着装是否合乎礼仪规范。一般来说，只要身着正装，保持清洁，穿起来给人以庄重大方的感觉即可。整洁并不完全为了自己，更是尊重他人的需要，因此这是良好仪态的第一要件。另外，着装要与口译身份相符，颜色不能太过鲜艳，要穿得传统和低调些，以示庄重。

在联络陪同口译工作中，口译与陪同工作都是必不可少的组成部分。尽管它们在客观上属于辅助性工作，但是它们却在发挥着举足轻重的作用。要做好联络陪同工作，既要充分注意二者之间的不同要求，又要认真掌握相关的礼仪规范，一丝不苟地予以遵守。

译练习　*Enhancement Practice*

第一项 Project 1
听力复述 Retelling
Listen to the following passages once and then reproduce them in the same language at the end of each segment.

English Passage：

Do you have a job? If you do, you'll know the world of work can be tough — long hours, tedious tasks and stress. // But it can bring benefits too, such as a regular salary and, sometimes, job satisfaction. Maybe that's why more people are now taking on a side hustle — another name for a second job. //

For some having two jobs is a necessity — a way to make ends meet and provide extra income. // But it now seems that more people want to put their skills and passions into practice to make money. These tend to be entrepreneurial young people who want to work on their own projects alongside their main source of income. //

According to Henley Business School, around one in four workers run at least one side hustle business, half of which were started in the past two years. Those aged 25 to 34 are most likely to be involved, with 37% thought to run a sideline of some kind. // It calculates that the average side hustle makes about 20% of their income through their second job. //

But what's interesting is that many millennials are turning their hand to new jobs not just for money and security. Research has found that almost three-quarters of people are following a passion or exploring a new challenge. //

Of course, having a side hustle means you are self-employed — or freelance — which can give you flexibility to work when you like, but it can be risky. // You sometime work on a zero-hours contract and may not get offered enough work. Or what was originally your passion may become more of a chore. However, this could be the best way to try out a new career or follow a passion while not giving up the day job. //

Chinese Passage：

郭沫若小时候很孝顺。有一次,妈妈得了一种"晕病",郭沫若不知从哪儿听说芭蕉花可以治这种病,就想弄一株来。可市面上这种花卖得很贵,并且难得一开,于是他就和哥哥一起跑到一座花园里去找。恰好那座花园里的芭蕉刚刚开了一朵大黄花,郭沫若和哥哥就把花偷偷地摘下来送给了妈妈。// 事后,妈妈虽然知道郭沫若这样做是孝顺她,可是儿子的行为让她很伤心,便教育了他一番,叫他以后要诚信做人。对这段往事,郭沫若一直牢记在心,直到后来成为中国的大学问家,也未曾忘记。//

第二项 Project 2
主题讨论 Discussion

Hold a 5-minute discussion with your partners on the topic "Celebrities and Heroes".

第三项 Project 3
听译练习 Listening and Interpreting

A. Sentence Interpreting

Listen to the sentences and interpret them into Chinese.

1. Confidence in yourself is the first step on the road to success.

2. Work is the grand cure of all the maladies and miseries that beset humankind.

3. The wide range of television programming and the prevalence of rental stores make TV-watching a popular activity.

4. Every country tends to accept its own way of life as the normal one and to praise or criticize others as they are similar to or different from it.

5. During its history, American society has usually given priority to an individual's ability and hard work rather than to class background or family connections.

B. Sentence Interpreting

Listen to the sentences and interpret them into English.

1. 获取知识的第一步是要知道自己的无知。

2. 我们要互相学习，互相帮助、取长补短。

3. 亚洲多样性的文化为其发展带来了旺盛的活力。

4. 博大精深的中国传统文化让这些外国青年感受到的是神秘和新奇。

5. 我们大家生活在同一个星球上，因此我们要共同对付人类生存和发展面临的挑战。

C. Dialogue Interpreting

Listen to the dialogue and interpret it into the target language.

An interview with an American student studying in China.

A：你好，凯特。你已经在中国待了半年了。一切还都好吧？

B：So far so good. But sometimes I feel my concept of being polite is quite different from yours.

A：你指哪方面？

B：Well, I have noticed that you Chinese use "please" as often as we Americans do on most occasions. But on some you don't.

A：这个发现很有意思啊！能举几个例子吗？

B：For example, Chinese teachers rarely say "please sit down" when their students have answered their questions and the traffic police here are also not accustomed to using "please" when they are on duty.

A：你说得有些道理。

B: And on the dinner table we say "please pass me the salt" instead of stretching out our arms to reach for it. So don't forget to say "please" wherever the situation requires it if you are in the United States.

A：知道了。你还注意到其他什么没有？

B: I believe we say "excuse me" more often and on more occasions than you. We say "excuse me" when we need to pass in front of someone, to have a party on the dinner table or when we want to excuse ourselves from company.

A：但我觉得中国人说得也挺多的。

B: The last one is "thank you." "Thank you" means that you appreciate what someone has done for you, very often very small and most ordinary things. So we Westerners thank people all day long.

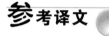 **参考译文 Reference Version**

对话口译 A：

A: David. As far as I know, even as a kid, you were performing illusions in your hometown. You began performing professionally at age 12 and became the youngest person ever to be admitted to the Society of American Magicians. By 16 you were teaching a course in magic at New York University.

B：是这样。

A: That's absolutely amazing. Now you are probably the best-known magician on this planet. People across the world are enthralled by your show.

B：谢谢。过奖了。

A: Well, is there anyone in this world who knows all the secrets of your magic?

B：没有。

A: No? Not even a single person?

B：对。

A: But you yourself know everything, right?

B：对,是这样。

A: How can you make sure other people don't know—you have to work with other people, right?

B：是的,但每个人只是各知一部分……他们需要知道部分内容,但不会有人知道全部内容。甚至搭建舞台也是这样,舞台是由不同的人一起搭成的,他们各搭一部分。没有人知道全部,这一点很棒。

A: Do you have any plans, like you tell everything to your kids in the future?

B：不想。我觉得保守魔术的秘密更好,更能推动人们自己去创新,想出新点子,而不是坐享其成。我想,我自己也是这样做的。

A: What kind of world are you living in? Do you think you're living in a sort of isolated world in some way?

B：不是的，因为我在和他人分享。我并不孤立，而是和人们分享这些故事，分享惊奇的感受。所以这根本不叫孤立，不过确有一些事情不是人人都能了解。

A：What do you mean?

B：这就好像歌手与人们分享音乐一样，人们并不用非得了解音乐的制造过程。他们不用亲眼看着声带是怎样振动的，也不用知道弹奏乐器有多难。重要的是你分享了这个结果，一个美妙的结果，我们的目的正在于此。

对话口译 B：

A：Hi, Mr. White.

B：你好，赵先生。近来我一直在思考件事，我想告诉你我的想法。

A：I'd like to hear them. And I'll be very happy if I can help you with anything.

B：现在越来越多的外国公司纷纷涌入中国，而一些沿海城市是人们投资的首选目的地之一。

A：You are absolutely right. Overseas investment in costal areas of China has quadrupled in recent years. There are many reasons for this rising investment fever. Apart from the fact that China is one of the fastest growing economies in the world, the Chinese central government and local governments focus a lot of their attention on opening the whole economy up to the outside world. Many institutional and individual investors overseas find it more profitable to invest directly in China than just to do trade with Chinese companies.

B：这种偏爱的原因何在，我不大明白。请你解释一下，我愿闻其详。

A：OK. Basically, direct foreign investment in China maximizes the strengths of both parties concerned. China has abundant natural resources, a growing consumer market, improving infrastructure and of course, a stable social and political environment with attractive investment policies. Foreign investors from developed countries or areas, on the other hand, have sufficient funds, advanced technology and managerial expertise.

B：你说得有道理。我有一些朋友有意在中国直接投资。对于最佳投资地点，你有何高见？

A：I suggest you invest in Hainan as it really is an ideal place for investment. The Hainan Free Trade Port is a special functional economic area with the highest level of openness in the world. Overseas products and funds will have free access within the port. This move reflects China's determination to further open up to the rest of the world.

B：太好了。接下来的一个问题是，目前中国许可的投资形式有哪些？

A：Among others you can invest in a joint venture with a Chinese partner, or set up a company solely funded and owned by a foreign investor.

B：你的解释让我茅塞顿开。如果我们决定在中国投资的话，想请你担任我们的顾问。

A：It's my honor. And I'm looking forward to the early arrival of that day.

篇章口译 A：

比尔·盖茨在 Reddit 的"问我任何问题"栏目上做了一场新冠病毒的专题问答。像往

常一样，Reddit 的网友们问了很多聪明的问题，这也是一个很好的机会，让大家基于事实来讨论这场大流行病，以及人们能做些什么来预防下一次的疫情。//

当被问及在这次疫情中最让他担心的是什么，又是什么给了他最大的希望，他回答说在当前阶段，很多富裕国家也出现很多新冠病例。// 如果采取正确的措施，包括检测、保持社交距离，那么在未来的几个月之内，这些富裕国家将能够避免大规模的感染。// 他很担心疫情带来的经济损失，更糟的是，他担心这将影响发展中国家。他们无法像发达国家那样进行隔离，医疗条件也要差得多。//

至于作为一个地球村，我们应当采取什么样的首要措施来更好地应对下一场大流行病，比尔·盖茨认为我们要具备迅速扩大诊断、药品和疫苗规模的能力。// 如果投资方向正确，现有的技术就能做到这一点。各国可以在这方面共同努力。// 他们创建了 CEPI，它在疫苗方面已经做了些工作，但还需要更多的资金支持，才能让全球具备随时量产的能力。// 没有人能预测一种新的病毒出现的概率。无论如何，我们知道一定会在某个时间发生流感或其他呼吸道病毒引起的疾病。// 我们为可能发生的战争与火灾做准备，现在，我们必须同样为流行病做好准备。// 好消息是，我们的生物工具，包括诊断、治疗和疫苗研发的新方法，让我们有能力建起一个强有力的应对系统，来应对自然引起的流行病种。//

篇章口译 B：

Welcome to Talk. Today we have with us a movie director from China Taiwan whose award-winning films have captivated audiences around the world. //

Ang Lee is one of the best-known Asian directors working in Hollywood at present. // His critically acclaimed film *Crouching Tiger Hidden Dragon* captured both the Oscar and Golden Globe Award for best foreign film. //

Lee began directing movies in the early 1990's and his early works focused on family dynamics and generation gaps in the Chinese family. // He went on to tackle a variety of other genres including the English classical drama *Sense and Sensibility*. // And in his latest film *The Hulk*, Lee takes on his first ever special effects block buster. // In fact, he does more than just direct that movie, at times Lee is the Hulk. // He wore a motion capture suit that recorded the movements he wanted the Hulk to have, from the raging hulk to the hulk in love. //

Lee's film resume demonstrates extraordinary range but he says the bottom line is that that they all deal with human emotion. // To find out why he decided to take on *The Hulk* and much more, Ang Lee joins us today in our studio. Now, Mr. Ang Lee. //

听译练习：

A：

1. 自信是成功的首要条件。

2. 工作是医治一切顽疾和厄运的最有效药物。

3. 电视节目丰富多彩，录像带出租店满目皆是，使许多人都将空闲时间花在看电视上了。

4. 有些国家总自以为自己的生活方式才是正确的，其他国家如果情况相似便加以赞扬，如果不同就横加指责。

5. 在美国历史的进程中，社会首先看中的是个人的能力和奋斗，而阶级背景和家庭出身则处于次要地位。

B：

1. The first step to knowledge is to know that we are ignorant.

2. We should learn from and help each other to make up for each other's deficiencies.

3. The diversified culture in Asia has invigorated and stimulated its development.

4. The profound traditional Chinese culture struck those foreign youngsters as mysterious and novel.

5. We must join hands in meeting the challenges to human existence and progress as we all share one and the same planet.

C：

A：Hello, Kate. You've been in China for six months. How is everything going with you?

B：挺好的，只不过有时候感觉我对礼貌的概念与你们有所不同。

A：On which aspect?

B：嗯，我注意到，在大多数场合，你们中国人和我们一样常常用"请"这个字，但在某些场合你们又不用。

A：That's an interesting finding. Could you mention some instances?

B：比如，中国老师在他们的学生回答问题后很少说"请坐"，中国交警在值勤时也不太用"请"这个字。

A：That might be true to some extent.

B：在餐桌上，我们说"请把盐递给我"，而不是自己伸手去拿。所以如果你们去美国，在需要说"请"时可千万别忘了。

A：I see. What else do you find?

B：嗯，我觉得美国人说"对不起"的时候比中国人多得多。当我们经过别人的面前、要离开宴会或餐桌，或是当我们要离开同伴时，我们都要说声"对不起"。

A：But I think we also use it a lot.

B：最后还有一个"谢谢"。"谢谢"意味着你在某人为你做了什么事后表示谢意，而那通常是件无足轻重、极其普通的事。所以，我们西方人真是从早到晚"谢"字不离口呢。

会展活动

第 の 单元

Unit

6

Exhibitions

背景知识
Background Information

With China's economy surging forward, various types of fairs or exhibitions have been successfully held in recent years. The events focus on international cooperation, self innovation, industry application, talents exchange, and capital connection with taking the vision and value as the main theme. By exhibitions, conferences and connecting activities, we present the vital development of our industry as well as the grand future, and the latest trend of development. Exhibitions serve as an important platform for promoting China's commercial and industrial development and the international exchange and cooperation. Fairs and exhibitions have become a fixed part in the field of marketing policies. Not only that fairs and exhibitions are a market instrument for the industry to present technological innovations of the branch, fair policy has also developed into an independent marketing instrument by means of which technological, social and communicative innovations with important target groups are to be worked out. This unit describes the importance of that kind of marketing instrument and the dealing with it.

In 2010, the World Expo was held in Shanghai. The Shanghai Expo was the most spectacular the world had seen — the first time an Expo had been held in a developing country. Shanghai Expo 2010 was the commercial, technological and cultural Olympics of 2010. It was four times the size of the 2005 World Expo in Aichi, Japan. 2010 was a critical time for many decision-makers and organizations as the demands and challenges were viewed and explored alongside the technologies and opportunities. The Shanghai Expo was a fantastic opportunity to broaden and deepen global communication and cooperation. The theme of the Expo "Better City, Better Life" was one in which we had much experience. The Expo provided a perfect opportunity to highlight Chinese creativity, diversity and innovation, and our contribution to dealing with global challenges such as sustainable development, including climate change.

对话口译

Dialogue A

 Vocabulary Work

Study the following words and phrases and translate them into the target language.

展位	与……建立贸易关系	结识	产品展示会
新闻发布会	加强	效果分析	appealing
cotton cheongsam			

 Text Interpreting

Listen to the following dialogue and interpret it into the target language.

A：Hi，Mr. Wang.

B：你好，伯纳特小姐。很高兴再次见到你。记得开展第一天你就来参观我们的展位了。

A：Mr. Wang，what are the results of the exhibition?

B：效果不错。

A：Could you give me some details?

B：我们和两个新客户建立了贸易关系，签了总量为 2000 万人民币的丝绸裙子的订单。我还新结识了 200 多个客户。

A：Oh，wow.

B：客户们提了十几条建议。在当地召开了产品展示会和新闻发布会。品牌得到了进一步的强化。这是效果分析。我期望 3—6 个月后展会的参观者会成为我们真正的买家。另外，我们从其他参展者身上学到很多东西。

A：You are right. I think you've done an excellent job. And besides，your cotton textiles are very appealing to me.

B：喜欢我们卖给你的产品吗？

A：Yes. The cotton cheongsams are selling well，especially the ones with the traditional Chinese patterns and characters.

B：很高兴听到这些。等我回国后会寄给你更多样的产品目录。

A：Thank you. In this exhibition，your products，presentation，and hospitality really impressed me. By the way，if your textile products have brighter colors，they will be more popular.

B：伯纳特小姐，很高兴你对我们的产品有这么好的印象。我会将你的建议转告给我们的总经理。希望我们能继续保持联系，并进一步合作。我给你的小册子上有我们的电话号码和电子邮件地址，请通报我们的产品销售情况。

A：I will keep in touch with you. Have a safe and happy journey home!

对话口译

Dialogue B

词汇预习 Vocabulary Work

Study the following words and phrases and translate them into the target language.

代表	纺织品	进出口公司	毛织品
棉布匹	服装	展品	handle
catalogue	pamphlet	询价	

口译实践 Text Interpreting

Listen to the following dialogue and interpret it into the target language.

A：Good morning. My name is Brown. I'm from Australia. Here is my card.

B：谢谢。布朗先生，见到您非常高兴。我叫欧阳华，叫我欧阳就可以了，我是渤海纺织品进出口公司的首席代表。

A：Pleased to meet you too，Ms. Ouyang. I travel a lot every year on business，but this is my first visit to your country. I must say I have been much impressed by your friendly people.

B：谢谢夸奖。您参观过展览厅了吗？展出的大部分是我们的产品，比如丝绸、毛织品、棉布匹和服装等。

A：Oh，yes. I had a look yesterday. I found some of the exhibits to be fine in quality and beautiful in design. The exhibition has successfully displayed to me what your corporation handles. I've gone over the catalogue and the pamphlets enclosed in your last letter. I've got some idea of your exports. I'm interested in your silk blouses.

B：我们的丝绸以质量好著称。丝绸是我们的传统出口商品之一。丝绸女衫色彩鲜艳、设计美观，在国外很受欢迎，需求量一直都很大。

A：Some of them seem to be of the latest style. Now I've a feeling that we can do a lot of trade in this line. We wish to establish relations with you.

B：我们双方的愿望是一致的。关于我们的财务状况、信用及声誉,你们可以向花旗银行了解情况,也可以向你们当地的商会或咨询机构了解情况。我们公司是国有公司,我们一向是在平等互利的基础上进行外贸交易,我们之间建立业务关系将对双方有利。我相信业务关系的建立也将使我们之间的关系更为密切。

A：That sounds interesting. I'll send a fax home. As soon as I receive a definite answer,I'll make a specific inquiry.

B：到时我们一定尽快报价。我希望我们之间能做成很多生意。

A：So do I.

篇章口译(英译汉)

Passage A (E-C)

 词汇预习 *Vocabulary Work*

Study the following words and phrases and translate them into Chinese：

address	Brown Crystal Sugar	per metric ton	F. O. B.
C. I. F.	C. F. R.	characteristics	quotation
concession			

译实践 *Text Interpreting*

Listen to the English passage and interpret it into Chinese at the end of each segment.

Mr. Kennedy，your letter of 15th August addressed to our Head Office has been passed on to us for attention and reply. // We now take pleasure in advising you that the price of Brown Crystal Sugar is at 5,000 USA dollars per metric ton F. O. B. Of course we also quote C. F. R. or C. I. F. prices if you so desire. // The price terms to be employed depend much on the characteristics of the goods as well as their specific transport requirement and shall always serve the best interest of buyers and sellers alike. // Taking everything into consideration，you'll find that our prices compare favorably with the quotations you can get elsewhere. //

For bulk goods such as Brown Crystal Sugar，it's the sellers who arrange the shipping space. It is more convenient for us, as well as for you. // You know that the cost of production has been skyrocketing in recent years. However, to get the business done, we can consider making some concessions in our price. But first, you'll have to give me an idea of the quantity you wish to order from us, so that we may adjust our prices accordingly. // We are expecting your order.

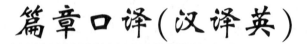

篇章口译(汉译英)
Passage B (C-E)

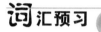
Vocabulary Work

Study the following words and phrases and translate them into English.

一流的	无柱式	现场服务	多功能
场馆	巩固	领导地位	确保

Text Interpreting

Listen to the Chinese passage and interpret it into English at the end of each segment.

上海新国际博览中心位于上海浦东，中国的商业中心，它拥有一流的设施，是中国领先的展览中心。//

上海新国际博览中心凭借其方便的交通地理位置、单层无柱式为特点的展馆设施以及多种多样的现场服务，博得了世界的广泛关注。// 作为一个多功能的场馆，上海新国际博览中心也是举办各种社会、公司活动的理想场地。// 自2001年11月2日正式开业以来，上海新国际博览中心已取得了快速的增长，每年举办60余场知名展览会，并正吸引着越来越多的展会在此举行。//

上海新国际博览中心的扩建已经完成，目前博览中心拥有17个无柱展厅，室内展览面积达200 000平方米，室外展览面积达100 000平方米。上海新国际博览中心的扩建进一步巩固了其在中国市场的领导地位，并确保上海作为东亚地区会展中心的领导地位。//

口译讲评

Notes on the Text

Dialogue A

1. Mr. Wang, what are the results of the exhibition? 王先生,这次展览效果如何? 本句中的 result 不宜直译为"结果",根据上下文,可以看出,这里是询问展览会的收获如何,因而译为"效果"更为贴切。

2. 品牌得到了进一步的强化。As a result, our brand has been strengthened. 这句话翻译时加了一个连接词 As a result。汉语中习惯省略句子的连接词,通过语境表达逻辑关系,而英语中的逻辑关系一定要通过连接词(transitional words)才能体现。因而,要根据两种语言的特点增减逻辑关联词。

3. And besides, your cotton textiles are very appealing to me. 本句中 appealing to 表示"对……有吸引力的"。appealing 表示"吸引人的,哀诉似的,恳求似的"。This dress is appealing to Susan. (这件衣服很吸引苏珊。)

4. 我给你的小册子上有我们的电话号码和电子邮件地址,请通报我们的产品销售情况。Our phone numbers and E-mail address are on the booklet I gave you. Please keep us informed about your selling of our products. 汉语原文是逗号连接的两个分句。汉语的逗号可以连接表先后关系的两个动作。英语中请某人做某事的结构一般单独成句,因而这里译作两句话。

Dialogue B

1. I must say I have been much impressed by your friendly people. 本句若是直译为"我被你们友好的人们深深地打动了",会显得十分生硬,可以按照中国人的表达习惯,翻译为主动式,即:你们这里的人非常友好,给我留下了深刻的印象。

2. 展出的大部分是我们的产品,比如丝绸、毛织品、棉布匹和服装等。译为 On display are most of our products, such as silk, woolen knitwear, cotton piece goods, and garments. 主语部分使用了一个介词短语开头的倒装句,符合英语的语法习惯,贴切地表示了原文的内容。

3. The exhibition has successfully displayed to me what your corporation handles. 展览会成功向我介绍了贵公司所经营的各种产品。handle 本为"处理、应用"之意,这里引申含义为"经营"。根据上下文,介绍展示对象的是"产品",因而本句补译一词"产品",更符合汉语的表达习惯。

4. 我们之间建立业务关系将对双方有利。Establishing business relations between us will

be to our mutual benefit. 本句中"对⋯⋯有利"，这里需要转换词性，译为"to our mutual benefit"。

Passage A

1. Your letter of 15th August addressed to our Head Office has been passed on to us for attention and reply. 商品买卖的合同信函及文件，语言应尽量严谨而凝练，避免过多口语化的用词。根据含义，可译为：您八月十五日致我总公司的信函已转交到我处作复。

2. We now take pleasure in advising you that the price of Brown Crystal Sugar is at 5,000 USA dollars per metric ton F. O. B. Of course we also quote C. F. R. or C. I. F. prices if you so desire. 我们高兴地通知您红砂糖的船上到岸价为每公吨 5000 美元。当然，如果您愿要 C. F. R. 或 C. I. F. 价，我们也可照办。注意本句中的几个贸易专业词。对外贸易中的商品单价通常由四个部分组成，即计量单位、单位价格、计价货币和价格术语。国际贸易中使用的价格术语很多，其中以 F. O. B. , C. I. F. 及 C. F. R. 三种价格术语最为常用。对于这三种价格术语，国际上有多种解释，现将这三种价格术语扼要解释如下：

   (1) F. O. B. 该价格叫装运港船上交货价，简称"船上交货"。F. O. B. 是 Free On Board 的缩写。采用这一价格术语时要在其后注明装运港名称。

   (2) C. I. F. 该价格叫成本加保险费、运费价。C. I. F. 是 Cost Insurance Freight 的缩写。采用这种价格术语的时候，应在 C. I. F. 后注明目的港名称。

   (3) C. F. R. 该价格叫成本加运费价。采用这种价格术语时，也应在 C. F. R. 后注明目的港名称。

3. Taking everything into consideration，you'll find that our prices compare favorably with the quotations you can get elsewhere. 如果把各种因素都加以考虑，你就会发现我们的价格比别处报的要便宜。本句中 favorably 并非表示"有利的"，而是"较为便宜的"。

Passage B

1. 上海新国际博览中心位于上海浦东，中国的商业中心，它拥有一流的设施，是中国领先的展览中心。Situated in Shanghai's Pudong district, the heart of Chinese business, Shanghai New International Expo Center（SNIEC）is China's leading expo center, boasting state-of-the-art facilities. 汉语是有好几个逗号连接的短句构成的长句子，翻译时首先应分析一下几个分句之间的逻辑关系，使用相应的从句和逻辑关联词，将这几个分句连成一句话或拆成几句。本句中，"位于上海浦东""中国的商业中心"都是附加成分，主干是"它拥有一流的设施，是中国领先的展览中心"。

2. 是中国领先的展览中心。本句中的"领先"不是指比赛中处于领先地位，而是先进的含义，因而不宜译为 leading，而应译为 state-of-the-art，表示"先进的，优质的"。

3. 作为一个多功能的场馆，上海新国际博览中心也是举办各种社会、公司活动的理想场地。SNIEC is a multi-functional venue that also caters to a diverse range of both social and corporate events. 本句中"也是"若译为 is 则不够生动。因为其中含有"适合"之意，所以译为 cater to 更为传神，且符合英语的语言习惯。

相关词语 *Relevant Words and Expressions*

商品交易会 commodity fair
主办商 organizer
注册 registration
展位/号 booth（number）
产品宣传手册 brochure
参展费用 exhibition cost
成品 finished product
参考/现行价格 reference/ruling price
办公用品 office supplies
珠宝展厅 jewelry exhibition hall
电子产品展厅 exhibition hall of electronics
日用品展厅 exhibition hall of consumer goods
纺织品与服装展厅 textile and garment exhibition hall
农产品展厅 exhibition hall of agricultural products
工艺品展厅 exhibition hall of handcrafts
家用电器展厅 exhibition hall of household electronic appliance

组委会 organizing committee
参展商 exhibitor
采购团 buying group
展示柜/架 display counter/shelf
产品目录 catalogue
展览品 exhibit
半成品 semi-finished product
零售价 retail price
食品展厅 foodstuff exhibition hall
高科技产品 high-tech product

口译技能 *Interpreting Skills*

译员的角色

联络陪同口译作为以口头方式传递源语信息的语际转换活动,在源语和目的语之间产生互动。在实际的联络陪同口译过程中,译员不仅仅是一个"传话筒",被动消极的"隐身人",完全的"中立者",口译过程中传递语言信息的工具,而是能"察言观色"的,具体情况具体分析,"见机行事",促进交际顺利进行的协调者。当然,这并不意味着译员可以忽略自己完整准确地翻译话语的责任,可以喧宾夺主,相反,译员要明了自己在口译过程中的角色。译员不应只专注源语信息的接收、理解和阐释,还应充分关注译语听众,了解他们的需要、接受能力、接受方式、审美价值取向等。

出色的口译者应该既能成功地完成口译活动本身(语言的转译),又能出色地扮演好谈话参与者的角色。由于听众在年龄、职业、受教育程度和个人爱好等方面存在着差异,所以为不同类型的听众口译时,译员的策略也应有所不同,主要体现在译语的专业化程度和语体风格等方面。例如,为来自医疗行业的被陪同者翻译"Acquired Immunity Deficiency Syndrome"(即 AIDS)时,译员完全可以译成"后天免疫缺乏症候群",而不用担心它无法为听众所理解,但若被陪同者是普通老百姓,译成"艾滋病"则更容易为听众所接受。再如,在展览会现场做联络口译时,译者既要负责在展览会中对产品的性质、特点进行详细的介绍,同时解答参观者现场提出的问题。译者要时时把握听众的反应来调整自己,普通听众的专业知识相对不足,专业素养相对不高,所以针对他们的口译要浅显易懂,利于他们对源语信息的听辨、理解和接受。

再以一实际口译场合发生的一幕为例。一位泥人厂老艺人在国外献技期间,向顾客们介绍:"我捏泥人用的泥都是从中国带来的。我们家乡的泥很好,随便什么水稻田里的泥都很好。我要它们方就方,要它们圆就圆。你们这里的泥不行,它们不听我的话。"这一段话如果直译的话,译者觉得不够婉转,故把原话后面部分译成 But I'm very sorry to say, the earth here is not suitable to make the clay figures. It just doesn't listen to me, although the people here are so friendly. 在座的人听了不但不恼,反而善意地笑了起来。

从以上译例中,可以看出口译员并没有逐字逐句地按照原文翻译。这乍看来是不"信"或不忠实。但这样有所取舍,灵活地翻译的效果却很好,更加符合译入语听众的语言文化思维习惯。

总之,在联络陪同口译或其他谈话口译过程中,译员应清醒地认识到自己的角色要求。作为口译谈话的积极参与者,译员应灵活机动地处理口译中出现的各种情况,促使谈话有序进行,排除交际困难,协调会谈双方的关系,有效地促进双方的成功交流。

 口译练习 *Enhancement Practice*

第一项 **Project 1**

听力复述 **Retelling**

Listen to the following passages once and then reproduce them in the same language at the end of each segment.

English Passage：

Since its initiation in 1985，Auto Shanghai is the earliest international trade auto show in China. In June 2004，Auto Shanghai became the first approved Chinese auto show by getting the identification successfully. // With the development of Chinese and international automotive industry and accumulating experience of 30 years，Auto Shanghai has grown into the most authoritative exhibition in China as one of the most influential international exhibitions. // Starting from 2003，authoritative industry associations with years of experience of hosting country-level big auto shows have involved into the exhibition as organizers to team up with the original organizer China Council for the Promotion of International Trade. //

Chinese Passage：

今天第十八届上海国际汽车展正式落下帷幕。// 上海国际汽车展每两年举办一次,现已成为中国最权威、规模最大、国际化程度最高的汽车工业展,成为中外汽车产业广泛交流与合作的重要展示平台,成为引导汽车消费、引领产业发展的重要载体。// 伴随着中国汽

车工业的欣欣向荣和中国汽车市场的迅猛发展,上海国际汽车展逐步成长为中国乃至全球最具赞誉的汽车大展之一。//

第二项 Project 2
主题讨论 Discussion

Hold a 5-minute discussion with your partners on the topic "Shanghai Expo 2010 in My Expectation".

第三项 Project 3
听译练习 Listening and Interpreting

A. Sentence Interpreting
Listen to the sentences and interpret them into Chinese.

1. We have been in this line of business for more than twenty years.
2. It would be very helpful if you could send us statistics on your sales.
3. We specialize in the export of Japanese Light Industrial Products and would like to trade with you in this line.
4. In order to acquaint you with the textiles we handle，we take pleasure in sending you by air our latest catalogue for your perusal.
5. We want to take this opportunity to talk to you about entering into business relations with you.

B. Sentence Interpreting
Listen to the sentences and interpret them into English.

1. 如果订货量大,我们就在折扣上给予优惠。
2. 只要价格合理,高质量的产品在我国是有市场的。
3. 若对此事或其他未及事宜有疑问,请随时跟我联系。
4. 我们在生意上有多年的往来。不知我们可否成为你们的产品在我国的独家代理?
5. 你们的产品给我留下了很深的印象,品种多样,又具有独创性,我相信在我地区很有市场潜力。

C. Dialogue Interpreting
Listen to the dialogue and interpret it into the target language.

A：This facility is great，don't you think?
B：是的,比去年好。他们这次做得很好。
A：I'm glad our booth is on the first floor. More people can see our display.
B：如果有人想找我们,他们可以察看场地分布图。它清楚地标示所有公司的摊位所在。
A：I can't see Comtex on this floor plan. Don't they have a booth here?
B：他们一定有。让我看一下那张场地图。在这儿,Comtex 在二楼,罗利摊位隔壁。
A：Oh，that will be uncomfortable for them.

B：对谁？对 Comtex？你说得对，那真的很不舒服的。

A：When you reserve a booth，you should check who your neighbors will be. Don't you think?

B：是的，或许是吧。

A：Where do you go for lunch around here?

B：我到对街去。靠近旅馆有一间不错的中餐厅。

A：Yes. Well，I think I'll go get lunch. Will you join me?

B：不，我留在摊位。我已吃过了。你要去中餐厅吗？

A：Maybe. I will look around.

参考译文 Reference Version

对话口译 A：

A：你好啊，王先生。

B：Hi，Miss Bernat. I'm so happy to see you again. I remember you came to our booth on the first day of the exhibition.

A：王先生，这次展览效果如何？

B：Not bad.

A：能否讲得具体些？

B：We have established business relationships with two new clients，who ordered 20 million RMB of silk skirts. I also got acquainted with more than 200 customers.

A：不错。

B：Customers made more than ten suggestions. There，I held a product show and a press conference. As a result，our brand has been strengthened. Here is the results analysis. I hope the visitors at the exhibition can be our real buyers in 3 to 6 months. What's more，we learned a lot from other exhibitors.

A：你说的对。我认为你们的工作完成得很出色。而且你们的棉织品对我很有吸引力。

B：Do you like the products we sold you?

A：是的。棉制旗袍很受欢迎，尤其是那些具有中国传统图案和文字的式样更受欢迎。

B：I'm glad to hear that. I'll send you a catalogue of our various products when I go back to China.

A：谢谢。在这次展览会中，你们的产品、展示，还有你的热情款待都给我留下了很深的印象。顺便说一下，如果你们的纺织品采用更亮一点的颜色，会更受欢迎。

B：I'm glad you have a good impression of our products，Miss Bernat. And I'll tell my general manager about your suggestion. I hope we can keep in touch and continue to cooperate. Our phone numbers and E-mail address are on the booklet I gave you. Please keep us informed about your selling of our products.

A：我会和你联系的。祝归国旅程安全愉快！

对话口译 B：

A：早上好！我叫布朗，澳大利亚人。这是我的名片。

B：Thank you. I'm pleased to meet you, Mr. Brown. My name is Ouyang Hua. Just call me Ouyang. I'm Chief Representative of Bohai Textile Import and Export Corporation.

A：见到你很高兴，欧阳。我每年出差跑很多地方，但是到中国来还是头一次。你们这里的人非常友好，给我留下了深刻的印象。

B：Thank you for saying so. Have you seen the exhibition halls? On display are most of our products, such as silk, woolen knitwear, cotton piece goods, and garments.

A：哦，对，昨天我去看过。有些产品质量好，设计又美观。展览会成功地向我介绍了贵公司所经营的各种产品。我已看过你上次在信中所附的目录和小册子，对贵公司的出口产品有了一些了解。我对你们的丝绸女衫颇感兴趣。

B：Our silk is known for its good quality. It is one of our traditional exports. Silk blouses are brightly colored and beautifully designed. They've met with great favor overseas and are always in great demand.

A：有些看来还是最新的式样。现在我感觉我们在这方面可以做不少买卖。我们希望同贵公司建立业务关系。

B：Your wish coincides with ours. Concerning our financial position, credit standing and trade reputation, you may refer to Citibank, or to your local Chamber of Commerce or inquiry agencies. As you know, our corporation is a state-operated one. We always trade with foreign countries on the basis of equality and mutual benefit. Establishing business relations between us will be to our mutual benefit. I have no doubt that it will bring about closer ties between us.

A：太好了，我会发一份传真回去。一收到肯定的答复，我就提供具体的询价。

B：We'll then make an offer as soon as possible. I hope a lot of business will be conducted between us.

A：我也一样。

篇章口译 A：

肯尼迪先生，您八月十五日致我总公司的信函已转交到我处作复。// 我们高兴地通知您红砂糖的船上到岸价为每公吨 5000 美元。当然，如果您愿要 C. F. R. 或 C. I. F. 价，我们也可照办。// 采用哪种价格，取决于产品的特点以及所需的运输条件，同时要使其符合买卖双方彼此的利益。如果把各种因素都加以考虑，您就会发现我们的价格比别处报的要便宜。//

同时，像红砂糖这一类的大宗货得由卖方安排舱位。这对你我都方便。// 近年来，红砂糖的生产成本迅速上涨。但为了成交，我们可以考虑做些让步，不过要请您先说明大概要订购多少，以便我们对价格作相应的调整。// 我们希望收到您方的订单。//

篇章口译 B：

Situated in Shanghai's Pudong district, the heart of Chinese business, Shanghai New

International Expo Center (SNIEC) is China's leading expo center, boasting state-of-the-art facilities. //

SNIEC has attracted worldwide attention, featuring a prime, easily accessible location, a pillar-free, single story structure and a wide array of expert on-site services. // SNIEC is a multi-functional venue that also caters to a diverse range of both social and corporate events. // Since its opening on November 2nd, 2001, SNIEC has been experiencing rapid growth. It now hosts more than 60 world-class exhibitions each year and this number is set to grow in the future. //

SNIEC's expansions have been completed. Currently, SNIEC has 17 exhibition halls with 200,000 square meters of indoor exhibition space and 100,000 square meters of outdoor exhibition space. SNIEC's expansions have cemented its market leadership in China and secured Shanghai's position on the forefront of East Asian exhibition destinations. //

听译练习：

A:

1. 我们经营这类商品已有二十多年的历史了。

2. 如果你们能将你们的销售统计资料寄给我们，那可就太有帮助了。

3. 鉴于我方专营日本轻工业产品出口业务，我方愿与贵方在这方面开展贸易。

4. 为了使贵方对我方经营的纺织品有所了解，特航寄我方最新目录，供细阅。

5. 我们愿借此机会同你们商谈与贵公司建立业务关系的事宜。

B:

1. If you place a large order, you will enjoy a profitable discount.

2. There is a ready market in my country for top quality products at reasonable prices.

3. Please feel free to contact me if you have any further queries on this or any other matter.

4. We have been business partners for years. Is it possible for us to become the sole agent of your products in our country?

5. I am deeply impressed by the diversity and creativity of your products. I am sure they have market potential in my area.

C:

A：这设备真好，你说是吗？

B：Yes, it is better than last year. They have done a very good job this time.

A：我很高兴我们的摊位在一楼，有更多人可以看到我们的展示。

B：If someone wants to find us, they can look at this floor plan. It shows where all the companies have their booths.

A：我没有在场地分布图看到Comtex。他们应该有摊位吧？

B：They must. Let me look at that. Here it is. Comtex. It's on the second floor, next to the Rolly booth.

A：对他们来说是很不舒服的。

B：For whom? Comtex? You're right. That would probably be uncomfortable.

A：当你要订一个摊位,你需要察看一下谁是你的邻居。你不这么认为吗？

B：Yes，maybe.

A：你在附近吃午餐吗？

B：I go across the street. There is a good Chinese restaurant next to the hotel.

A：是的。嗯,我想要吃午餐了。你要跟我一起吗？

B：No，I'll stay here at the booth. I ate earlier. Are you going to the Chinese restaurant?

A：或许是吧。我会到处看看。

商贸展销

第 **7** 单元

Unit **7**

Trade Shows

背景知识
Background Information

Trade shows are sponsored by trade associations for specific industries, and there are thousands of associations running shows globally every year. A trade show is an exhibition for companies in a specific industry to showcase and demonstrate their new products and services. It puts all the services associated with international trade under one roof and enables buyers and sellers to interact frequently and efficiently. Manufacturers, agents, importers and wholesalers display and sell their merchandise to professional buyers.

A year-long series of short-term trade shows of various kinds bring together domestic and international business people and allow them to view samples, to negotiate and place orders. The convenience of one-stop shopping eliminates the necessity of travelling around to find suitable suppliers and greatly helps to increase trade opportunities.

Exhibiting at a trade show is an excellent way to find potential clients to help your business grow. According to the survey, 86% of show attendees at the trade show are the decision-makers or those who will influence buying decisions. Trade shows are also economical ways of getting sales. It is reported that closing a sale that begins with contact at a trade show runs about half the cost of closing a sale that doesn't have the exhibition advantage. Under the circumstance of today's economic globalization, trade shows have become increasingly popular and it's easy to find one that fits your industry and your company's needs. You'll improve your trade show experience by planning ahead. Equally important, you need to pick a trade show that has lots of exhibitors to draw attendees.

对话口译

Dialogue A

 Vocabulary Work

Study the following words and phrases and translate them into the target language.

销路好	candle stand	釉彩玻璃	业务范围
bronze-made	报价	shipment	取决于
旺季	sample	delivery	提前交货

 Text Interpreting

Listen to the following dialogue and interpret it into the target language.

A：Excuse me, your exhibits look very attractive to me. I'd like to ask about these candle stands.

B：请进来看。我们的烛台在海外市场销路很好，主要出口到北美和东欧。我们刚接了三份订单。

A：Oh, is that so? But what kind of materials are they made of?

B：嗯，有些是用一种特殊的金属制成的；有些是用釉彩玻璃制成的。

A：I see. So, you've only got these colors? The color seems a bit too loud for our customers. I think they prefer something a little quiet. By the way, do you do custom color?

B：目录上只列了我们部分的产品。其实我们可供应产品的种类很多。当然我们也接受定做的产品，这属于我们的业务范围。

A：That's good. I am particularly interested in those bronze-made stands. So, what's your pricing on them? I don't need to remind you that the market is very competitive these days.

B：你会觉得我们的报价非常合理。至于定做的产品，你也知道，其价格一般要高于我们平时的报价。我们的报价是 CIF 30 美元 1 个。

A：I think I can accept that. Do you have a minimum order, say 1,000 pieces for a shipment?

B：我们当然可以做更小的量，但是我们的价格取决于订货的量。

A：I understand. When can we get our sample, then?

B：秋季是我们的旺季,不过我想两个星期够了。

A：That would be fine. Will the sample be free for us?

B：样品不是免费的,除非你订一批货试一下。但我得提醒你,定做产品的交货时间通常要长一点。

A：That's OK. I'd love to give your product a try, but I expect the delivery before Christmas shopping season.

B：应该没问题。如果你下订单早的话,我们一般可以提前交货。

对话口译

Dialogue B

 词汇预习 *Vocabulary Work*

Listen to the following dialogue and interpret it into the target language.

product range	foremost	velvet	supplier
符合	设计	独特	trial order
订单	客户	offer	valid

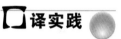 **译实践** *Text Interpreting*

Listen to the following dialogue and interpret it into the target language.

A：Hello, Mr. Lin. It's good to be back to this annual show. Hope we will find something more interesting this time. Are these your latest hand-made products?

B：很高兴又见到你了,特纳先生。这些是我们的新产品,它们目前在日本和韩国都很走俏。

A：That's very nice. Could you show us your catalogues? We'd like to have a close look at your product range to see what we are likely to order.

B：当然可以。如果愿意的话,我们可以给你们看一下我们出口产品的录像,这样你们可以对我们的产品有更好的了解。

A：Great! Um, your products certainly look very attractive on the video. But our foremost concern is the price. Would you please just give us a quote for these velvet slippers?

B：当然可以。我们的报价是每100双FOB价400美元,CIF价600美元。

A：I'm afraid your price is not competitive at all as compared with our other suppliers.

Will you bring the price down a bit if we place a large order?

B：特纳先生，你也知道我们的价格完全符合国际市场的行情。再说我们产品的质量是其他厂家无法比的，并且你们也看得出我们拖鞋的设计很独特。

A：The design is truly nice，but the price is still a bit high for us.

B：那么，你们打算订多少货？按照惯例，买得越多，价格越便宜。

A：I think we will place a trial order first. But if you can offer us a more favourable price，we might consider to place a larger order.

B：考虑到你们是我们的老客户，我想我们最多可以降价4%。

A：I'm glad to hear that. Well，Mr. Lin，one more thing，how long will you keep the offer valid?

B：一般是四天。

A：All right. We'll let you know if we decide to place an order of a certain amount.

B：没问题。希望我们很快能再次见面。

篇章口译(英译汉)

Passage A (E-C)

 词汇预习 *Vocabulary Work*

Study the following words and phrases and translate them into Chinese.

spa	high-spending	feature	seminar
complimentary	massage	cosmetic surgery	well-being
designated	presentation		

口译实践 *Text Interpreting*

Listen to the English passage and interpret it into Chinese at the end of each segment.

The Spa Show，is the UK's only dedicated consumer event held annually in November. // The show targets a high-spending audience that enjoys spa holidays and treatments. // Exhibitors include destination spas from around the world，spa products and treatments. // The show also features seminars，advice and complimentary treatments such as Hot Stone，Tuina massage. //

The Spa Show now co-locates with the Body Beautiful Show，which was previously a cosmetic surgery based exhibition. // The new combined show creates a broader opportunity for visitors to look at well-being, beauty and travel opportunities. // A new attraction of the show is the addition of treatment rooms which will allow exhibitors to conduct their treatments in privacy. // In the designated area, smaller companies are allowed to sell their products directly to the consumer. // The show is expected to attract approximately 150 exhibitors and 10,000 visitors each year. // Fantastic features, presentations and seminars make it the 'must-do' event of the year. // The show has helped companies promote their products, services and develop trade contracts. //

The spa show has seen rapid development over the last 3 years and it is believed that the event will reach its full potential with the kind of established international network. //

篇章口译（汉译英）

Passage B (C-E)

词汇预习  *Vocabulary Work*

Study the following words and phrases and translate them into English.

零配件	五金	通讯	车库门系统
饮料	提供现货	采购商	佣金

译实践 *Text Interpreting*

Listen to the Chinese passage and interpret it into English at the end of each segment.

南方国际金属公司主要出口五金和电子的零配件。// 目前与十几家厂家有业务联系,主要分布在浙江的宁波。// 公司的产品主要销往美国、加拿大、德国、瑞典、希腊及印度。//

我们的零配件主要用于通讯、车库门系统,以及食品、饮料设备。// 如果你们想更多地了解我们公司的产品,我们可以提供产品目录及免费样品。// 你们也可以上我们公司的网站以便对我们的业务有全面的了解。//

我们公司经营的原则是向顾客提供质优价美的产品。// 如果你们对我们的产品感兴趣的话,我们可以给你们提供最优惠的价格。// 而且我们给采购商的佣金比其他供应商要高。// 我们的报价完全符合世界市场的行情。// 如果你们现在下订单的话,我们可以提供现货。//

口译讲评

Notes on the Text

Dialogue A

1. 有些是用釉彩玻璃制成的。这里的 glazed 是过去分词,表示"上了釉的……",如"上釉的陶器",英语译为 glazed pottery。但是 glazed 与玻璃搭配时,须译成"釉彩的"。国外教堂的门窗以釉彩玻璃居多。

2. Do you do custom color? 这里的 do 是比较口语化的用语,表示"生产、做"。若用 produce,显得比较书面化,不符合日常交流的语境。其他例子,如 We mainly deal in home furnishings,but also do office furniture.(我们主要经营家居装饰,但也经营办公家具。) custom 这里指"定做的",如 custom table-cloth(定做的桌布)。

3. 我们的报价是 CIF 30 美元 1 个。句子中的"报价"是名词,这里既可用名词 quotation,也可用动词 quote。CIF 是 Cost,Insurance and Freight 的缩略形式,表示"到岸价"。

4. 我们的价格取决于订货的量。这里"订货的量"可译成 the quantity you want 或 the size of the order,但无须将"货"对号入座般译出来。这里的 size 是指"订货数量的多少",不能机械地理解为"单子本身的大小"。

5. 但我得提醒你,定做产品的交货时间通常要长一点。"交货"译成 delivery,而不是 give the goods。"准时交货"应译成 to keep the delivery date。

Dialogue B

1. 这些是我们的新产品,它们目前在日本和韩国都很走俏。"走俏"或"销路好"在英语中可以说 go down well 或 sell well。表示"有销路",我们可以说 There is a market for sth.,如 There may be a market for these antique chairs in our country.(这些古董椅子在我们国家也许有销路。)

2. 我们的报价是每 100 双 FOB 价 400 美元;CIF 价 600 美元。这里 FOB 是 Free on Board 的缩略形式,指"离岸价"。一般 CIF 比 FOB 的报价要高。

3. I'm afraid your price is not competitive as compared with our other suppliers. competitive 是指"竞争力","价格不具竞争力"也就是说"价格太高了"。表示价格"合理,优惠"英语可用 reasonable,favourable。还有,"最优惠的价格;最好的价格",可以说 the best price。如 We always give our old customers the best price.(我们总是给老客户最优惠的价格。)

4. 我们最多可以降低 4%。在业务洽谈中,双方经常会讨价还价。比较常用的术语有"降低多少价格"或"打几折",一般英语的表达是 a reduction of... %;...% reduction;

reduce the price by . . . %; make the price . . . % off; a discount of . . . %; . . . % discount。

5. . . . how long will you keep the offer valid? valid 是指"有效期"。在业务洽谈中，一方报盘后，另一方一般不会当场接受，而是考虑几天后再给出答复。因此，报盘的一方会给对方一定的考虑时间，但一般时间不会长。"报价的有效期多长？"在英语中可译成 How long will you leave your offer open? / How long will you keep your offer valid? / How long will your offer remain good?

Passage A

1. The Spa Show, is the UK's only dedicated consumer event held annually in November. 这里的 dedicated consumer event 应理解成 an event dedicated to the consumer。口译时可译为"致力于消费者的活动"；或采用口译中增词的技巧将其译为"专门服务于消费者的活动"。

2. Exhibitors include destination spas from around the world, spa products and treatments. destination spas 根据意思应译成"矿泉（spa）疗养地"（如日本的箱根；中国海南的兴隆），而不是按照原语的词序译成"目的地 spa"。spa 是指"矿泉"，这个概念的英文表达已为中文讲话者熟知并采用，因此口译时无须译成中文。类似的例子还有 WTO，APEC 等。

3. Tuina massage. Tuina 是中文"推拿"的拼音表达，是指中式的按摩。因此这里口译时不用将后面的 massage 再译出来，可直接译成"推拿"。

4. The Spa Show now co-locates with the Body Beautiful Show. Body Beautiful Show 可直译成"美体展"。

5. . . . to look at well-being, beauty and travel opportunities. 可译成"使观众可以看看有关健康、美容及旅游方面的机会"。这里可适当加词，如"关于……方面的……"，使译文更完整，也显得比较口语化。well-being 根据上下文应译成"健康"，beauty 在这里更多是指"美容"。因此，口译时一定要理解并翻译原语的意思，因为口译时译员几乎没有时间作进一步的解释。

Passage B

1. 南方国际金属公司。一般来说，公司的名称按照原语的词序采用直译。"南方金属公司"可译为 South International Metal Company。又如"世界知识产权组织"，可直译为 World Intellectual Property Rights Organization。

2. 我们公司经营的原则是向顾客提供质优价美的产品。"我们公司经营的原则……"可译为 Our business principle is to... "公司"在这里不用译。"质优价美的产品"则可译为 high-quality goods at reasonable prices。这里"价美"是"公道，合理"的意思。

3. 而且，我们给采购商的佣金比其他供货商要高。"采购商、供货商"是贸易中的两个术语。分别译为 buyer 和 supplier。

4. 我们的报价完全符合世界市场的行情。"符合世界市场的行情"可译为 be in line with the world market。"行情"在中文里是比较口语化的用语，在此无须死译为 situation。如"最近股市行情如何?"英语为 How's the stock market recently? 口译时,译员应在有限的时间内及时处理原语与目的语之间不同的表达。

5. 如果你们现在下订单的话,我们可以提供现货。"提供现货"可译为 supply from stock。stock 表示库存品、存货。如:这家店备有大批食用油存货。英语为:This store has a large stock of cooking oil. "产品或商品有/无存货"在英语中表达为 be in/out of stock.

相关词语 *Relevant Words and Expressions*

国内市场 domestic market   外销 export market
展品 exhibit   周转快的商品 fast-moving items
总销售额 gross sales   保险单 insurance policy
宣传介绍资料 literature   维护;保养 maintenance
厂商 manufacturer   净利润 net profit
上门服务 on-site service   外部采购 outsourcing
生产线 production line   维修 repairs
底价 rock bottom price   促销 sales promotion
规格 specifications   标准展位 standard booth
交易 transaction   保修期 warranty period

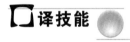

口译技能 *Interpreting Skills*

文化差异的应对和处理

各种不同文化背景的人群,对于外部事物的感知和解释也受着各自文化的影响和制约。译员所搭建的交流桥梁是否成功,则取决于译者是否能够跨越文化障碍,积极主动地吸收、理解、转化并输出语言。译员必须在听众和发言人之间传情达意,借助于语言、手势或面部表情,根据听众对译语的反应,对译文进行调整,共同传达谈话意图。

一名称职的联络陪同口译员不同于一般大多端坐于严肃的会议厅之中的会议口译。陪同口译员与宾主双方的交往常常更为直接和随意,相处的时间也常常较长,口译时涉及的内容更可能是天南地北,无所不包。例如,一名出色的旅游陪同口译不仅需要具备出色的口译能力,同时也能对名胜古迹的历史与文化略有了解。试想游览西湖时,如果源语讲话人问起与西湖有关的诗词歌赋,而陪同口译却一无所知,场面就会显得尴尬。相反,如果口译员能够向听众吟咏苏轼的"欲把西湖比西子,淡妆浓抹总相宜",并给出较为准确的译文:I like to think of the beautiful Xishi and compare this Western Lake to her. She can use heavy make-up or light either way; the man who sees her is happy. 无疑口译现场则会显得熠熠生辉。

在陪同口译这种多元化的语言文化环境中,源语说话人所涉及的话题很有可能是译者之前所没有接触或者准备过的。倘若说话人提起美国"黄丝带"的风俗传统，而译者对此即使一无所知，但仍可以通过言语行为的文化或心理内涵、微妙的语义变化、委婉的意愿表达等，借助已有的知识和经验对讲话人的意义迅速地加以修补。

另外，口译员对于不同民族和文化之间的差异要有敏锐的意识。一句在某种文化中充满友情的话，直接翻译到另外一种语言中，就可能会引起误解和不快。看几个例子。

在接待远道而来的外宾时，中方主人出于礼貌和关心，往往会说："欢迎欢迎，一路辛苦了。"我们不能直译为：Welcome. You must be tired all the way? 在英语思维习惯上，要对满脸倦容的人表示关切，而不是打招呼的问候。按英语习惯可以这样说：You've had a long trip. 或 Did you have a long flight?

如果接待的外宾年纪较大，中文还有这样的说法："您年纪这么大，身体还是这么健康。"而英语国家没有类似的表达习惯。在他们的文化里，人们忌讳直接说对方年纪大。不能译成：You are old but still look so healthy. 这样不但没有丝毫关心问候之意，却使别人以为你嫌他年老，轻易之间，就开罪了他。可以这样译：You look great. 或 You look wonderful.

在参观或者会谈等场合，常听见中方的人说"请多提宝贵意见"。若直译为 Please give us your valuable comments. 在这里，中方的"宝贵"一词仅是客套而已。如果如上直译，就会让听者觉得如果意见算不上宝贵的话就请免开尊口。正确的译法应是：Please give us your comments. 或 We welcome your comments.

在宴席上，中国人出于自谦，往往会说"今天的菜不好，请多多包涵"。在英语国家的人看来，这种自谦客套的说法反而流于做作和虚伪。故不宜直译为：Pardon me for the poor foods today. 若用餐开始讲这句话，英语应说 Enjoy yourself. 若用餐完毕，则应该说：Hope you've enjoyed yourself.

在陪同结束时，中方往往会说："怎么样，今天就谈到这里吧?"如果直译成：Well, shall we stop here for today? 会显得生硬而突兀。应该翻译为：Thank you for... Shall we call it a day? 这样会显得委婉得多。

丰富的文化背景和相关专业知识会有助于口译员的临场发挥。而同时口译员必须充分关注到个体的独特性和文化的复杂性，在陪同口译的过程中，既关注源语说话人的言词和举动，也要留意听者的反馈和神情，灵活应对，才能做到游刃有余。

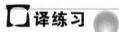 **译练习** *Enhancement Practice*

第一项 Project 1

听力复述 Retelling

Listen to the following passages once and then reproduce them in the same language at the end of each segment.

English Passage：

Interior Lifestyle Show is an international showcase of home textiles and interior decoration products. It features an impressive variety of high-end products from bedding,

kitchen and bath textiles to ready-made window coverings. // At the show, you can meet a wide range of high-quality visitors, such as retailers, wholesalers, contractors and designers. //

Companies at the show have all promised to provide complete customer satisfaction in quality products once you place an order. Thousands of individual meetings are arranged for business people coming from around the world. // Billions of dollars of business can be done at the show. Therefore, Interior Lifestyle Show is viewed as the most successful of its kind each year. //

Chinese Passage：

中国西部国际博览会自 2000 年创办以来不断发展壮大,成为集"商品展销、经贸交流、招商引资、理论研讨"于一体的大型综合性国际博览会。// 通过这一展会全面吸纳了西部地区改革开放以来的发展成就,展示西部丰富的资源、发展的优势和潜力,// 进一步融通了西部区域合作,加强了西部与东部、与世界经济的合作交流。// 与此同时,每年一些国际经济组织、世界 500 强跨国公司、主流商会与团体都积极参加西博会,为展会注入了新的活力。//

第二项 Project 2
主题讨论 Discussion

Hold a 5-minute discussion with your partners on the topic "Prospects of Trade Shows".

第三项 Project 3
听译练习 Listening and Interpreting

A. Sentence Interpreting

Listen to the sentences and interpret them into Chinese.

1. You'd better tell the factory to make products strictly according to our sample.
2. We are much impressed by your product demonstration，but still we need to consider it before we place an order.
3. We are willing to give your new products a try, but what concerns us most is after-sales service.
4. Your leather jackets are well received in our market and I hope you could quote us a lower price this time.
5. We urge you to contact your forwarding agent to arrange an early shipment so that our clients can get the goods ready before Easter.

B. Sentence Interpreting

Listen to the sentences and interpret them into English.

1. 至于质量,我们的产品出厂前必须经过严格的检验。
2. 你询问的产品目前无货,等下一批货来时我们会通知你们。

3. 我们公司主要经营各种体育用品,从运动服装到运动器械都有。

4. 我们大部分的原材料在中国内地采购,而生产主要在沿海城市。

5. 如果你们能保证长期的、一定数量的订货,我们可以给你们打 10% 的折扣。

C. Dialogue Interpreting

Listen to the dialogue and interpret it into the target language.

A：Your rugs look very attractive. May I look at your sales catalogues?

B：当然可以。我们的地毯在世界市场上卖得很好。但不是所有的品种都列在上面。

A：That's all right. Are they available in all patterns?

B：大部分都有。如果你不满意花样的话,我们也接受定做。

A：Oh, that's really nice. What kind of material is it? Is it silk?

B：不是 100% 的真丝,30% 的真丝和 70% 的新型合成纤维。

A：Oh, really? Where are your rugs produced, in Shanghai or elsewhere?

B：我们公司在上海,厂家在昆山,许多合资企业都在那里。

A：I see. But what we are most concerned about is the quality, for our users are very particular about the craftsmanship.

B：我们可以向你保证质量。我们的产品都达到 ISO9002 的标准。

A：Well, that seems nice. But how long will it take to fulfill an order?

B：那要看你们订单的大小了。一般我们都能准时交货。

A：I am wondering if you could arrange a visit to your factory for us?

B：我们很乐意安排。请告诉我们你们什么时候有空以便我们安排时间。

A：We will. So, we can reach you at either of these two numbers?

B：是的。你们任何时候,甚至晚上都可以与我们联系。

参考译文 Reference Version

对话口译 A：

A：劳驾,你们的展品看上去挺吸引人的。我想问一下有关你们烛台的情况。

B：Please come in and have a look. Our candle stands sell well in the overseas market and they are mainly exported to North America and East Europe. We've just got three orders.

A：噢,是吗? 你们的烛台是用什么材料做的?

B：Well, some are made of a special kind of metal, while some are made of glazed glass.

A：明白了。所有的颜色都在这里吗? 这些颜色对我们顾客来说有点太艳了,我想我们的顾客偏爱素色。顺便问一下,你们定做颜色吗?

B：Only part of our products are listed here in the catalogue. In fact, we can supply a wide range of candle stands. We certainly do custom products. It's within our business scope.

A：太好了。我对那些铜制的烛台尤为感兴趣。它们的价格如何？我无须提醒你市场的竞争很厉害。

B：You will find our price most favourable. But for custom products, as you know, the price is normally higher than our usual quotations. We quote CIF thirty dollars per piece.

A：我想这个价格我可以接受。你们是否有最低订货的限度，比如说一次发货 1000 个？

B：We could certainly do smaller amounts, but our price is subject to the quantity you want.

A：明白。那么我们什么时候可以拿到你们的样品？

B：Autumn is our busiest season, but two weeks will be enough, I guess.

A：太好了。给我们的样品是免费的吗？

B：No, unless you place a trial order. But I have to remind you that it usually takes custom products longer time before delivery.

A：那没关系。我们很愿意试一下你们的产品，但是你们必须在圣诞购物旺季前交货。

B：It shouldn't be a problem for us. We can normally advance the time for delivery if you place an order earlier.

对话口译 B：

A：你好，林先生。能来到一年一度的展销会真好。希望这次能找到一些我们更感兴趣的东西。这些是你们最新的手工产品吗？

B：Nice to see you again, Mr. Turner. These are our new products and they go down well both in Japan and South Korea at present.

A：不错！能给我们看一下你们产品的目录吗？我们想好好了解一下你们产品的范围，看看我们大概可以定哪些货。

B：Sure. If you like, we could show you the video of all our exported products so that you can get a better knowledge of them.

A：太好了！嗯，你们的产品在录像上看上去很吸引人。但是我们最关心的是价格。你能给我们这些丝绒拖鞋的报价吗？

B：Certainly. We quote 400 dollars per one hundred pairs FOB, while 600 dollars CIF.

A：恐怕你们的价格与我们其他的供应商相比一点都不具竞争力。如果我们下大订单的话，你们能否将价格降低一点？

B：Mr. Turner, as you know, our quotation is well in line with the world market. Besides, our quality is unparalleled and you may also find our slippers are original in design.

A：设计真的不错，但价格对我们来说还是高了点。

B：So, what's the quantity you intend to take? As a rule, the larger the order, the lower the price.

A：我想我们先订一批货试一下。如果你们能给我们更优惠的报价，我们也许会考虑下更大的订单。

B：Considering you are our old client，we can make the price 4% off. That's the most we can do.

A：噢，林先生，还有一件事要问一下，你们报价的有效期多长？

B：Normally four days.

A：那好。我考虑一下，如果我们决定要订购一定的量，我们会告诉你们的。

B：No problem. We are looking forward to seeing you soon.

篇章口译 A：

    Spa 展是英国专门服务于消费者的活动，每年 11 月举行。// 展销针对那些喜欢 Spa 度假和疗法的高消费观众。// 参展商分别来自世界各地的 Spa 旅游目的地、Spa 产品制造商以及 Spa 医疗机构。// 展销还以举办研讨会，提供咨询及诸如烫石，推拿免费疗法为特色。//

    Spa 展与"美体展"在同一地点举办。"美体展"曾经是一个以整容手术为主的展览。// 合而为一的新展销使观众可以看看有关健康，美容及旅游方面的机会。// 展销的新亮点是新扩建的治疗室，这使得参展商可以单独对顾客进行治疗。// 在规定的区域内，小公司可以直接向顾客销售产品。// Spa 展每年吸引了大概 150 家参展商和 10 000 名观众。// 非凡的特色服务、展示及研讨会使 Spa 展成了一年一度必办的展销。// Spa 展有助于各公司推销自己的产品，同时服务也可以促成贸易合同的签署。//

    Spa 展在过去三年发展迅速。相信展销活动在互联网的基础上将充分发挥其潜力。//

篇章口译 B：

South International Metal company mainly deals with hardware and electronic components. // At present，we have business contact with over ten manufactures, mainly in Ningbo Zhejiang. // Our products are largely exported to the US, Canada, Germany, Sweden，Greece and India. //

Our components are used in telecommunication, garage door system, food and beverage equipments. // We can offer catalogues and free samples if you want to know more about our products. // You may also log onto our company website to get an over-all understanding of our business. //

Our business principle is to provide high-quality goods at reasonable prices to our customers. // If you are interested in our products, we can give you our best price. // Also, the commission we offer to the buyer is higher than other suppliers. // Our quotation is in line with the world market. // If you place an order right now, we can supply from stock. //

听译练习：

A：

1. 你们最好告诉厂家严格按照我们的样品来做。

2. 你们的产品演示给我们留下了深刻的印象，但我们在下订单前还得考虑一下。

3. 我们很愿意试一下你们的新产品,但我们最担心的是售后服务。

4. 你们的皮夹克在我们市场上很受欢迎,希望这次你们给我们的报价能低一点。

5. 我们迫切要求你们与你们的货代联系一下早点装货,这样我们的客户可以在复活节前拿到货。

B:

1. As for the quality, all our products must pass strict inspection before they go out.

2. The item you are inquiring is out of stock right now, but we'll contact you when we have our next supply.

3. Our company is specialized in handling all kinds of sports articles from sports wear to sports equipment.

4. Most of our raw materials are sourced in China's inland and production is mainly based in costal cities.

5. We would give you a 10% discount if you can guarantee a regular order of a certain amount.

C:

A: 你们的地毯看上去很吸引人。我可以看一下你们的销售目录吗?

B: Sure. Our rugs have been selling well in the world market. But not all the items are listed here.

A: 没关系。你们的花样齐全吗?

B: Mostly. We also take customization if you are not satisfied with the pattern.

A: 那太好了。你们的地毯采用什么面料? 是真丝的吗?

B: Not 100% silk. 30% silk and 70% a new type of synthetic fiber.

A: 噢,是吗? 你们的地毯是哪里产的,上海还是其他地方?

B: Our company is Shanghai-based, while the factory is in Kunshan, home to many JV companies.

A: 明白了。但我们最关心的是质量,因为我们的用户对质量很挑剔。

B: You can be assured of our quality. Our products are up to the standard of ISO9002.

A: 嗯,那很好。你们完成一个订单需要多久?

B: It depends on the size of your order. Generally, we can make the delivery on time.

A: 我想你们能否安排我们参观一下你们的工厂?

B: We'd love to. Please let us know when you will be free so that we could set up the time for you.

A: 我们会的。这两个电话中的任何一个都可以联系到你们?

B: Yes. You may contact us anytime, even in the evening.

商务谈判 单元 第 8

Unit

Business Negotiation

背景知识
Background Information

Business negotiation is a bargaining situation in which two or more players have a common interest to cooperate, but at the same time have conflicting interests over exactly how to share.

Firstly, you have to know what you really want, why and how badly you want or need it, and at what point you're willing to walk away without getting it. Secondly, you have got to know what the other party wants and why it's important to them. You should be fully aware how much they need or want and what would make them really happy. There is no such thing as "take it or leave it" in international business. Everything is negotiable. But it all depends on the expertise of the negotiators.

International business negotiation is known as the zero-sum game. One side's gains are directly the other side's losses. Your counterpart attempts to achieve the maximum concessions while leaving you just enough to keep you interested in the deal.

The target of international business negotiation is to achieve the desired results. Therefore, at the beginning, you should make a high offer and negotiate for the best target. Normally speaking, people who firmly maintain the desired objectives to the end can get the best deal. If you meet with negotiators who always use harsh language, you don't have to be angry because it means they want to buy your products.

The main content of negotiation on international business includes price, quality, term of payment, packing and shipping, and insurance.

对话口译

Dialogue A

 词汇预习 *Vocabulary Work*

Study the following words and phrases and translate them into the target language.

加快	苏州工业园	合资企业	项目计划
positive	preferential policy	investor	基础设施
免除	所得税	registered capital	factory facility
厂房	期限		

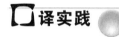 口译实践 *Text Interpreting*

Listen to the following dialogue and interpret it into the target language.

A：Mr. Liu, we see you are aggressively pursuing foreign direct investment.

B：是的。我们正在加快发展的步伐,因此我们对你们准备在苏州工业园区与我们合作建立合资企业的项目计划很感兴趣。

A：Oh, that's very nice. The investment climate in China certainly looks positive these days. But we want to know what preferential treatment foreign investors could enjoy in this area?

B：我们当地政府正在努力创造良好的投资环境,包括大规模的基础设施建设。外商投资者如果在工业园区注册公司的话,可以减免所得税。此外,合资企业还可以享受低息贷款甚至政府资助的培训。

A：It sounds very encouraging. If that's the case, we are more confident in investing in this project.

B：你们的投资肯定会有很高的经济回报。那么你们准备在这个项目上投资多少?

A：We will invest 45 million US dollars for a start, I think. And how much should the registered capital be?

B：这个投资数目非常令人满意。至于注册资本,它至少占总投资的50%。

A：What do you think is the right proportion of investment for our two parties? Is there a lower limit for foreign investors?

B：投资比例是灵活的。一般来说,外商的投资不得低于30%。

A：This shouldn't be a problem on our side. In fact，we'd like to make it 60％ if you can take care of factory facilities while we provide technology.

B：那完全可以。事实上，我们已经有厂房了。

A：That's great. How long will the term of such a joint venture be，then?

B：我们建议 10 年。如果我们双方愿意的话，合资期限可以延长。

A：Very well. OK，so far，so good. But it seems there is much to deal with before we sign the agreement.

B：别担心。让我们去好好喝一杯，将细节问题留给我们的助手去处理。

对话口译

Dialogue B

 ## 词汇预习 *Vocabulary Work*

Study the following words and phrases and translate them into the target language.

agent	sole agent	promote	Greater China
reputation	销售额	sales network	拓展
开拓	营业额	合作伙伴	月开支
publicity			

 ## 口译实践 *Text Interpreting*

Listen to the following dialogue and interpret it into the target language.

A：Mr. Hu，we are looking for a sole agent to promote our products in Greater China. As we understand，your company has a good reputation as an agent in the furniture market.

B：的确如此。我们在这一行已经做了 15 年了。我们主要为欧洲的家具供应商做代理。目前我们的年销售额已达到 245 万美元，大大超出了我们的主要竞争对手。

A：I'm very much impressed by your sales volume. But what concerns us most is your sales network.

B：哈里森先生，我们不断在拓展我们的业务。目前除了现有的中国东部和南部的市场外，我们最近在中国的北部开拓了一些新的市场。

A：Well，that sounds great. We'd love to work with experienced agent like your company.

B：如果你们委任我们做独家代理，我们可以使你们的营业额在目前基础上增加 50%。

A：The figure seems very attractive. Then what commission do you expect?

B：一般说来，我们收取销售额的 7%。但既然你们是我们新的合作伙伴，我想收取销售额的 6% 加上 2,000 美元的月开支。

A：6% sounds reasonable，but I'm afraid we can't cover the monthly expense. And I need to know the annual order you can guarantee.

B：那么我们就收取 6% 的佣金，加上一些促销费用。如果你能接受的话，我们每年可以保证订购 1,000 件。

A：Well，based on the quantity you'll order, we can give you a certain amount for publicity.

B：这个条件我们可以接受。那我们的代理期限多长呢？

A：At the initial stage，we should say one year. But of course, the contract can be renewed.

B：我理解。如果我们双方都同意这些条件的话，那么什么时候签约呢？

A：I think we could sign the agreement in two days.

B：很好。那我们休息一下，喝点咖啡吧。

篇章口译(英译汉)

Passage A (E-C)

 词汇预习 *Vocabulary Work*

Study the following words and phrases and translate them into Chinese.

liberalize	forum	dispute	negotiating membership
trade barrier	trading system	consumer	accession

 口译实践 *Text Interpreting*

Listen to the English passage and interpret it into Chinese at the end of each segment.

　　The WTO (World Trade Organization) is an organization for liberalizing trade. It's a forum for governments to negotiate trade agreements. // It's a place for them to settle trade disputes and operates a system of trade rules. // Essentially, the WTO is a place where member governments go, to try to sort out the trade problems they face with each other. // The first step is to talk. The WTO was born out of negotiations, and everything the WTO does is the result of negotiations. //

At present, the WTO has more than 160 members, accounting for over 90% of world trade. // Over 30 others are negotiating membership. Decisions are made by the entire membership. //

When countries have faced trade barriers and wanted them lowered, the negotiations have helped to liberalize trade. // But the WTO is not just about liberalizing trade, and in some situations its rules support maintaining trade barriers—for example to protect consumers. // The WTO also helps producers and exporters know that foreign markets will remain open to them. // The WTO has helped to create a strong and prosperous trading system. //

篇章口译（汉译英）

Passage B (C-E)

  Vocabulary Work

Study the following words and phrases and translate them into English.

外国直接投资	积极的	沿海城市	批准
金融	地产	欧盟	研发中心

Text Interpreting

Listen to the Chinese passage and interpret it into English at the end of each segment.

中国正在努力改善其投资环境以吸引更多外资。// 中国目前的外国直接投资达到了1400亿美元，但还不够。// 因此，中国政府正在采取积极的措施鼓励沿海城市和一些主要的城市吸收更多外资。// 中国政府已批准了4万4千个新的外商投资项目。//

迄今为止，中国的外国投资领域已从工业扩大到金融、地产、商业、外贸及服务业。// 根据最新的调查，欧盟对中国的投资迅速上升，然而来自美国的实际投资有所下降。// 东南亚依旧是主要的投资来源，并且投资结构已有改善。// 外国投资者对高科技领域及研发中心的投资表现出极大的兴趣。// 此外，在通信设备、计算机、电子产品及运输设备生产方面的投资大幅度增加。//

口译讲评

Notes on the Text

Dialogue A

1. We can see you are aggressively pursuing foreign direct investment. 这里 aggressively 应根据上下文灵活译为"积极地",而非"侵略地"。又如 Chicago is aggressively seeking opportunity for international business.（芝加哥在努力寻求国际商务的机会。）foreign direct investment 是"外国直接投资",其缩略形式为 FDI,运用于各种场合。中文报刊中也经常出现这个术语的缩略词。如"2020 年中国的 FDI 达到了 1630 亿美元"。

2. 因此我们对你们准备在苏州工业园区与我们合作建立合资企业的项目计划很感兴趣。由于中、英句子结构的差异,本句口译时应先译句子后面的部分,即 We are quite interested in...。"项目计划"可译成 project proposal;"苏州工业园区"译为 Suzhou Industrial Park。学员练习口译时,要充分了解主题的背景知识并不断扩大词汇库。这里学员需了解有关投资合作的基本知识及建立合资企业的相关术语。

3. 可以减免所得税。这里"减免"是"减"和"免"两个概念,应译为 reduction of income tax and even tax exemption。

4. And how much should the registered capital be. registered 意为"注册的,挂号的",如：registered capital（注册资本）, a registered letter（挂号信）a registered lawyer（注册律师）。

5. 我们建议 10 年。如果我们双方愿意的话,合资期限可以延长。这里要注意 suggest 的用法,可直接译作 suggest ten years 或 suggest it（should）be ten years。由于口译时间有限,在中译外时容易犯语法错误,因此语言知识能力的不断提高非常重要。"合资期限"这里可直接译作 period,而不要再重复前面的 term of such a joint venture。因此,口译时译员一定要学会随机应变,选择的译语要简单、达意,且不能占用太多讲者的时间。

Dialogue B

1. 的确如此。"的确如此"是口语化的用语,这里可译成 Yes, indeed. 或 Exactly. 联络陪同口译时要注意语域（register of language）,即：书面语还是口语,正式语还是非正式语等。

2. I'm very much impressed by your sales volume. be impressed by 表示"对……印象深刻"或"……给我留下了深刻印象"。这里可译成：你们的销售额令我印象深刻。

3. ……,我们最近在中国的北部开拓了一些新的市场。"开拓市场"可以译作 explore the new market。如果要表示"扩大市场",则可用 expand the market。expand 是表示"扩大，拓展"，如"业务拓展"（business expansion）。

4. Then what commission do you expect? 这个句子可简单译成：你们打算要多少佣金？如果将中文回译到英文，则还可译作 And the commission you expect? 或者 What about the rate of commission you want to charge?

5. 这个条件我们可以接受。"这个条件"在口译时无须死译成 this condition/term。整句可译成 That's acceptable. 这样，句子显得简洁且口语化。

Passage A

1. The WTO is an organization for liberalizing trade. WTO 是 World Trade Organization 的缩略形式，中文为"世界贸易组织"，简称"世贸组织"。中文讲话中有时也采用 WTO，因此英译中时也无须翻译，就直接保留 WTO，这样译员可以有更多时间口译其他的信息。

2. Over 30 others are negotiating membership. Decisions are made by the entire membership. 这里的 negotiating membership 应译为"谈判成员国"。虽然 membership 表示"成员"，在此译作"成员国"，意思显得更明白、完整。毕竟这里的"成员"代表国家，而非个人。entire membership 可相应译作"所有成员国"，虽然其本意是"全体成员"。

3. When countries have faced trade barriers and wanted them lowered，the negotiations have helped to liberalize trade. barrier 表示"障碍，隔阂"，一般 trade barrier 译作"贸易壁垒"。tariff barrier 则为"关税壁垒"。口译时译员一定要熟悉某个领域的行话，熟悉讲话者和听众的话语。

4. The WTO has helped to create a strong and prosperous trading system. trading system 是"贸易体系"。system 还可表示"系统"，但这里是指"体系"，也是约定俗成的表达。WTO 的核心是 multilateral trading system，也就是"多边贸易体系"。

Passage B

1. 中国正在努力改善其投资环境以吸引更多外资。"投资环境"在英语中为 investment environment。但英语讲话者有时也用 investment climate 来表示"投资环境"。因此，译员要熟悉同一概念的不同表达法，并且需掌握大量的同义词。

2. 中国目前的外国直接投资达到了 1 400 亿美元，但还不够。这里"达到"在英语中的表达可以是 reach，arrive at，be，但现在比较流行用 stand at。因此，译员要时时关注流行的用语。

3. 因此，中国政府正在采取积极的措施鼓励沿海城市和一些主要的城市吸收更多外资。这个句子中的动词比较多，如"采取""鼓励""吸收"。由于中英文中动词时态的表示和衔接方式差别很大，语言转换时要充分意识到这些差别。

4. 迄今为止，中国的外国投资领域已从工业扩大到金融、地产、商业、外贸及服务业。本句中列举的内容较多，口译练习时学员要学会快速有效地将所列举的"金融、地产、商业、外贸及服务业"这些内容笔录到笔记本上，以免口译时遗漏其中的任何一项。

5. 根据最新的调查，欧盟对中国的投资迅速上升，然而来自美国的实际投资有所下降。这里"欧盟对中国的投资迅速上升"口译成英语时可直接用介词词组 a rapid increase of European Union investment to China。但这样句子并不完整，因此可使用 there 引导的句型,译成:There has been a rapid increase of European Union investment to China.

相关词语　*Relevant Words and Expressions*

津贴 allowance
自主权 autonomy
可行性报告 feasibility study
保税区 free trade zone
意向书 letter of intent
生产厂家 manufacturer
市场调研 market research
常驻代表处 representative office
销售价格 selling price
经济技术开发区 economic and technological development zone

审批 approval
营业执照 business license
外汇 foreign exchange
高科技园区 high-tech park
劳动密集型 labor-intensive
市场潜力 market potential
项目建议书 project proposal
销售渠道 sales channel
独家经销 sole distribution

口译技能　*Interpreting Skills*

记忆理解(1)

口译做得成功与否,在很大程度上取决于译员的记忆能力。也许有人要问:"译员不是可以记笔记吗? 翻译的时候看着笔记不就行了吗?"

事实上,译员所做的笔记往往只是一段话的大体框架,其他的细节部分都需要通过记忆来补充。译员的水平越高,对笔记的依赖就越小。因为笔记就像是一把双刃剑,使用得当的话,会对记忆起到极大的促进作用;若使用不当的话,则会起到不小的反作用。

很多同学在初学口译的时候,常常觉得各种各样的口译笔记符号非常"神奇",非常有趣,因而在口译练习过程中过多地专注于笔记,试图记下发言人的每一句话。结果却发现自己虽然记下了许多东西,发言人究竟讲了些什么,反而不清楚了。

经验丰富的译员都明白,实战口译中笔记只是一种辅助手段,而起关键作用的则是头脑记忆。因此,良好的记忆能力是口译过程中一个至关重要的环节,而口译训练也常常是从记忆力训练入手的。

说到记忆力训练,我们首先要弄清楚记忆究竟是什么。简而言之,记忆就是人们将日常生活、学习、工作中获得的大量信息进行编码加工,使其储存在大脑里,需要时再将相关信息从大脑里提取出来,应用于实践的一个过程。譬如,遇到多年未见的老同学,你能立刻叫出他的姓名;在特定场景下,突然想起幼时学过的一首儿歌……这些都是记忆的具体表现。

根据记忆过程中信息保持时间的长短不同,科学家们将人的记忆分为"长时记忆(long-term memory)"和"短时记忆(short-term memory)"两种。

所谓"长时记忆"，即人们在成长过程中不断积累起来的专业知识、生活常识、经验教训及种种经历等等，属于一种储存性的永久记忆，有时也被称为"潜在记忆"或"被动记忆"。

"短时记忆"亦称为"操作记忆"或"积极记忆"，则是一种操作性的暂时记忆，大脑暂时性地将信息保存起来，随后虽然有一小部分可能会转化为长久记忆，但大部分内容还是很快就被遗忘了。

科学研究表明，即便被感知的信息是有意义的，人的短时记忆最多也只能容纳由 20 多个单词组成的句子，或者一组 10 位数的数字，而且保持时间也很难超过 1 分钟，短时记忆有着很大的局限性。

口译活动要求译员不仅能在有限的时间内处理大量信息，而且能有效地保持信息。它要求译员在听完一段文字后立刻把听到的内容口译出来，对译员的"短时记忆"要求极高。因此，记忆是每个译员在培训过程中必须要解决的首要问题。

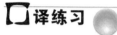 **Enhancement Practice** 口译练习

第一项 Project 1

听力复述 Retelling

Listen to the following passages once and then reproduce them in the same language at the end of each segment.

English Passage：

China's textile producers and exporters have welcomed the textile agreement reached between China and the European Union (EU). The deal will create a positive, stable trade environment for both Chinese and European companies. // According to the deal, the EU has agreed to stop investigations on 10 categories of textile products from China. Both China and the EU have agreed to settle future textile trade disputes through "consultations". // Such an approach is of great significance for global textile and garment sectors in their transition to a new trade situation. It is hoped that Chinese textile firms will further improve their international competitiveness to avoid trade disputes and strengthen cooperation with their EU counterparts. //

Chinese Passage：

随着中国经济的快速发展，尤其是加入 WTO 后，中国各个领域中的国际商务谈判越来越多。// 国际商务谈判涉及的因素很多，但价格则几乎是所有商务谈判的核心内容。// 谈判双方在利益上的得与失主要通过价格升降而得到体现。因此，在商务谈判中，应以价格为中心，坚持自己的利益。// 此外，由于各国的文化背景不同，谈判者还应运用不同的文化模式，掌握与各国打交道的有效策略。//

第二项 Project 2

主题讨论 Discussion

Hold a 5-minute discussion with your partners on the topic "Cultural Factors in International Business Negotiation".

第三项 Project 3

听译练习 Listening and Interpreting

A．Sentence Interpreting

Listen to the sentences and interpret them into Chinese.

1. We are greatly interested in investing in technology-intensive projects in your free trade zone.

2. We are fully aware that investment always involves high risks，but the chances of success are also great.

3. As a foreign investor，we should make better use of local manpower and resources to create a win-win situation.

4. We will give you an allowance for advertising to help you promote sales.

5. As our exclusive agent in this area，you are not allowed to sell similar products of our competitors.

B．Sentence Interpreting

Listen to the sentences and interpret them into English.

1. 外国投资者在中国投资基础设施建设可以享受极大的优惠待遇。

2. 我们城市在地方政府的大力支持下最大限度地扩大其吸收和利用外资的机会。

3. 我们与当地的经销商,批发商和零售商都有着长期的良好的业务关系。

4. 我们会尽一切努力使你们的产品打入亚洲的市场,并争取所有潜在的客户。

5. 作为你们的代理,我们还会处理售后服务以确保产品在市场上的良好声誉。

C．Dialogue Interpreting

Listen to the dialogue and interpret it into the target language.

A：We've found that your company is a local partner for global buyers.

B：是的。基本上来说,我们是国外采购商和地方厂家的联系人。

A：I see. How long have you been in this business?

B：差不多有八年了。我们与我们的供货商有着很好的关系。

A：So you think your suppliers can give us the best quote for the products we need?

B：如果你们能保证订货的量,并且发货后能及时付款的话,我想他们会的。

A：Fair enough. My understanding is that you deal with everything from samples to the finished products and final shipment on your end?

B：非常正确。我们的工程师还会代表你们公司去厂家检验质量。

A：Very good. But the packing must be up to our standard.

B：当然。厂家会完全按照你们的要求去做。

A：Then the commission you want to charge?

B：销售额的 5％。低了我们不做。

A：It seems a little high for us. But if that's the case, we don't cover travel expenses.

B：你们不用支付差旅费。但你们必须及时将佣金电汇到我们公司的账户上。

A：No problem. Well, we will come back next week with our agreement ready.

B：好的，到时见。

参考译文 Reference Version

对话口译 A：

A：刘先生，看得出你们在积极寻求外国直接投资。

B：Yes, indeed. We are accelerating our development pace, so we are quite interested in your project proposal for establishing a joint venture with us in Suzhou Industrial Park.

A：那很好。中国目前的投资环境确实不错。不过我们想了解一下外国投资者在你们这里投资可以享受哪些优惠政策呢？

B：Our local government is working hard to create a better environment for foreign investment, including large-scaled infrastructure construction. If foreign investors register their companies in the industrial park, they could enjoy the reduction of income tax or even tax exemption. Besides, joint ventures can also enjoy low-interest loan and even government-funded training programs.

A：这听上去很令人鼓舞。如果是这样的话，那我们对这个项目的投资更充满信心了。

B：Your investment will surely bring high economic return. How much do you intend to invest in this project?

A：我想我们准备在起步阶段投资 4 500 万美元。那么注册资本应该是多少？

B：That's a pleasant amount. As for the registered capital, it should make up at least 50％ of the total investment.

A：那么我们投资双方出资的比例应该是多少？对外商有没有投资下限？

B：It could be flexible. Usually, it is no less than 30％.

A：这对我们来说不成问题。其实我们愿意出资 60％，如果你方能负责提供工厂设施而我方则提供技术。

B：That's not a problem. As a matter of fact, we've already acquired a factory building.

A：太好了。那么，像我们这样的合资企业，它的期限多长？

B：We would suggest ten years. And the period can be prolonged if we both want to.

A：很好。看来目前一切都很顺利。不过，在签协议前还有很多事要处理。

B：Don't worry. Let's have a good drink and leave the details to our assistants.

对话口译 B：

A：胡先生，我们在找一家独家代理商在大中华地区推销我们公司的产品。据我们了解，你们公司在家具市场上做代理有着良好的声誉。

B：Yes，indeed. We've been in this business for fifteen years and mainly act as the agent for European furniture suppliers. Our sales now stand at 24. 5 million US dollars，much greater than our major competitors.

A：你们的销售额令我印象深刻。不过，我们最关心的是你们销售网络的情况。

B：Mr. Harrison，we've never stopped expanding our business. We've recently explored some new markets in northern China alongside of our existing markets in the east and the south.

A：哦，那挺不错。我们很乐意与你们这样有经验的代理商合作。

B：If you appoint us as your sole agent，we can increase your turnover by 50％ on the current basis.

A：这个数字听上去挺诱人的。那么，你们打算要多少佣金？

B：Normally，we charge a commission of 7％ on sales. But since you are our new partner，we'd like to make it 6％ plus ＄2,000 for monthly expenses.

A：6％听上去挺合理的，但是恐怕我们不能支付你们要求的月开支。而且我想知道你们每年能保证订多少货。

B：Then we can take a commission of 6％ plus some subsidy for sales promotion. If you think it's acceptable，we can guarantee an annual order of 1,000 pieces.

A：好吧，基于你们要订购的量，我们可以给你们一笔适当的费用用于宣传。

B：We can accept that. And in our case，how long will the term of your agent be?

A：初始阶段就一年吧。但合同可以续签。

B：I understand. When will we sign the contract if we both agree on the terms?

A：我想两天后我们可以签约。

B：Good. Let's take a break and have some coffee.

篇章口译 A：

　　世贸组织是一个促使贸易自由化的组织。它是政府间谈判贸易协定的论坛。// 世贸组织是政府间解决贸易争端、运行贸易准则体系的地方。// 世贸组织本质上是各国政府解决相互间面临贸易问题的一个场所。// 第一步是要谈判。世贸组织的性质是谈判，而世贸组织所做的一切都是谈判的结果。//

　　目前为止，世贸组织拥有一百六十多个成员国，占世界贸易的 90％。// 其中三十多个是谈判成员国。一切决定由所有成员国做出。//

　　当国家间面临贸易壁垒并希望降低这些壁垒时，谈判有助于贸易自由化。// 但是，世贸组织的作用不仅仅使贸易自由化，同时在某些情况下它的准则会支持现有的贸易壁垒——比如说为了保护消费者。// 世贸组织还帮助制造商和出口商了解国外市场是否对他们开放。// 世贸组织有助于创立一个强大而又繁荣的贸易体系。//

篇章口译 B：

China is working hard to improve its investment climate to attract more foreign investment. // China's current foreign direct investment (FDI) stands at US＄140 billion，but still is not sufficient. // Therefore, the Chinese government is taking proactive measures to encourage coastal cities and some major cities to take in more foreign investment. // The Chinese Government has approved 44,000 new foreign-invested projects. //

To date，foreign investment in China has extended from industry to finance, real estate，commerce，foreign trade and service. // According to the latest survey，there has been a rapid increase of European Union investment to China，but a moderate decrease of actual investment from the United States. // Southeast Asia still remains a major foreign investment source and the structure of investment has been enhanced. // Foreign investors are showing strong interest in investing in high-tech fields and research and development centers. // Also, investment in telecom equipment，computer，electronics and transportation equipment manufacturing has increased substantially. //

听译练习：

A：

1. 我们很有兴趣在你们的保税区投资技术密集型的项目。

2. 我们完全知道投资风险很高,但是成功的机会也很大。

3. 作为外国投资者,我们要很好地利用当地的人力和资源以创造双赢的局面。

4. 我们会给你们提供一笔广告津贴用作促销。

5. 作为我们在这个地区的独家代理,你们不可销售我们竞争厂家的产品。

B：

1. Foreign investors can enjoy great preferential treatment if they invest in infrastructure construction in China.

2. Our city is maximizing its opportunity of absorbing and utilizing foreign capital under the great support of the local government.

3. We have long-term good business relationship with local distributors，wholesalers and retailers.

4. We will do everything we can to help your products penetrate the Asian market and reach our potential customers.

5. As your agent, we will also deal with after-sales service to ensure the good reputation of the product.

C：

A：据我们了解,你们公司是全球采购商的地方合作伙伴。

B：Right. Basically, we act as a middleman between foreign buyers and local manufacturers.

A：明白了。你们做这一行有多长时间了?

B：Almost eight years. We have very good connections with our suppliers.

A：那么你觉得他们可以给我们需要的产品最合理的报价？

B：I think they will，if you can guarantee the quantity of your order and make the payment right after the shipment.

A：很合理。那么，我的理解是你们公司负责从样品到成品和发货。

B：Absolutely. And our engineers will go to the factory to check the quality on your behalf.

A：很好。但是包装必须符合我们的标准。

B：Sure. They will do exactly as you require.

A：那么，你们收取多少佣金？

B：5％ of the sales. We couldn't do less than that.

A：这个价有点高。如果是这样的话，我们不负责差旅费。

B：No，you don't have to. But we need you to wire the commission to our company account with no delay.

A：没问题。我们下星期再来你们公司，我们会准备好协议的。

B：Fine. See you then.

第

9

单元

旅游观光

Unit

9

Sightseeing

背景知识
Background Information

Tourism is the act of travel for predominantly recreational or leisure purposes, and also refers to the provision of services in support of this act. According to the World Tourism Organization, tourists are people who travel to and stay in places outside their usual environment for no more than one consecutive year for leisure, business and other purposes not related to the exercise of an activity remunerated from within the place visited. Tourism has become an extremely popular, global activity.

As a service industry, tourism has numerous tangible and intangible elements. Major tangible elements include transportation, accommodation, and other components of a hospitality industry. Major intangible elements relate to the purpose or motivation for becoming a tourist, such as rest, relaxation, the opportunity to meet new people and experience other cultures, or simply to do something different and have an adventure.

Tourism is vital for many countries, due to the income generated by the consumption of goods and services by tourists, the taxes levied on businesses in the tourism industry, and the opportunity for employment and economic advancement by working in the industry. For these reasons government agencies may sometimes promote a specific region as a tourist destination, and support the development of a tourism industry in that area.

The terms tourism and travel are sometimes used interchangeably. In this context travel has a similar definition to tourism, but implies a more purposeful journey. The terms tourism and tourist are sometimes used pejoratively to imply a shallow interest in the cultures or locations visited by tourists.

对话口译

Dialogue A

词汇预习 *Vocabulary Work*

Study the following words and phrases and translate them into the target language.

book a hotel	旅行社	itinerary	登记入住
海洋公园	浅水湾	新界	港岛
舢板	点心	豪华套房	升级

口译实践 *Text Interpreting*

Listen to the following dialogue and interpret it into the target language.

A：您好,我们有各种路线,不知道您想去什么地方玩?

B：I am going to Hong Kong. I know that it has grown from what was a simple fishing village into the world's fourth largest banking and financial center and eleventh largest trading economy. It must be a wonder to see.

A：我同意您的看法。香港是个日益繁荣、充满活力的商业中心。在这里,你既能享受到现代生活带来的愉悦,又有不计其数的东西勾起对历史和过去的回忆。您准备在那里待多久?

B：I hope to stay there for five days. Can you recommend me a best route and help me book a better hotel?

A：当然可以。明天正好有一个团要前往香港,他们将在位于市中心的喜来登大酒店住宿。您觉得可以吗?

B：That's good! Sheraton should be pretty good. But what's the itinerary like?

A：第一天登记入住后,主要是休息。第二和第三天,您将参观香港著名的海洋公园,欣赏浅水湾美景,从太平山顶俯瞰维多利亚港,游览新界。最后两天自由活动。

B：That sounds good! Hong Kong is known as a "shopping paradise". Do we have time to enjoy shopping there?

A：您有兴趣的话,可以在最后两天自行前往。我想您会在香港的中心——港岛——买到很多好东西,这里购物、美食、娱乐和户外活动应有尽有。

B：Do we have many activities at night?

A：没有。晚上您可以尽情自由活动,那里的夜晚总有一些东西能迷住您:乘游轮夜游海港, 乘舢板,乘高速船摆渡,逛逛充满东方风情的市场,尝尝大排档里的美味或是正宗粤菜馆 里的茶和点心,这些只是一部分。

B：Ha! Ha! That's what I expect. I know Hong Kong won't let me down. May I know how much this trip costs?

A：一个人4800元。如果您想升级为豪华套房的话,每晚再加300元。

B：Please upgrade to a suite. Here's the money.

A：谢谢。不过请您明天一定要提前10分钟到此集合,我们的导游将会向各位解说日程安排。车子八点出发去机场,逾时不候。

B：I will be on time. Thank you!

对话口译

Dialogue B

词汇预习 Vocabulary Work

Study the following words and phrases and translate them into the target language.

靠过道座位	靠右窗的座位	front cabin	emergency exit
conveyor belt	overweight	luggage claim	Baggage Claim Area
terminal	登机口	departure	duty-free shop

译实践 Text Interpreting

Listen to the following dialogue and interpret it into the target language.

A：你好,我想确认机位,总共两位。

B：Your passport and tickets, please. Do you have any seat preference?

A：请把我们座位排在一起。最好有一个靠过道,或者靠右边的窗户也可以。

B：Just a moment please... We have two second-row aisle seats in the front cabin near the emergency exit. Is it all right with you?

A：很好。我不喜欢第一排,因为不能把包放在前排的座位下。

B：Please put your luggage on the conveyor belt. Bring with you the valuables. How many pieces altogether? Is there anything fragile in it?

A：一共三件。没有什么易碎品。我们自己打包的,超重了吗?

B：Let me see... I'm sorry but you're five kilograms overweight. Would you like to pay extra or do you have someone else taking your luggage?

A：我可以拿出一些东西放在手提行李里吗？

B：Sure. Your luggage claim is attached to the back of your tickets. You will be able to retrieve your checked luggage from the Baggage Claim Area of the airport when you get off. The flight number，the flight's origination city and the baggage carousel number will be posted on a terminal screen. Anything else I can help?

A：非常感谢，但是现在我们应该去哪个登机口呢？

B：Gate No. 7 on the second floor. You can go up the escalator on the left and turn right. Please be there thirty minutes before departure.

A：飞机准时吗？

B：I'm sorry. The departure will be delayed for an hour because of heavy fog still not clearing up. But you can enjoy a cup of coffee or shop around. I bet you will find some interesting things in our duty-free shops.

A：谢谢你的建议。我太太是购物狂。她不会觉得无聊的。再见。

B：Bye. Enjoy yourself.

篇章口译(英译汉)

Passage A (E-C)

 Vocabulary Work

Study the following words and phrases and translate them into Chinese.

folk music	vibrant	fuse	genre
mainstream	fabulous	busker	reveler
harp	emblem	medieval times	band
impromptu			

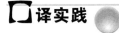 *Text Interpreting*

Listen to the English passage and interpret it into Chinese at the end of each segment.

　　Irish music is a folk music which has remained vibrant throughout the 20th century，when many other traditional forms worldwide lost popularity to pop music. // In spite of its well-developed connection to music influences from Britain and the United States，Irish music has kept many of its traditional aspects. // It has occasionally also been modernized，however，and fused with rock and roll，punk rock and other genres. // Some of these fusion artists have attained mainstream success，at home and abroad. //

Whether you want to walk around an outdoor field，or go to a spot of jazz in a fabulous club，music is at the heart of social life in Ireland. // Buskers line the streets，festivals set small towns and villages ablaze and traditional music sessions entertain revelers in pubs across the country. //

Unique and distinctive，the harp holds a special place in Irish musical life and has come to symbolize the harmony of people and music in Ireland. // It's the earliest musical instrument mentioned in Irish literature and has been used as an official emblem for Ireland since medieval times. // Today，it's on Irish passports and stamps. // Irish massive musical successes include some bands and artists you may have heard of：U2，Enya，Westlife and so on. // Festivals are a major part of Irish cultural life and impromptu traditional sessions have become the stuff of legend. //

篇章口译（汉译英）

Passage B (C-E)

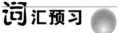 **Vocabulary Work**

Study the following words and phrases and translate them into English.

布达拉宫	统治时期	修复	梁柱
佛像	壁画	经文	联合国教科文组织
世界文化遗产			

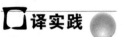 **Text Interpreting**

Listen to the Chinese passage and interpret it into English at the end of each segment.

坐落在拉萨市中心的布达拉宫，占地 41 公顷，是 7 世纪松赞干布统治时期建造的。// 它最初是第 33 任赞普松赞干布为迎娶唐朝文成公主而兴建的。// 它由白宫和红宫近一万间房间组成，是历代达赖喇嘛居住和处理政务的地方。// 最初的宫殿已被毁坏，今天看到的是后来重建而成的。// 白宫是五世达赖于三百多年前修建的，而中央的红宫则是由五世达赖的追随者后来建造的。// 这座宫殿共 13 层,有一万多根梁柱。// 这座城堡式的宫殿是座宝藏,内有许多佛像、壁画、经文和珍宝。// 布达拉宫是西藏文化的宝贵遗产,现已被普遍认为是西藏的象征,被联合国教科文组织列为世界文化遗产。//

口译讲评

Notes on the Text

Dialogue A

1. Hong Kong is a thriving and vibrant commercial center where you can find the delights of modern living alongside an abundance of reminders of its historic past. 这一句充分显示了英语"形合"的特点,delight,modern living,reminders 等名词化的手法使句子十分精练,涵盖了很多内容。在口译时,既要把内容充分译出,又要尽量保持原有的语言美。

2. ... the fantastic viewpoint of Victoria Peak:这里指的是维多利亚港的夜景。从太平山顶俯瞰时为最美,所以得名,在口译时将此意译出为佳。

3. ... tasting delicacies at Dai Pai Dong, or tea and dim sum in a typical Cantonese restaurant. 在香港很多东西的名称采用了粤语的音译,时间久了也就固定了下来。

4. 如果您想升级为豪华套房的话。"豪华套房"译为 deluxe suite。常见的宾馆客房的翻译有几种:deluxe room (豪华房);executive suite(行政套房);grand deluxe suite(超级豪华套房);twin beds room(标间);king bed room(大床房);balcony room(有阳台的房间)等。

5. 车子八点出发去机场,逾时不候。The bus will leave right at 8 for the airport and will not wait for latecomers. 此处对逾时不候做了灵活处理,两个动作共享同一个主语,保证了句子的连贯。

Dialogue B

1. Do you have any seat preference? 是询问顾客选择座位时的偏好,在电影院、音乐厅、剧院售票处等,这样的问句也同样适用。口译时可以按照汉语的习惯译为:你喜欢什么样的座位?

2. Bring with you the valuables. the valuables 是指贵重物品,最好随身携带,例如 hand carry the valuables/put the valuables in carry-on luggage。

3. luggage claim 是行李的存根,是提取行李的凭证。如果发生行李丢失的情况,可以凭此存根获得赔偿。"提取行李"可以译为 claim luggage or retrieve luggage。

4. 我太太是购物狂。My wife is a shopaholic. 可按照词缀法译出 shopaholic 一词。-aholic 和-oholic 两个词缀泛指对某件事过于痴迷的人。例如:bookaholic 爱书成癖者;cashaholic 爱财成癖者;chocoholic 吃巧克力上瘾者;workaholic 工作狂等。

Passage A

1. Irish music is a folk music which has remained vibrant throughout the 20th century, when many other traditional forms worldwide lost popularity to pop music. 这里有几处需要词性转译，即根据上下文需要，将形容词转译为名词，将名词转译为动词。vibrant 转译为"勃勃生气"；popularity 转译为"受到青睐"。

2. Some of these fusion artists have attained mainstream success, at home and abroad. fusion artist 虽然非常流行，但对应的中文翻译却还无定论，"混搭艺术家"的说法还只停留在时下年轻人的口中，所以这里采取了意译，即"致力于音乐融合的艺术家"。

3. ... festivals set small towns and villages ablaze. 节日让小型城镇和村庄都充满了激情。set...ablaze 这里是指"使……情绪激动或者使气氛达到高潮"之意。又如：He is ablaze with enthusiasm. 他热情高涨。

4. U2、西城男孩都是爱尔兰知名的乐队，影响深远；恩雅是爱尔兰著名女歌手，她的歌声被称为"天籁之音"。

5. ... impromptu traditional sessions have become the stuff of legend. 即兴演出的传统音乐部分也成了节日上重要的传统项目。这里 stuff of legend 译为传统项目。

Passage B

1. 它最初是第 33 任赞普松赞干布为迎娶唐朝文成公主而兴建的。It was built to honor the marriage of the 33rd King to Princess Wen Cheng of the Tang Dynasty. "赞普"是对吐蕃之王的称呼，这里译为 King。此处使用了 honor 一词，与 in honor of 意思相同，有"庆祝"之意，又如：The Foundation is holding a dinner at the Museum of American Art in honor of the opening of their new show. 基金会在美国艺术博物馆举办晚宴庆祝新展览的开幕。

2. 最初的宫殿已被毁坏，今天看到的是后来重建而成的。"重建"可以译为 rebuild, reconstruct, renovate, restore 等，这里用 restore 或者 renovate 有"恢复原样"的意思，更为合适。

3. 这座城堡式的宫殿是座宝藏，内有许多佛像、壁画、经文和珍宝。Housed in this castle-like palace are a wealth of Buddhist statues, murals, religious scriptures. 这里用了倒装，在词序上与中文原句保持了一致，有利于口译者的快速思维。a wealth of 意思是 a large number of，是较为正式的用法。

4. 联合国教科文组织（UNESCO）1946 年 11 月正式成立，同年 12 月成为联合国的一个专门机构。总部设在法国巴黎。其宗旨是通过教育、科学和文化促进各国间合作，对和平和安全做出贡献。1972 年，联合国教科文组织在巴黎通过了《保护世界文化和自然遗产公约》，成立联合国教科文组织世界遗产委员会，其宗旨在于促进各国和各国人民之间的合作，为合理保护和恢复全人类共同的遗产做出积极的贡献。中国自 1985 年 12 月 12 日加入《公约》的缔约国行列以来，截至 2021 年，经联合国教科文组织审核被批准列入《世界遗产名录》的中国的世界遗产共有 56 项，数量上位居第二，仅次于意大利。

相关词语 *Relevant Words and Expressions*

班机号 flight number
标签 tag
度假胜地 holiday resort
风景区 scenic spot
机长 captain
靠窗座位 window seat
领取行李 luggage claim
签证 visa
行李托运 check luggage

避暑胜地 summer resort
乘务员 flight attendant
兑换率 exchange rate
海关 customs
景点 place of interest
礼品店 gift shop
蜜月度假胜地 honeymoon resort
行李车 luggage cart
自然景观 natural scenery/attraction

名胜古迹 places of historical interest/relics and scenic beauty
人文景观 places of historic figures and cultural heritage
野生动物保护区 wildlife conservation area

口译技能 *Interpreting Skills*

记忆理解（2）

在上一讲中,我们知道"记忆"可分为"长时记忆"和"短时记忆"两种,而在口译过程中,短时记忆则是译员最为仰赖的。虽然有些人天生就"记性好",可以在短时间内记住比别人都多的信息,但后天若训练得法,也是可以有效提高短时记忆的。改善短时记忆最关键的一个环节就是要"积极地听",也就是说要做一个 active listener,同时将理解和记忆紧密地结合在一起。理解是记忆的前提与保证,记忆是理解的辅助与提高,二者相辅相成。

口译过程粗略地可以分为两个阶段:一个是记忆理解阶段,另一个是表达阶段。在记忆理解阶段,主要解决的是"听什么""如何理解"以及"如何记住理解内容"的问题。记忆和理解是齐肩并进的,在听源语的时候,绝对不能专注于每个单独的单词,而是要有意识地将句子划分为若干意群来听,譬如下面的例子。

例1:

In survey after survey, / traditional relationships / among parents, children, and siblings / are identical as the most important aspect of life. // Families are seen as more important / than work, recreation, friendships, or status. // Researchers have been asking Americans / about their families / for over half a century, / and Americans have always replied that / the family takes priority / over everything else in their lives. //

一些经验丰富的译员习惯于一边听发言人的讲话一边默默地计数,一个意群计一个数,这样听完一段话后对源语的大致意思就心中有数了。就像上面这个例子,按照意群逐个听完后，既做到了理解，也做到了记忆，于是译文就可以很自然地"流"出来了：

一次又一次的调查表明，/ 父母关系、子女关系、兄弟姐妹关系等 / 这些传统关系 / 还是生活的重要方面。// 家庭的重要性 / 胜过工作、娱乐、友谊和地位。// 研究人员询问 / 美国人的家庭观念 / 询问了半个世纪，/ 而美国人总是这样回答，/ 说他们看重家庭 / 胜过生活中的一切。//

其实无论是听句子、段落抑或是文章，译员首先需要弄明白其主语、谓语、宾语和状语，即什么人、什么事、什么地方和什么时间。我们来看这样一段有趣的英文：

I have six honest serving men.

They taught me all I knew.

Their names were what and where and when,

And why, and how, and who.

归根结底，记忆理解阶段的本质就是要正确地找出这 six honest serving men，为下一阶段，即表达阶段奠定好基础。

 译练习 *Enhancement Practice*

第一项 Project 1

听力复述 Retelling

Listen to the following passages once and then reproduce them in the same language at the end of each segment.

English Passage：

Traveling involves so much stress! // Preparation is especially hard—trying to arrange the transportation, accommodation, and time off from work. // Packing isn't easy. How can you possibly know everything you may or may not need in a place that's largely unknown to you? // Assuming you ever reach your destination, you have to communicate with people who often don't speak your language and you have to navigate your way around an area you have no idea about. // How are you supposed to relax under such conditions? // And all that money you're spending! For what? I don't get it at all. //

Chinese Passage：

鼓浪屿与厦门一水相隔，山上怪石嶙峋，海风扑面，涛声和雷声交织，因而得名。// 鼓浪屿终年绿树成荫，被誉为"海上花园"。这里没有车辆，岛上全靠步行。// 鼓浪屿被称为"万国建筑博览"，在弹丸之地的小岛上荟萃了上千座风格各异、中西合璧的中外建筑。// 这里有我国传统的飞檐翘角的庙宇，有闽南风格的院落平房，// 有被称为"小白宫"的八卦楼，有小巧玲珑的日式房舍，也有 19 世纪欧陆风格的西方领事馆等等。//

第二项 Project 2

主题讨论 Discussion

Hold a 5-minute discussion with your partners on the topic "Why People Love Traveling".

第三项 Project 3

听译练习 Listening and Interpreting

A. Sentence Interpreting

Listen to the sentences and interpret them into Chinese.

1. Sweden is a unique country that occupies a long piece of land stretching from north to south.

2. Familiarize yourself with local laws and customs of the countries to which you are traveling，since in a foreign country you are subject to its laws.

3. The best season for viewing the northern lights in Greenland is between mid-August and late March when the nights are long and the air is clear.

4. The shows are every 15 minutes until about midnight，and last maybe 2-3 minutes depending on what song they are using.

5. The dog sledding tours vary from short two-hour trips to ones that last several days, and a rough standard for prices is $ 700 for a two-hour tour.

B. Sentence Interpreting

Listen to the sentences and interpret them into English.

1. 不要把无人看管的行李留在公共场所。

2. 如果你主动融入当地人中,你会对这个国家和人民更多些了解。

3. 酒店的屋顶、墙壁、床和餐桌都用冰制作,因此只有冬季才开张营业。

4. 乘船黄浦江游览往返共 60 公里,途经港口城市上海的一些标志性建筑。

5. 不论你对什么感兴趣,文化遗迹或是自然风光,或是两者的结合,你都能在中国找到意外的惊喜。

C. Dialogue Interpreting

Listen to the dialogue and interpret it into the target language.

A：May I see your passport?

B：在这里。

A：What's the purpose of your visit?

B：观光旅游。

A：How long are you staying? Do you have a return ticket?

B：10 天。我 28 号返回,这是我的回程票。

A：Good. Do you have anything to declare?

B：没有。我没带新鲜水果、蔬菜、肉类和腌制品。

A：That's fine. Please open your luggage.

B：好的。

A：What's in this box?

B：这是一些点心,有太阳饼什么的。

A：Could you please step over to the counter on the right and open the box for inspection?

B：好的。

A：And what is this?

B：蛋黄酥。

A：Egg yolk? I'm sorry but products with egg yolk are banned from entry. We have to confiscate them.

B：唉! 对不起,你们留着吧。

参考译文 Reference Version

对话口译 A:

A：How do you do! We have all kinds of routes. What kinds of places would you like to visit?

B：我想去香港。我知道香港是从一个普通的小渔村发展起来的,现在已成为了世界第四大银行金融中心,拥有世界排名第十一的贸易经济。那里太神奇了,值得一看。

A：I agree. Hong Kong is a thriving and vibrant commercial center where you can find the delights of modern living alongside an abundance of reminders of its historic past. How long do you plan to stay there?

B：我想在那里待五天。你能推荐最佳路线给我吗? 还有请帮我安排好一点的酒店。

A：Sure. We happen to have a group leaving for Hong Kong tomorrow. They will stay in Sheraton Hotel which is right downtown. Would that work?

B：好啊! 喜来登挺好的,只是日程怎么安排呢?

A：On the first day, after you check in, you'll have a good rest. On the second and third day, you'll be going to visit the better known highlights like the stunning Ocean Park, the fantastic viewpoint of Victoria Peak, the beautiful Repulse Bay and New Territories. The last two days are free.

B：听起来不错! 香港被称为"购物天堂",我们有时间尽情购物吗?

A：If you like, you can go on your own during the last two days. I guess you'll find nice things in its heart—Hong Kong Island, which has all the shopping, gourmet, entertainment and outdoor activities.

B：晚上有很多活动吗?

A：No, you will enjoy free time at night. There will always be something to enchant you at night: taking a night time harbor cruise, a trip in a sampan, high speed ferry, shopping in an oriental market, tasting delicacies at Dai Pai Dong, or tea and dim sum in a typical

Cantonese restaurant，to name just a few.

B：哈哈！这正是我所期望的。我知道香港不会让我失望的。请问这一路线多少钱？

A：Forty eight hundred per person. If you want to upgrade to a deluxe suite，you only pay 300 *yuan* extra per night.

B：请升级一下。给你钱。

A：Thank you! Please be sure to meet here ten minutes earlier tomorrow. Our guide will go through the detailed itinerary with you. The bus will leave right at 8 for the airport and will not wait for latecomers.

B：我一定按时，谢谢。

对话口译 B：

A：Hi! I want to check in for two，please.

B：请出示护照和机票。你喜欢什么样的座位？

A：Please put us together. It's better to have one aisle seat，or one right-side window seat.

B：请稍等……前舱第二排靠近安全门的地方有靠过道的座位，可以吗？

A：Yes，please. I don't like the first row since you can't stow your bag under the seat in front of you.

B：请把你们的行李放到传送带上来。贵重物品随身携带。一共有几件行李？内有易碎物品吗？

A：Three pieces total. We packed them ourselves but we haven't packed any fragile items in. Are we overweight?

B：我看看……对不起，你们的行李超重 5 公斤。你们是补差额，还是有其他人帮你们拿？

A：Can I take something out and hand carry?

B：当然可以，你们的行李存根贴在机票后。下飞机后，您可以在机场行李提领区取回您托运的行李。候机楼屏幕上会显示航班号码、起飞的城市以及行李传送带号码。还有什么需要我帮忙的吗？

A：Thanks a lot，but which boarding gate should we go to?

B：七号登机口，在二层。你们从左边的扶梯上去，然后右转。请在起飞前 30 分钟到那里。

A：Is the plane on time?

B：非常抱歉。因为浓雾未散，飞机将延后一小时起飞。您可以喝杯咖啡，或者到我们的免税店逛逛，我相信您一定会找到一些有趣的东西。

A：Thank you for your advice. My wife is a shopaholic. She won't be bored. Bye bye.

B：再见。祝你们愉快。

篇章口译 A：

　　当世界上其他地方的传统音乐形式不如流行音乐受青睐时，爱尔兰的民族音乐却在整个 20 世纪都保持着勃勃生气。// 虽然受到与其息息相关的英美音乐的影响，它仍然保持了许多传统元素。// 但是，偶尔它也会被现代化，与摇滚、朋克摇滚或其他流派相融合。//

一些致力于音乐融合的艺术家蜚声海内外,取得了巨大的成功。//

无论你想到户外走走,还是去一个时尚酒吧欣赏爵士乐,音乐都是爱尔兰社交生活的中心。// 街头艺人为街道增添了气氛,节日让小型城镇和村庄都充满了激情,传统音乐更是让全国的酒吧都充满了魅力。//

独特而有特色的竖琴在爱尔兰乐器中占有特殊地位,同时也象征了爱尔兰人民和音乐的和谐。// 它是爱尔兰文学中提到的最早的乐器,而且自中世纪起便成了爱尔兰的正式象征标志。// 现在爱尔兰的护照和印章上都印有竖琴。// 爱尔兰的音乐成就还体现在其众多著名的音乐组合和音乐人上,比如 U2、恩雅、西城男孩等。// 节日是爱尔兰人文化生活的主要部分,而即兴演出的传统音乐部分也成了节日上重要的传统项目。//

篇章口译 B:

The Potala Palace in downtown Lhasa is a 41-hectare complex which came under construction during Songtsan Gambo's 7th-century reign. // It was built to honor the marriage of the 33rd King to Princess Wen Cheng of the Tang Dynasty. // Consisting of White Palace and Red Palace, with nearly 10,000 rooms, it was where the Dalai Lamas lived and handled political affairs. // The original palace was damaged but restored to the way it looks today. // The white buildings were built more than 300 years ago by the 5th Dalai Lama and the central, red building was built by the disciples of the 5th Dalai Lama. // The palace is 13 stories and has over ten thousand pillars. // Housed in this castle-like palace are a wealth of Buddhist statues, murals, religious scriptures, and treasures. // As a precious legacy of Tibetan culture, the Potala Palace is now the most widely recognized symbol of Tibet. It is a UNESCO-endorsed world cultural heritage site. //

听译练习:

A:

1. 瑞典地形南北狭长,独一无二。
2. 到了国外,你就必须遵守当地法律,因此去旅游前,你要熟悉当地的法律和风俗。
3. 格陵兰观赏北极光的最佳时间是 8 月中旬至 3 月下旬。这时,天空晴朗,夜晚也相对较长。
4. 表演每 15 分钟一次,直到午夜,因选用歌曲不同,每次表演时间为 2 到 3 分钟不等。
5. 狗拉雪橇之旅短则两个小时,长的可以持续几天,价格大概在两小时 700 美金左右。

B:

1. Do not leave your luggage unattended in public areas.
2. As long as you consciously blend yourself into local people, you will get further understanding of the country and its people.
3. A hotel limited to wintertime with its roof, walls, beds and restaurant tables all made of ice.
4. A cruise on the Huangpu River involves a 60-km-long round trip, which runs past some of the major landmarks of Shanghai as a port city.

5. No matter what you are interested in，whether it is cultural relics，natural attractions or the combinations of both，in China you will find an unexpectedly pleasant surprise.

C：

A：请出示你的护照？

B：Here you are.

A：你这次访问的目的是什么？

B：Sightseeing.

A：你会停留多久？你有回程票吗？

B：10 days. I will return on 28th and this is the ticket.

A：好的。你有需要申报的物品吗？

B：No，I don't have fresh fruits，vegetables，meat and salted preserves here.

A：那就好。请你打开行李。

B：Here you go.

A：这个盒子里是什么？

B：Some snacks like sun pastry.

A：麻烦请到右边的柜台，打开让工作人员检查。

B：Sure.

A：这是什么？

B：Egg yolk shortbread.

A：蛋黄？很抱歉，含有蛋黄类的食品不准携带入境，我们必须没收。

B：Alas! I'm sorry. You keep them.

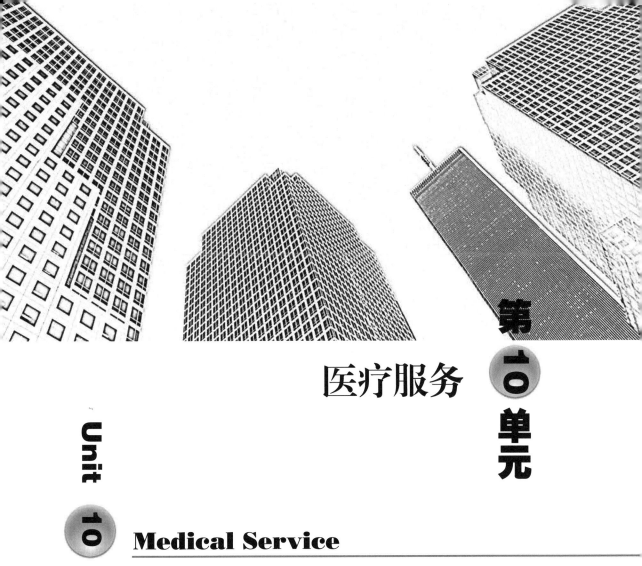

医疗服务

Medical Service

背景知识
Background Information

Medical science refers both to an area of science and a group of professions. It is, in the broadest sense of the term, the science and practice of the prevention and cure of human diseases, and other aliments of the human body or mind. However, it is often used only to refer to those matters dealt with by physicians and surgeons, excluding such areas as dentistry and clinical psychology.

Medical science usually contains two aspects: as both an area of knowledge and as an application of that knowledge. It comprises various specialized sub-branches, such as cardiology, neurology, or other fields such as sports medicine, research or public health.

Medical science, in the modern period, is the mainstream scientific tradition which developed in the Western world since the early Renaissance. Many other traditions of health care are still practiced throughout the world; most of these are separate from Western medicine, which is also called biomedicine, allopathic medicine or the Hippocratic tradition. The most highly developed of these are traditional Chinese medicine, including Traditional Tibetan medicine, and the traditions of India and Sri Lanka. Various non-mainstream traditions of health care have also developed in the Western world.

Human societies have had various different systems of health care practice since at least the beginning of recorded history. The earliest type of medicine in most cultures was the use of plants and animal parts.

Since the 19th century, only those with a medical degree have been considered worthy to practice medicine. Clinicians, licensed professionals who deal with patients, can be physicians, physical therapists, physician assistants, nurses or others. The medical profession is the social and occupational structure of the group of people formally trained and authorized to apply medical knowledge. Many countries and legal jurisdictions have legal limitations on who may practice medicine.

对话口译

Dialogue A

 词汇预习 *Vocabulary Work*

Study the following words and phrases and translate them into the target language.

sore throat	vomit	发肿	油腻的
燕麦粥	药方	药丸	insect bite

 口译实践 *Text Interpreting*

Listen to the following dialogue and interpret it into the target language.

A：请进来，坐下。您叫什么名字？您哪儿不舒服？

B：My name is Allen James. I have a headache and a sore throat and my chest hurts. In fact I was in aches and pains all over. During the night my stomach began to ache and I felt like vomiting. I could get no sleep at all.

A：我听听您的胸。做深呼吸。这种情况有多久了？您吃过什么药了吗？

B：Two or three days now. No，I haven't taken any. Has the pain in chest anything to do with the upset stomach?

A：不，两者没有关系。张开嘴，让我瞧瞧您的舌头。我看到您喉咙发红且明显发肿。我再来给您量量体温。胃还痛吗？

B：It' a little better than this morning，but it still aches.

A：您在发高烧，摄氏 39 度。我想您是得了流感。现在正流行流感呐。胃没有什么大问题，您不必担心。要是您觉得病情加重了，就请来门诊。

B：What do you think I ought to do? Will it take long to recover?

A：拿这张药方去配药，然后马上上床睡觉。您需要卧床几天。还有我必须提醒您，暂时不要吃油腻的食物，两三天内吃容易消化的食物，如燕麦粥和牛奶。这以后您想吃什么就吃什么。不过，短期内即使想吃也不要吃太多。

B：Excuse me，I'd like to have this prescription filled.

C：请等一等。我马上就给您配药。对不起，这张处方上的药品已经用完了。您是否愿意购买其他牌子的同类药品呢？它们是同一种药，质量相同，但价格却低得多。

B：OK. I'll take this brand. How often am I supposed to take it?

C：饭前半小时服这种药丸，一天三次。

B：By the way, what do you suggest for insect bites?

C：试试这种药吧，这是新产品，十分有效。每日涂抹四次。

B：OK. I see. Thank you for your help.

对话口译

Dialogue B

词汇预习　Vocabulary Work

Study the following words and phrases and translate them into the target language.

骨科医生	elbow	rib	肱骨
骨折	石膏托	愈合	口服药
弹力绷带			

译实践　Text Interpreting

Listen to the following dialogue and interpret it into the target language.

A：你好，我是骨科医生。你哪里不舒服？

B：Well, I was knocked to the ground by a car about an hour ago, and when I got up, my left arm and elbow were grazed and injured. And now, I have a pain in my ribs.

A：请躺在这里，尽量放松。让我检查一下吧。你哪儿疼啊？请你指出最疼的部位。你用过任何止痛药吗？

B：It's hard to say. It hurts all over. I was sent here directly without taking any painkillers.

A：我按这儿，你疼不疼？

B：Ouch! The pain is very bad when you press here. Have I broken my elbow?

A：你的肘部好像骨折了。护士将送你去照一张 X 光片。片子照好之后，马上拿过来让我看看。

B：OK. See you later.

（Ten minutes later, the patient brings back the X-ray plates.）

B：Here's my X-rays. Do you think it is serious, Doctor?

A：X 光片显示肱骨下段骨折。我们在你肘部和肩膀上打个"U"型石膏托。

B：How long will I have to have it? Is there anything else I should do?

A：可能要两个月时间。你最好将患肘放在高于心脏的部位上,经常活动你的指关节。彻底恢复需要一段很长的时间。你需要定期来门诊检查。

B：Should I take some medicine，doctor?

A：是这样,我会给你开一些草药,这样你的伤口会愈合得快一点。另外,你还需要服用一些口服药。这是药方。待会儿你拿到药房去配药。请按说明服药。

B：I'm afraid I've sprained my left ankle. It's swollen and very painful and I would like you to see if it's all right.

A：别紧张,只是扭伤,护士会为你缠上弹力绷带。每天在热水和冷水中交替三次,疼肿就会消失。照我的建议去做,我确信你会好的。

篇章口译(英译汉)

Passage A (E-C)

 Vocabulary Work

Study the following words and phrases and translate them into Chinese.

pharmacist	mild painkiller	nasal decongestant	indigestion
nausea	diarrhea	office call	emergency room treatment
deposit			

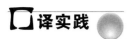 *Text Interpreting*

Listen to the English passage and interpret it into Chinese at the end of each segment.

Getting ill away from home is a very frightening thought，but it's something you can sometimes be prepared for. // Unless you are planning to immigrate into Britain, check with your country's own health services or your health insurance agency before you leave home. // People who take medication regularly should bring enough with them for their entire stay. //

In Britain pharmacists in one town will not fill prescriptions from other towns, nor those from other countries. // If you run out of medicine while you are in Britain, you'll have to be examined by a doctor and get a new prescription. // Some medication—such as aspirin and other mild painkillers，cold medicines and nasal decongestants, vitamins, cough syrups and sore throat tablets, as well as medication for indigestion, nausea and diarrhea—is available without a prescription. // You can even get these drugs over the counter at convenience stores or supermarkets. //

If you need a doctor for your illness, you should be prepared to pay for office calls, emergency room treatment and even hospital stays, as most doctors and hospitals will want you to pay when you are treated. // Hospitals usually require a deposit of money or the name of someone who will promise to pay in case you don't. // In any case, make arrangements with your health or travel insurance company before you leave, or take some extra money with you in case of an emergency. //

篇章口译(汉译英)

Passage B (C-E)

词汇预习 *Vocabulary Work*

Study the following words and phrases and translate them into English.

传染病	寄生物质	光学显微镜	绦虫
传播(疾病)	传染源	肺结核	天花
麻疹	疟疾		

译实践 *Text Interpreting*

Listen to the Chinese passage and interpret it into English at the end of each segment.

引起传染病的寄生物质在体积上大小各异,相差很远。// 像病毒这样的寄生物质小到在光学显微镜下也难以看到。但其他一些寄生物质,比如绦虫却有一米长。//

传染病的防治靠的是对它们传播途径的了解。主要有三种控制疾病的途径。//

首先,消灭传染源。比如,发现和治愈所有肺结核病人可防止肺结核的传播,隔离所有天花病人可防止天花的传播。//

其次,消除疾病的传播媒介。比如,消除一个地区的所有蚊子就使疟疾失去了传播媒介。//

此外,清洁卫生的食物和水供应以及对苍蝇的控制都有利于防止疾病传播。//

再者,要注意对个体和人群的保护。采用免疫法对付天花、麻疹等传染病很有效。// 要用药物防病。使用一定的硬件设施,比如蚊帐可以使人们免受蚊蝇的侵害,从而防止疟疾。//

口译讲评

Notes on the Text

Dialogue A

1. 您哪儿不舒服？这一句有多种英语译文，如：What's your complaint? What is the trouble with you? Is there anything wrong? 等。

2. have a sore throat. 可译为"喉咙发炎"，而 inflamed eyes, a nose inflamed by an infection 则分别可译为红肿的眼睛，发炎而红肿的鼻子。

3. the upset stomach. 可译为肠胃不适或反胃。

4. 开处方。可译为 give/write out a prescription，配药可译为 fill/make up/compound a prescription。在医院看病，一般由医生开处方，药剂师配药。

5. 提醒某人不要做某事。通常译为 warn somebody against something。

Dialogue B

1. graze. 可译为擦破皮，如 graze one's arm or leg。其他描述受伤的动词包括 twist（扭伤腕部等）、sprain（扭伤，尤指腕和踝）、dislocate（脱臼）、fracture（骨折）、burn（烧伤）等。

2. 照一张 X 光片。可译为 go to the X-ray Department 或者 take an X-ray。

3. 你最好将患肘放在高于心脏的部位上。这句话意思为"你最好让患肘保持在高于心脏的部位上"，因此可译为 You'd better keep your elbow higher than your heart。

Passage A

1. 英国的国民健保制度（National Health Service，简称 NHS）为具有社会福利性质的公益制度。自第二次世界大战后，50 年代便开始实施，迄今已有七十年之久。目前由 NHS 负担的费用大约包括：家庭医师的诊疗费、住院医疗费（但部分住院费用与项目仍需自费）、产前检查与生产医护费用等。由于英国实行诊断与配药分开的医药制度，在英国只有很偏远没有药房的地方才会允许医生配药。在就诊后，可持医师所开处方至药店买药，除了 16 岁以下儿童、19 岁以下全日制学生、老人、残障人士或孕（产）妇已获医药免费证明外，须自行负担药费。

2. 在英国一般的药可以在药房或超市买到。有些药品不能自己随便买，一定要有医生签了名的处方，才能到药房买。

3. You can even get these drugs over the counter at convenience stores or supermarkets. over the counter 是指无须处方（可直接购买）。

4. If you need a doctor for your illness, you should be prepared to pay for office calls, emergency room treatment and even hospital stays. 这里 office calls, emergency room treatment 和 hospital stays 都属于需要医生治疗的情况，因此翻译时可灵活地将其前置，

可译为：如果你需要医生给你看病，或门诊，或急诊，或住院，你都要做好付费的准备。

Passage B

1. 常见的传染病还包括 AIDS / HIV（艾滋病）、chickenpox（水痘）、influenza（流感）、mumps（腮腺炎）、rabies（狂犬病）、scarlet fever（猩红热）等。

2. 体积上大小各异，相差很远。其实就是指体积相差很大，口译时可精练地译为 vary greatly in size。

3. 发现和治愈所有肺结核病人。这句中"病人"可以用可数名词 case（患者、病例）来表达，另如"一位伤寒患者"可译为 a case of typhoid。

4. 要注意对个体和人群的保护。实质是指保护个体和人群，可译为 protect individuals and groups。在口译时有时可运用意译法，在译文中删去不符合译出语思维习惯和表达方式的词以避免译文累赘。

5. 硬件设施。不必按照字面意思逐字译为 hardware facilities，而可直接译成 facilities。

 相关词语 **Relevant Words and Expressions**

病床 hospital bed	病房 ward
挂号处 registration office	观察室 observation ward
候诊室 waiting room	护理部 nursing department
急诊病人 emergency case	急诊室 emergency room
门诊病人 out-patient	门诊部 out-patient department
内科 medical department	实习医生 intern, interne
手术室 operation room	外科 surgical department
小儿科 pediatrics department	药剂师 pharmacist, druggist
诊室 consulting room	住院病人 in-patient
住院部 in-patient department	住院处 admitting office
住院医生 resident physician	

主治医生 physician/surgeon in charge, attending doctor, doctor in charge

 **口译技能** **Interpreting Skills**

公共演讲技能(1)

作为一名联络陪同口译员，声音的重要性是大家公认的。如果人们很难听见你的声音，那么口译过程将会中断。当你必须在公共场合进行口译的时候，你必须有一个好嗓子，因为可能当你要口译时，周遭却非常吵闹。而一个好的陪同口译员却要讲述要点、突出重点、描绘细节，总之，在整个过程中要保证声音能被目标语听众清晰地听到。

如果你是在一个需要扩音设备的地方从事口译工作,那么检查室内设备成了你要提前到场的原因之一。你需要检查话筒是否正常。通过话筒你的声音可以传到多远。你要知道你自己的声音应该多大。在检验时,要保证音量足够大,这样当人们一进入会场就会立刻被吸引。确保音响系统可以顾及室内的每一个角落。如果音响遥控器不在你的手边,你可以通过调整嘴与麦克风之间的距离,或是增加或减弱你自己的声音来调节音量。但尽可能不要使用后一种方法,因为这样很容易让你的嗓子疲劳。

针对这一问题,我们有一些具体的自我训练方法。首先试着把自己的声音录下来,然后听听自己的声音——有什么发现吗?你多半会大吃一惊,"我听上去是这样的吗?"也许你们对自己的声音会感到沮丧,在心里可能会说:"这不可能是我!我觉得我的嗓音更深沉(更响亮、更圆润……)。"其实一些著名的演说家和演员的嗓音也不是很理想。但我们现在没有时间去接受几年的专业培训。所以我们将从嗓音的几个因素开始注意这一问题。

一、音质

你的嗓音首先为人们所注意的就是音质,是刺耳带鼻音、单薄还是洪亮。如果要与他人沟通思想与感情,你的嗓音一定要符合两点要求:(1)容易听懂,(2)有抑扬顿挫。我们也没有必要学得像电视里的新闻播音员那样,重要的是准确形象地进行口译表达。

二、音量

很可能,要让别人理解你所说的话,最重要的因素就是你的音量了。首先是距离的因素:听众离得越远,你的声音就该越高。当你把声音传向远处时,你会自然地调高音量。就像你在楼底冲着你楼上的朋友喊一样。但是,我们也千万不要忘记同样的道理也适用于短距离。对你自己而言,你的声音总是要比你的听众所听到的响。具体练习方式:深吸一口气,然后用吹气的方式把它呼出来,就像吹蜡烛一样。反复练习这两个动作,帮助自己在不扯开嗓门的情况下也能提高嗓音。

三、语速

你知道自己说话有多快?自己计时算一下,在一段的开头做个记号,大声朗读一分钟,然后数数你读过的字数。一般应该是每分钟150字左右。在一般的口译表达中,语速和表达内容是密切相关的。对口译内容很熟的译员在说不同内容时语速也会不一样。例如,他们在说主要思想和关键点时的语速要比说笑话和总结时慢。

四、音调和抑扬顿挫

没有什么比变换音调更能改进你口译表达的整体效果了。但是刚开始的人往往不会充分利用他们的最好音调和抑扬顿挫。相反,他们总是用一种音调进行表达。即使他们说得很容易理解,有时也会让人感到无聊。更严重的是,声音变化不够多会导致没法表达意思的细微差别,而有时真正的沟通却正是建立在这一点上的。让我们做一个简单的练习:我们来试试看一个简单的"噢"(Oh)字能表示多少种意思。我们可以用10种不同的方式来说这个词。自己试一试,用不同的音调和抑扬顿挫说"噢",表示下列的意思:

——现在我懂了。

——我不能等了。

——我很失望。

——你想让我相信这个吗?

——太棒了!

——这很精明，但不够光明正大。

——小心！

——真疼啊！

——真讨厌！

——可怜的小东西。

五、节奏

1. 停顿起到断句的作用。正如标点符号逗号、句号分隔开书面的东西一样，长短不同的停顿把话分成一个个的意群。随意的停顿会把听众弄糊涂且严重影响你的表达效果。确保停顿在意群之间而不是在其中。

2. 通过停顿来强调。例如，当你在说完一句很重要的话之后停顿，你其实是在告诉听众，这是重点。请注意，在某些情况下，恰到好处的停顿比什么话都能更有效地传递你的意思。

3. 不要害怕停顿。有人会觉得停顿会让他们忘记要说什么。还有时，他们会害怕在停顿时听者会盯着他们看。所以他们不停顿，代之以一串"嗯""啊"之类无意义的词（这反而是口译最避讳的东西，因为这会使你的听众对你失去信任）。不要害怕停顿，从来就没有谁因停顿而被攻击。

口译练习 *Enhancement Practice*

第一项 Project 1

听力复述 Retelling

Listen to the following passages once and then reproduce them in the same language at the end of each segment.

English Passage：

In the United States, obesity has risen at an epidemic rate during the past 30 years. Research indicates that the situation is worsening rather than improving. Recent results of a National Survey show that an estimated 61 percent of US adults are either overweight or obese. // Diet and physical activity are the two primary behavioral factors believed to be associated with overweight. // The choices a person makes in eating and physical activity contribute much to overweight and obesity. The latest survey shows that calorie intakes have increased in adults and that recreational activity is low for many Americans. // It tells us again that Americans need to do better in choosing a healthy diet and a sensible plan of physical activity. //

Chinese Passage：

改革开放以来，我国的医疗卫生取得了长足进步和显著成效，人民的健康水平大幅提高。// 但是，发展的同时也产生了一些新的问题，滋生了不良现象：医疗费用居高不下，医

生拿回扣,卫生资源不合理等等,这些都引起全社会的极大关注。// 这时医改来了,是为解决这些问题而来的。应该说,来得是及时的。// 但是,能否真正给百姓带来益处? 多大益处? 还要看医改怎样进行。//

第二项 Project 2
主题讨论 Discussion

Hold a 5-minute discussion with your partners on the topic "Reform of China's Medicare System".

第三项 Project 3
听译练习 Listening and Interpreting

A. Sentence Interpreting

Listen to the sentences and interpret them into Chinese.

1. The purpose of APC Pharmaceutical Company is to help realize humanity's quest for longer, healthier, happier lives.

2. World Health Organization's main priority is to promote health equity, and so contribute to the well-being of all the world's people.

3. HIV/AIDS is a global crisis that, despite recent advances in treatment, requires even more than before, urgent action on an unprecedented scale.

4. If an American citizen becomes seriously ill or injured abroad, a US consular officer can assist in locating appropriate medical services and informing his family or friends.

5. A traveler going abroad with any preexisting medical problems should carry a letter from the attending physician, describing the medical condition and any prescription medications.

B. Sentence Interpreting

Listen to the sentences and interpret them into English.

1. 今天,中医以其独特的疗效和科学本质赢得了全世界的广泛赞誉。
2. 中医注重无病防病,强调以食补保健来延缓衰老,减少疾病。
3. 我国积极发展中医,鼓励中西医结合诊断和治疗。
4. 这是一种尚未被人类完全认识的新型传染病,还没有特效的诊断办法和治疗手段。
5. 国家已安排 35 亿元人民币,用于全国疾病预防控制机构的基础设施建设和中国疾病预防控制中心工程建设。

C. Dialogue Interpreting

Listen to the dialogue and interpret it into the target language.

A：您有什么不舒服?

B：I had a rash recently. There is a lot of eruption on my body, trunk, arm, leg and scalp, especially my trunk. I am itching all over.

A：请解开衬衫，让我检查一下。这疹子有多久了？受冷或吹风时病症加重吗？

B：I've had it for a month. Yes, it does. I also have nausea and diarrhea sometimes.

A：起皮疹前您吃过鱼或虾吗？

B：No, I didn't. I'm allergic to seafood and I always avoid eating that.

A：您过去有没有得过这样的病？

B：Yes. I had something like this about three years ago. But it's never been bad before, and I didn't go to see a doctor.

A：您的病在什么情况下发生？

B：I really don't know. This time it might be overwork.

A：您家族中有没有患此病的人？

B：Yes, my father had the same skin disease, and so did my uncle. It is a genetic disease, isn't it?

A：是的。这是一种多因素的遗传性疾病，有遗传和环境两方面因素才发生临床表现。您不必担心，可以治好的。请问您喝酒吗？

B：Yes, I drank a lot in recent months.

A：哦，我明白了。首先您应该对治疗充满信心，然后您要好好照顾自己，避免着凉。经常用温水洗澡，保持皮肤清洁。

B：Thank you for your advice. I will do as you told me. Goodbye.

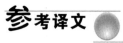 **Reference Version**

对话口译 A：

A：Come in, please. Sit down. What's your name? And what's the matter?

B：我叫艾伦·詹姆斯。我头痛，喉咙发炎，胸口疼。事实上我全身酸痛。夜里开始感到胃痛、想吐。我一夜都没有睡着。

A：Let me listen to your chest. Breathe deeply. How long have you been like this? Did you take any medicine for it?

B：有两三天了。没有吃过药。胸痛与反胃有什么联系吗？

A：No, it has nothing to do with it. Open your mouth and let me see your tongue, please. I can see your throat is bright red and markedly swollen. Now, let me take your temperature. Do you still have a stomachache?

B：比早上好些，不过我还是觉得痛。

A：You are running a high fever, 39 degrees centigrade. I think you've got the flu. There's a lot of it going around. There's nothing serious with your stomach, so you don't need to worry about that. If you feel worse, please come back to the clinic.

B：你看我该怎么办呢？很久才会恢复吗？

A：Get this prescription filled and go straight to bed. You should stay in bed for a few days. Now then, I must warn you against greasy food for a while. For two or three

days eat only soft food such as oatmeal and milk. After that you can eat what you want，but don't overeat for a while even if you have an appetite.

B：劳驾,我要配这张处方。

C：Wait a moment please. I'll take care of it right away. Sorry，the drugs on this order are exhausted. Would you prefer to take similar medicines of another brand? They are of the same medication，same quality，but at a much lower cost.

B：好的,我就要此类药。我应该隔多少时间用一次药?

C：Take the capsules three times a day thirty minutes before meals.

B：顺便问一下,虫咬了用什么药好?

C：You might try this. It's a new product and is very effective. Rub this medicine on your skin four times a day.

B：好的,我明白了。谢谢你的帮助。

对话口译 B：

A：Hello. I'm an orthopedic surgeon. What seems to be the problem?

B：唉,我大约 1 小时前被汽车撞倒在地,从地上爬起来时,我发现左臂和肘部擦破皮了,现在肋骨还有点痛。

A：Please lie down here and relax. I'll just take a look. Where does it hurt? Please point to the spot where you feel the most pain. Have you taken any painkillers?

B：这很难说清楚,好像浑身都痛。我直接被送到这儿来了,没有服过止痛药。

A：Does it hurt when I press here?

B：哎呀! 你一按这儿我就疼得要命。我的肘部骨折了吗?

A：It seems to be so. The nurse will send you to the X-ray Department. When the X-rays are ready，bring them back to me to examine.

B：好的,那么待会儿再见吧!

（十分钟后,病人取回 X 光片。）

B：这是我的 X 光片。医生,严重吗?

A：The X-ray reveals a fracture of the lower humerus. We'll give you a U-type plaster cast on your elbow and shoulder.

B：这石膏托需要戴多久? 我还需要注意什么事吗?

A：Probably two months. You'd better keep your elbow higher than your heart and move your finger joints from time to time. Complete recovery will take a rather long time. You will have to come here for periodical check-ups.

B：大夫,我是否需要服用点什么药呢?

A：All right. I'll give you some herbal medicine to help you heal quickly. In addition，I will prescribe you some medicine to be taken orally. Here is a prescription. Take it to the chemist's. Please take the medicine according to the instruction.

B：我恐怕扭伤了左踝关节。现在又肿又疼。想请您看看是否要紧。

A：Take it easy. It's just a sprain. The nurse will put on a supporting bandage. Put your foot in hot and cold water alternatively three or four times a day, and the pain and swelling should go. Follow my advice and I'm sure you are going to be all right.

篇章口译 A：

一想到在异乡患病就会令人不寒而栗，不过有时你也可以为这类事的发生预先做些准备工作。// 除非你计划移民到英国，不然出国前你可以到国内卫生部门或健康保险公司去检查身体。// 定期服用药物者应该带足可供自己在国外整个逗留期间需要服用的药剂。//

在英国，某城镇的药剂师不会为另一城镇或另一国家所开的处方配药。// 如果你在英国期间用完了药，你得让医生作检查，开新的处方。// 购买有些药，如阿司匹林这类轻微止痛药、感冒药、鼻通药、维他命、止咳药、咽喉药，以及医治消化不良、恶心、腹泻等现象的药都无须处方。// 你甚至可以在便利商店或超市的柜台上随意购买。//

如果你需要医生给你看病，或门诊，或急诊，或住院，你都要作好付费的准备，因为大多数医生和医院都要病人就诊时付费。// 医院通常要求你付上一笔押金，或要求你告诉院方某个可以代你付费的人的姓名。// 不管怎样，你都应该在出国前与你的医疗或旅游保险公司做出某种安排，或者多带些钱出国，以防万一。//

篇章口译 B：

The agents or parasites that cause infectious disease vary greatly in size. Some parasites, like viruses, are so small that they cannot be seen under an optical microscope. Other parasites, like the tapeworm, may be more than a meter long. //

Prevention of infectious diseases depends on knowing how they are transmitted. There are three main ways in which diseases can be controlled. //

First, remove the source of infection. For example, finding and curing all cases of active lung tuberculosis prevents further infection. Isolating all cases of smallpox prevents further spread of the disease. //

Second, cut the transition media of the disease. For instance, killing all mosquitoes in an area could undermine the transition of malaria. //

Moreover, safe food, sanitary water supplies and eradication of flies help to prevent the spread of diseases. //

Third, protect individuals and groups. Immunization is very effective in dealing with smallpox, measles and other infectious diseases. Certain types of medicine can be used as means of prevention. Some facilities, like mosquito net could protect people from being bitten by mosquitoes and flies, thus being free from malaria. //

听译练习：

A:

1. APC 医药公司的目标就是帮助人类实现梦寐以求的理想：延长寿命，增强体质，幸福生活。

2. 世界卫生组织的首要任务是保证医疗的公正性,使世界各国人民都享有健康。

3. 艾滋病是个世界性的危机。尽管最近在治疗方面取得了一些成绩,但仍然比以往任何时候需要采取大规模的紧急应对行动。

4. 如果一位美国公民在国外患了重病或受了重伤,那么美国领事馆官员会帮助其接受合适的医疗服务并告知其亲属或朋友。

5. 如果旅行者在出国前就接受药物治疗的话,他就应该携带医生描述其治疗情况和药物处方的信。

B:

1. Today, traditional Chinese medicine has won worldwide acclaim owing to its unique effectiveness and scientific nature.

2. Traditional Chinese medicine places emphasis on the early prevention of diseases, advocating the food treatment approach, that is, efforts should be focused on maintaining good health through the intake of nourishing food to defer senility and reduce the risk of contracting diseases.

3. China has made energetic efforts to develop TCM, encouraging the combination of Chinese and western medicines in diagnosing and treatment.

4. This is a brand new contagious disease yet to be fully understood to mankind. There is neither a conclusive method of diagnosis, nor an effective cure.

5. The central government has allocated RMB 3.5 billion yuan for infrastructure development of a national disease control system, and for the construction of the China Center for Disease Control and Prevention.

C:

A: What's your complaint?

B: 近来我发皮疹了。我身上有好多皮疹,躯干、胳膊、腿和头皮,尤其是躯干。我浑身发痒。

A: Please unbutton your shirt and let me examine you. How long have you had this rash? Does it get worse when you feel cold or when it is windy?

B: 已经一个月了。是的。我有时还会觉得恶心并且腹泻。

A: Did you eat any fish or shrimps before the rash began?

B: 没有。我对海鲜过敏,总是避免食用。

A: Did you ever have any trouble like this before?

B: 得过。3 年前也像这样起皮疹,但没有这次重,而且也未找大夫看过。

A: Under what conditions does your trouble occur?

B: 我不太清楚,这次可能是太劳累了。

A: Has any one in your family ever had such a problem?

B: 有,我父亲有同样的皮肤病,我叔叔也是。这病是遗传的吗?

A: Yes, it's a multifactorial genic disease, which requires both polygenic and environmental factors for its clinical expression. But don't worry, you can be cured. Please tell me, have you been drinking?

B: 是的,这几个月我喝了不少酒。

A：Oh，I see. First you should have much faith in treating this disease. Then，you'd better look after yourself. Avoid catching colds. Take a bath with warm water frequently to keep the skin clean.

B：谢谢您的忠告。我一定遵照您说的去做，再见。

饮食文化

第二单元

Unit

Catering Culture

背景知识

Background Information

Cuisine is a specific set of cooking traditions and practices, often associated with a specific culture. Religious food laws can also exercise a strong influence on cuisine. A cuisine is primarily influenced by the ingredients that are available locally or through trade. For example, the American Chinese dish chop suey clearly reflected the adaptation of Chinese cuisine to the ingredients available in North America. Chop suey is a Chinese dish which literally means mixed pieces. Now chop suey as found in North America is not an authentic Chinese dish, but part of American Chinese cuisine and Canadian Chinese cuisine. It is also a relatively new addition to Indian Chinese cuisine.

The last century has produced enormous improvements in food production, preservation, storage and shipping. Today almost every locale in the world has access to not only its traditional cuisine, but also to many other world cuisines as well. New cuisines are constantly evolving, as certain aesthetics rise and fall in popularity among professional chefs and their clients.

In addition to food, catering trade is also often held to include beverages, including wine, liquor, tea, coffee and other drinks. Increasingly, experts hold that it further includes the raw ingredients and original plants and animals from which they come.

There are also different cultural attitudes to food. For example, in India, consumption of food is regarded as an offering. Thus the stomach is considered to be the holy fire and all the food consumed is an offering to the holy fire. In Japan, tea drinking is a fine art and there is an elaborate ceremony about it. Not drinking tea in the right way is considered to be an act of barbarism.

对话口译

Dialogue A

 Vocabulary Work

Study the following words and phrases and translate them into the target language.

筷子	刀叉	烈酒	清酒
鱼香肉丝	savory	香酥鸭	香料
猪油	蒸	炸	蘸酱
gravy			

 Text Interpreting

Listen to the following dialogue and interpret it into the target language.

A：Nice to see you again, Mr. Zhou. It's very kind of you to have invited me here.

B：我也很高兴再次与您相见,您能光临是我们的荣幸。不要客气,桌上菜,请自便。

A：Chinese people are known for their hospitality. Now I've experienced it by myself.

B：您是用筷子还是刀叉呢? 两者我们都为您准备了。

A：When in Rome, do as the Romans do. The use of chopsticks has been part of Chinese food culture. I think I'll try chopsticks and see if I can manage.

B：好的。那您是喝绍兴酒还是茅台呢? 绍兴酒属米酒一类,品之香味诱人,有点像日本的清酒。茅台是我国最负盛名的烈酒,上口不上头。

A：I prefer Shaoxing Wine. Thank you.

B：好的。现在我们来尝尝菜肴吧。这是鱼香肉丝,是一道著名的川菜。川菜选料范围大,调味及炊技变化多样。川菜最大的特点是口味重,以麻辣著称。

A：Very savory. Sichuan cuisine has always been my favorite. I was told that the number of Sichuan dishes has surpassed 5,000. It can be said that one who doesn't experience Sichuan food has never reached China.

B：你对中国饮食文化颇有研究啊。这是香酥鸭,请趁热吃。

A：Great! It's tender and crisp. Do you know how it is cooked?

B：先加各种香料蒸,然后用猪油炸脆。在油炸时,可以准备蘸酱,将含有橄榄油、酱油、辣椒片、红糖和蒜头的蘸酱放在小碗中。

A：Oh，it must take a long time to cook！What is this dish called？

B：这是红烧扣肉菠菜。吃这道菜时喝上一杯绍兴酒特别香。

A：That's a good idea. The dish is thick in gravy，bright in color，mellow and delicious to the palate. Thank you again for such a nice dinner！

B：不客气。亲朋好友相聚，美酒佳肴相敬，实属人生之最大快乐也。希望您在中国过得愉快。

对话口译
Dialogue B

词汇预习 **Vocabulary Work**

Study the following words and phrases and translate them into the target language.

sauté sliced beef	炸特色菜	色、香、味	古老肉
with oyster sauce	炸	烤	
清炒虾仁	原汁原味	能引起食欲的	
点心		炖	

译实践 **Text Interpreting**

Listen to the following dialogue and interpret it into the target language.

A：I've been in Guangzhou for several days and I found the food here is very nice.

B：你喜欢这里的饭菜我很开心。粤菜强调轻炒浅煮，选料似乎不受限制。你最喜欢的是什么呢？

A：Umm，sauté sliced beef with oyster sauce is my favorite. Dishes like shark fin soup，steamed sea bass，and roasted piglet are also very tasty.

B：这些都是广东菜的特色菜啊。我也很喜欢。广东菜的特点多以清淡、生脆、偏甜为主。

A：Before I came here，I've heard of China as a "Kingdom of Cuisine". But many dishes are so delicious that they are beyond my expectation.

B：是的，中国人对"吃"很讲究，我们从"色、香、味"三个方面来评价烹饪水平。

A：Really？Then I think sauté sliced beef with oyster sauce is a perfect combination of the three.

B：是的，古老肉和清炒虾仁也是广东名菜。广东菜对炒、炸、烤、炖都非常重视。清蒸和快

炒最常被用来保持原料的原汁原味。广东大厨也非常注重菜肴外观的艺术性。

A：Now，I know why the Canton dishes are so delicious.

B：你吃过广东点心吗？很能引起食欲。经典的点心有包子、饺子和饭团，其中有牛肉馅的、鸡肉馅的、猪肉馅的、虾仁馅的和蔬菜馅的。许多点心餐厅还提供蒸时蔬、烤肉、粥和汤。

A：Dim sum? I haven't got such a chance to try them but I am very interested.

B：广东点心可以是蒸也可以是炸。点心一般个头较小，通常一碟点心有三或四个，所以可以品尝到不同的品种。那我们一起去尝尝吧？

A：I'd love to. That really makes my mouth watering. Where can we find those snacks? I didn't find any near my hotel.

B：我会和你一起去的。今天一定让你大快朵颐。

A：Great! Please wait a moment. I must take my camera with me.

B：好的，我在楼下等你。

篇章口译（英译汉）

Passage A (E-C)

词汇预习 *Vocabulary Work*

Study the following words and phrases and translate them into Chinese.

distinctiveness	landscape	mouthwatering	ingredient
forage	speciality	delicacy	ingest
digest			

译实践 *Text Interpreting*

Listen to the English passage and interpret it into Chinese at the end of each segment.

　　Welsh food has a long-established reputation for distinctiveness and quality, making it popular among consumers across the world. // Wales prides itself on supplying some of the finest produce in the world. // Its very landscape reflects freshness, quality and variety. From unique cheeses and wines, famous Welsh beef and lamb to fresh fish and seafood, Wales has it all. // However what's the usual diet for the daily life? // In hotels around Wales, you will be served with the most mouthwatering breakfast—local eggs and bacon combined with the more unusual ingredients—Laver bread and Cockles. // Afternoon tea can be served with Bara Brith (a fruit bread) or Welsh cakes. The traditional meat for dinner in the evening is Welsh Lamb. // When you have tasted these daily meals and slightly touched on the Welsh people's daily life, you must eagerly "forage" the local specialty. // Here we will give you a full picture of welsh food and culture on our website, from monthly delicacy, unique cheese to world famous whisky and beer. // The description of the food and drink in Wales will give another angle to "taste" the local culture. // When you ingest and digest the delicious Welsh food to your heart's content, you also "ingest and digest" "the delicious Welsh culture" at the same time. //

篇章口译（汉译英）

Passage B (C-E)

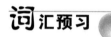 **Vocabulary Work**

Study the following words and phrases and translate them into English.

| 四大菜系 | 熔炉 | 移民 | 精美的烹调 |
| 美食家 | 素食 | 清真 | |

Text Interpreting

Listen to the Chinese passage and interpret it into English at the end of each segment.

上海菜肴虽没被列入四大菜系中，但其烹调风格却集各派菜肴烹调之长。// 上海是集多种文化和民俗的"小熔炉"。// 大多数上海人的祖辈是"移民"，他们为追求新生活来到上海。// 他们各自把当地的烹饪技术带到了上海，使上海烹调技术得以发展和提高。// 于是，上海的菜肴烹调成了世界上最精美的烹调之一，获得国内外美食家的好评。// 现在人们能"不出上海，吃遍全球"。// 世界各地的"移民"带来了富有各地风味的菜肴。// 在上海，不但有许多供应不同地方烹饪风味的餐厅，如有专以山东、广东、淮扬、四川、北京、浙江、河南、湖南和福建菜肴为特色的饭店，而且还有以素食、清真和欧亚各国烹饪为特色的餐馆等。//

口译讲评

Notes on the Text

Dialogue A

1. 中国的白酒度数很高,一般都在 35 度以上,英语中把酒精含量在 14％以上的称为烈酒,英文是 spirits or liquor,如威士忌、杜松子酒、雪利酒、白兰地等。

2. 茅台是我国最负盛名的烈酒,上口不上头。"上口"是指口味好,可处理为 delicious 或 tasty,而"不上头"是指不会因喝酒而使人眩晕,英语中正好有一形似意同的表达方式,即:not go to someone's head。

3. 品之香味诱人。"香味"可以译为 aroma。fragrance 多指植物的香味,而食物和饮料的香味宜用 aroma。

4. The dish is thick in gravy, bright in color, mellow and delicious to the palate. 这句有几处排比结构,译成汉语时也应尽量保留原句的句型特色。当然,在口译时迫于时间压力,能将原文意思准确流利地表达出来,已属过关,但还是应当在平时口译练习中尽可能考虑到意合和形似两方面。此句如处理为"这道菜汁浓、色艳、香醇、美味",则原句的意和形都能得到很好的体现。

Dialogue B

1. 中国人对"吃"很讲究。"吃"并非指吃的动作,而是指所吃的食物,因此不能译为 eating,而应当处理成 food 或 what to eat;另外"讲究"是指重视,因此可以译为 pay attention to。

2. 古老肉和清炒虾仁也是广东名菜。"菜"是指具体的两道菜,因此可以译为 dishes。

3. 广东菜对炒、炸、烤、炖都非常重视。"广东菜"并非指一道一道的菜肴,而是指广义上的广东菜的烹饪方法,因此可以处理为 Cantonese cuisine。

Passage A

1. Wales prides itself on supplying some of the finest produce in the world. the finest produce 在文中是指威尔士所生产出的最美味的食品。

2. However what's the usual diet for the daily life. 若按原句结构直译成"然而,日常生活的常规饮食是什么",显得过于生硬,不如意译成:然而,威尔士人日常吃些什么呢?

3. In hotels around Wales, you will be served with the most mouthwatering breakfast——local eggs and bacon combined with... mouthwatering 充当定语修饰 breakfast。由于 breakfast 后面跟着一长串列举早餐食物的内容,因此可以将该定语置于句末,译成独立的小短句"这准让你垂涎三尺",比较符合汉语的表达习惯。

4. daily meals 宜译为家常便饭。

Passage B

1. 上海菜肴虽没被列入四大菜系中。"四大菜系"是指中国的扬、粤、川和鲁四大菜系，它们分别以重油香甜、酥脆鲜嫩、麻辣爽口和咸鲜汁浓为各自的特色。

2. 上海是集多种文化和民俗的"小熔炉"。"多种文化"是指不同区域不同种类的具体的文化类型，所以在译"多种文化"时，可以处理为 various cultures。

3. 他们各自把当地的烹饪技术带到了上海。"当地的"是指他们在移民上海之前的居住地，相当于"原籍地"，因此这里"当地的"可以译成 native。

4. 现在人们能"不出上海，吃遍全球"。"吃遍全球"是指吃遍全球的美食。另外，口译时可将"不出上海"后置，处理成介词短语 without leaving Shanghai。

5. 在上海，不但有许多供应不同地方烹饪风味的餐厅，如有专以山东、广东、淮扬、四川、北京、浙江、河南、湖南和福建菜肴为特色的饭店，而且还有以素食、清真和欧亚各国烹饪为特色的餐馆等。此句比较长，在口译时可先迅速抓住它的主要结构，为"在上海，不但有如以……菜肴为特色的饭店，而且有以……烹饪为特色的餐馆"。若是按原文结构译成英语，会出现三次 restaurant（原文先后出现餐厅、饭店、餐馆）。要译得地道些，不如将原文形式变为"上海的餐馆不但提供……地方特色菜，而且还提供……特色菜肴"，使之更符合英语的表达习惯。

相关词语 *Relevant Words and Expressions*

白灼 scald
烘烤 bake
爆 quick-fry
清炒 plain-fry
清蒸 steam
勾芡 dress with starchy sauce
炒米粉 fried ground rice noodles
冷拼盘 assorted hors d'oeuvres platter
麻婆豆腐 spicy and hot bean curd
回锅肉 twice-cooked pork slices in brown sauce
鱼香肉丝 fish-flavored shredded pork in hot sauce
三鲜汤 consommé with three delicious ingredients (shredded chicken, ham and bamboo shoots)

焖，炖；煨 stew；simmer
焙 roast；broil
炒 stir-fry, sauté
煎 pan-fry
红烧 braise with soy sauce/ in brown sauce
餐前开胃点心（或酒）appetizer
炸酱面 noodles with fried brown sauce paste
糖醋排骨 sweet and sour spare ribs

口译技能　*Interpreting Skills*

公共演讲技能（2）

在陪同口译的工作实践中,经常会需要译员和谈话的一方进行一些预热的交流。除了那些最为正式的场合,幽默都是一个非常关键的沟通因素,但是在你决定使用多少幽默和其类型之前,你必须考虑你自己的风格。

1. 在沟通表达中运用幽默的一些基本准则

需要注意:社会习俗(Customs)、观众分析（Audience analysis）

适合场合(Occasion)、个人风格（Personal style)等问题。

2. 是否使用幽默

在你决定运用一个幽默之前问问自己下列问题:

这个笑话真的好笑吗?（Fun or not?）我能舒畅地把这个笑话说出来吗?（Fluency?）我的听众会喜欢吗?（People like it or not?）该笑话适合我的演讲目的吗?（Serve my purpose?)我的听众都能听懂吗?（People get it or not?）该笑话和演讲的基调相符吗?（Consistency?）

如果其中任何一个问题的答案是"不",那么保险一点——不要它。有个定律一定要遵从:有疑问,就不要。如果你可以对所有的问题说"是",就可以使用这个幽默,并使它成为你沟通表达的一部分。最危险的幽默是取笑他人的幽默,请避免下面的话题:

宗教(religion),人种(race),性行为(sex),智力(I. Q.),出生地(birth place),身体缺陷(physical deficiency),性取向(sexual orientation),宗教领导人(head of any religion),外表(appearance),政治倾向（political preference)

3. 让幽默为你服务

一个能打动听众的说故事者有许多加强幽默的方法,如面部表情、多变的语句和手势,以及恰当的停顿,但即使你不是个天生的喜剧家,你也可以成功地讲述故事。以下是加强幽默的几点建议:

（1）别为你的没有经验说抱歉。永远别说像"我不是块戏剧演员的料"或"我笑话说得不好,但我会尽力而为"之类的话,这会在你开始说之前就毁了你的幽默。

（2）只要最基本的东西。如果你笑话里有很多不必要的细节,听众会失去兴趣。它只需要人物、时间和其他让这个笑话出彩的东西。

（3）开心一些,微笑,显出高兴的样子,你的情绪会感染听众,这样使你更容易获得笑声。

（4）说笑话时看着听众的眼睛。每看着一位听众,略微停留一会儿,扫视全场。

（5）笑话要短,太长了会破坏其幽默。

（6）留给听众足够的时间欣赏笑话。如果你匆忙打断笑话,那么你花了这么大劲取得的效果就会打折扣。

（7）说的要慢,要清楚。确保听众都能听懂你笑话的每一个字——特别是妙言之处。

口译练习 **Enhancement Practice**

第一项 Project 1
听力复述　Retelling

Listen to the following passages once and then reproduce them in the same language at the end of each segment.

English Passage：

In my home country Canada，there are some Chinese restaurants serving traditional Chinese food，but I was not courageous enough to go inside and taste them. // But after a short stay here in Shanghai，I found myself loving Chinese food. // Eating in China is quite different from eating in Canada. // In my country，people often go outside eating in large restaurants. The menus offer a wide choice with excellent seafood like lobsters and clam，and also a range of ethnic foods. // However，most restaurants in China have their own features. // Some mainly serve the dishes of Sichuan Cuisine like hot pot series，and some offer delicate local snacks. People with different tastes can find their favorite foods in different places. //

Chinese Passage：

北方人主食饺子，一般喜欢吃菜肉馅的。//而南方人喜欢吃馄饨，其形似饺子，但更像元宝，其馅与饺子相同。//馄饨在三国时出现在中国南方，以后逐渐地流传到全国各地。馄饨通常下入汤内，与汤一起吃。//上海人很喜欢吃馄饨，馄饨是普通话的发音，广东话的发音是 wonton，这词现在已成了一个英文单词，实际上它源自广东话。//

第二项 Project 2
主题讨论 Discussion

Hold a 5-minute discussion with your partners on the topic "Chinese Food and Chinese Culture".

第三项 Project 3
听译练习 Listening and Interpreting
A. Sentence Interpreting

Listen to the sentences and interpret them into Chinese.

1. Questions about food should not be lifted out of its cultural context.
2. The United States is a country of immigrants，so there is an immense variety in its catering culture.
3. In fact，our strong rejection of certain meats is not founded in physiology but in aesthetics.

4. Health food includes natural food with minimal processing，that is，there are no preservatives to help it last longer or other chemicals to make it taste or look better.

5. Coffee shops are usually less expensive and less dressy than fine restaurants，and so are pizza places，pancake houses，sandwich shops and family restaurants.

B. Sentence Interpreting

Listen to the sentences and interpret them into English.

1. 色、香、味一直被看成是中餐烹饪的基本要素。

2. 湖南菜口味很重,用烟熏肉的做法是最为显著的特点之一。

3. 上海烹调的一个显著特点是,一年中不同的季节用不同类型的药品原料做滋补食品。

4. 菜系的差异由多种因素所致,其中包括地理位置、气候条件、交通状况、人口迁移、海外文化。

5. 南翔汤包皮薄如蝉翼,却饱含醇香的汤汁,吃的时候不要一口吞下以免烫嘴。

C. Dialogue Interpreting

Listen to the dialogue and interpret it into the target language.

A：Mr. Wang，we are tourists from USA. We hope to get some ideas about Chinese food and dietary habits. Would you tell us something about it?

B：非常高兴有机会跟你们谈我们中国的饮食文化。现代中国已享有"烹饪王国"之美称。

A：Can you introduce to us some of the major cuisines in China?

B：中国有鲁菜、川菜、粤菜、扬州菜四大地方菜系。必须指出这种区域划分并无严格的地理界限。

A：So which cuisine does Beijing food belong to?

B：北京菜虽属鲁菜,却也融入了一些川菜的特色,并受到蒙古菜的影响。

A：Could you tell me the different features of each of the four major cuisines in China?

B：乐意效劳。粤菜以生淡和独特风味而著称;川菜以辣味而闻名;鲁菜以海鲜为特征;而扬州菜的烹调风格则以用料广泛、味道微甜而著名。

A：Chinese people like to eat Jiaozi during the Spring Festival，and I'd love to learn how to make Jiaozi. Do you know how?

B：当然知道,我经常同家人一起包饺子。包饺子有很多步骤,首先是和面,然后到第二步,即准备饺子馅。

A：What goes into the fillings?

B：有各种各样的,但通常都是些剁碎的猪肉或绿色蔬菜。第三步是做饺子皮。

A：Then comes the tricky part—filling the Jiaozi, am I right?

B：对了,你只需放少量的馅在饺子皮里,然后把饺子皮的边缘折在一起成一个半月形,最后把边缘压紧,这就好了。

A：Sounds complicated! I'll try my best to learn it.

B：你愿意的话我可以来教你。

参考译文 Reference Version

对话口译 A：

A：周先生,很高兴再见到您。非常感谢您邀请我到这里。

B：Nice to see you too and it's a pleasure to have you here. Make yourself at home and help yourself to the dishes.

A：以前就听说中国人十分好客,今天我亲身体验到了这一点。

B：Would you like to use chopsticks or knife and fork? We have prepared both.

A：入乡随俗。筷子是中国饮食文化的一部分。我想试试筷子,看看行不行。

B：Well. Would you like Shaoxing Wine or Maotai Liquor? Shaoxing Wine is made from rice; it possesses an inviting aroma and tastes like Japanese sake. Maotai is China's best-known liquor. It is delicious and yet doesn't go to the head.

A：我比较喜欢绍兴酒。谢谢。

B：OK. Now let's try the food. This is pork shreds with fish seasoning, a famous dish of Sichuan cooking. Sichuan Cuisine features a wide range of materials, various seasonings and different cooking techniques. With a rich variety of strong flavors, Sichuan food is famous for its numerous varieties of delicacies, dominated by peppery and chili flavors and best known for being spicy-hot.

A：非常鲜美。川菜是我的最爱。我听说川菜的品种在 5,000 种以上。可以说没尝过川菜就等于没来过中国。

B：You are quite a scholar on Chinese culinary culture. Here's the crispy duck. Please have it while it's piping hot.

A：不错,又嫩又脆。您知道这是怎么做的吗?

B：Steam it with various spices and then fry in lard to crisp it. While the duck is being fried, prepare the dipping sauce. Combine the olive oil, soy sauce, chili flakes, brown sugar and garlic in a small bowl.

A：那做这道菜一定很费时间啦! 这又是什么?

B：Braised pork slices trimmed with spinach. It's especially tasty to have it with a glass of Shaoxing Wine.

A：这个主意不错。这道菜汁浓、色艳、香醇、美味。再次感谢您招待我这么丰盛的一餐。

B：You are welcome! Fine food and good drink, taken in the company of good friends, constitute one of our supreme pleasures in life. I wish you a pleasant stay in China.

对话口译 B：

A：我到广州已经好些天了,我发现这里的饭菜很好吃。

B：I'm glad to hear that you enjoy the food. Cantonese cuisine emphasizes light cooking with seemingly limitless range of ingredients. What do you like most?

A：嗯,我最喜欢蚝油牛肉。鱼翅汤、清蒸海鲈和烤乳猪也非常美味。

B：Oh，these are typical dishes of Cantonese cuisine. I also like them. Cantonese cuisine features light，crisp and sweet taste.

A：来中国之前，我就听说中国是"烹饪王国"，但这里的菜实在很好吃，超出了我的想象。

B：Yes，we Chinese people have been paying a lot of attention to what to eat，and we judge cooking from three elements known as color，aroma and taste.

A：真的吗？我觉得蚝油牛肉是三者的完美结合。

B：That's right. Other famous dishes include sweet-sour pork fillet with chili，plain sauté shrimps，and so on. Cantonese cuisine stresses frying，deep-frying，roasting and braising. Steaming and stir-frying are most frequently used to preserve the ingredients' natural flavors. Canton chefs also pay much attention to the artistic presentation of their dishes.

A：我现在可知道了，广东菜为什么那样好吃。

B：Have you tasted the local dim sum，a Cantonese term for snacks？They are very appetizing. Classical dim sum includes buns，dumplings and rice rolls，which contain a range of ingredients，including beef，chicken，pork，prawns and vegetarian options. Many dim sum restaurants also offer plates of steamed greens，roasted meats，congee and soups.

A：点心？我很感兴趣，但至今还没有机会品尝。

B：Dim sum can be cooked by steaming and frying. The size of dim sum is usually small and it is normally served as three or four pieces in one dish. Because of the small portions，people can try a wide variety of dishes. Then let's go to try some？

A：我很乐意去。听得我都流口水了。我们在哪里能找到这些小吃？我在宾馆附近没看见过。

B：I will go with you. You can eat to your heart's content today.

A：那太好了。请等我一下，我去拿相机。

B：OK，I will wait for you downstairs.

篇章口译 A：

　　威尔士饮食以其特色和品质而声名远扬，受到了世界各地人们的欢迎。// 威尔士为能生产出世界上最美味的食物而感到自豪。// 威尔士美丽的风景体现出其饮食的新鲜、品质和多样化。独特的奶酪、酒、著名的威尔士牛羊肉和新鲜的鱼类和海鲜，在威尔士应有尽有。// 然而，威尔士人日常吃些什么呢？// 在威尔士的酒店里，早餐一般都会为你奉上当地的鸡蛋和咸猪肉并且加入了较为独特的配料——莱佛面包和鸟蛤，这准让你垂涎三尺。// 下午茶是巴拉伯里斯水果面包或威尔士蛋糕的组合。而传统晚餐的肉类是威尔士羊肉。// 吃完了家常便饭并稍微接触了当地威尔士人的生活后，你一定是迫切地想搜索当地的风味小吃。// 在此我们为你展现威尔士饮食文化的全景图，罗列每月珍馐美味，独一无二的奶酪，世界著名的威尔士威士忌和啤酒等种种美味佳肴。// 通过对威尔士饮食的介绍给你另一种角度去感悟当地的文化。// 当你在尽情品味和消化威尔士美食的时候，同时也在品味和消化"美味的威尔士文化"。//

篇章口译 B:

Shanghai Cuisine, which is not ranked among the four main cuisines of China, has comprised all the favors of the whole ranges of cuisines. // Shanghai is a miniature "melting pot" of various cultures and customs. // The grandparents of most Shanghainese were "immigrants", who came to Shanghai for a new life. // They brought to Shanghai their native cooking styles, which enriched and enhanced Shanghai cuisine. // Thus it makes Shanghai Cuisine one of the most delicate cuisines in the world. It is highly appraised by gourmets both at home and abroad. // Now people can entertain themselves with all tastes of cuisines without leaving Shanghai. // All "immigrants" have brought their particular style of cooking to Shanghai. // The restaurants in Shanghai not only serve many different regional cuisines, such as Shandong, Guangdong, Huai-Yang, Sichuan, Beijing, Zhejiang, Henan, Hunan, and Fujian foods, but also provide vegetarian, Muslim and other palatable exotic dishes from Europe and Asia, etc. //

听译练习:

A:

1. 有关食物的问题不能脱离文化背景。

2. 美国是一个移民国家,因此它有着丰富多彩的饮食文化。

3. 其实,我们之所以拒食某些肉类并非基于生理原因而是出于美学原因。

4. 保健食品包括那些加工程度极低的天然食品,也就是说,这些食品中不含用以延长食品保鲜期的防腐剂,不含用以改善食物味道的食用味素或用以美化食物的食用色素。

5. 咖啡厅通常比高级餐馆便宜,装潢也没有高级餐馆那么讲究,比如比萨饼店、薄煎饼店、三明治店和家庭餐馆等都属于这类价格较为便宜、装潢较为朴素的餐饮场所。

B:

1. Color, aroma and taste have been regarded as the basics of Chinese culinary art.

2. The preparation of meats by smoking is one of the most prominent features of richly flavored Hunan cuisine.

3. One prominent feature of Shanghai cuisine is that tonic foods are prepared by using different types of medicinal ingredients for the various seasons of the year.

4. Many factors are involved in the distinct regional differences in cuisine such as geography, climate, transportation, migration, and influence from overseas cultures.

5. The Nanxiang Soup Dumpling is dainty with a thin and translucent wrapper, filled inside with mashed meat and tasty soup. Don't eat one in whole or you will risk burning your tongue.

C:

A:王先生,我们都是来自美国的游客,我们很想了解一下中国菜和中国人的饮食习惯。你能先跟我们谈谈吗?

B:With pleasure. Modern China enjoys a worldwide reputation as the "Kingdom of cuisine".

A：你能给我们介绍一些主要的菜系吗？

B：Shandong，Sichuan，Guangdong，and Yangzhou cuisines are the four most famous Chinese cuisines. It should be pointed out that these designations are not hard and fast geographical boundaries.

A：那么北京菜属于哪个菜系？

B：Beijing food，for instance，falls within the realm of Shandong cooking，but includes some Sichuan dishes and Mongolian-influenced specialties.

A：你能谈谈每一菜系的特点吗？

B：My pleasure. Cantonese cuisine is famous for raw and lightly-cooked foods and their original flavors. Sichuan cooking is noted for its hot flavors. Shandong cuisine is characterized by its seafood dishes and the Yangzhou cooking style is known for its wide variety of ingredients and sweetish flavors.

A：中国人喜欢在春节吃饺子。我很想学包饺子。你知道怎么做吗？

B：Oh，yes. I often make Jiaozi with my family. There are several stages. The first one is making the dough. Then you go on to the second stage，which is preparing the filling.

A：有什么馅的？

B：It's quite variable but usually finely minced pork or whatever green vegetable is available. The third one is to make wrappers.

A：一切就绪后就到了最复杂的一个环节——包饺子，是吗？

B：Yes. You only put quite a small amount of filling on the wrapper and then fold together the edges of the wrapper to form a half moon shape，and press the edges well together. That's it.

A：听起来好复杂。我会尽力学。

B：I'd be happy to teach you if you like.

第12单元

体育健身

Unit 12

Sports

背景知识
Background Information

Everyone hopes to live happily in the world. Physical exercises are indispensable to a happy life. There is a famous saying: "Life lies with exercise." Although lack of regular physical exercises may not cause one to die, doing exercises will certainly help us live longer and more healthily.

Why, then, are physical exercises so important to our health? First, physical exercises can improve blood circulation, speeding up the supply of nutrients and oxygen to every part of the body and the removal of waste from the blood through sweating and exhalation.

Secondly, physical exercises can promote a healthy metabolism. It helps with the digestion and absorption of food, thus giving everyone a good appetite.

Thirdly, physical exercise can help consume excessive fat in the body and prevent us from putting on too much weight, therefore keeping them in good shape.

Finally, after physical exercises we usually have a good rest and a sound sleep at night, refreshing us for the next day's work.

In conclusion, physical exercises do not only keep us fit and strong, but also help us to be successful in our lives. It is, therefore, strongly suggested that people, old and young, spare some time to take an active part in various kinds of physical exercises.

对话口译

Dialogue A

Vocabulary Work

Study the following words and phrases and translate them into the target language.

skipping meals	store fat	布局	infield and outfield
bases	投球手和击球手	跑垒	the batting stance
the backswing and stride			

Text Interpreting

Listen to the following dialogue and interpret it into the target language.

A：Hello，Tang. How is it going?

B：你好,迈克尔。还不错。不过说真的,这几天我感觉有点累。工作太辛苦了,没有精力去锻炼。

A：Oh，that is just an excuse，I'm afraid. You can always find some time to exercise.

B：我一工作起来就要连续好几个小时,经常忙得连吃午饭的时间都没有,可是我还是越来越胖。

A：Tang，you know that work is not the same as exercises because it is stressful but not relaxing. And skipping meals will not help you lose weight. In fact your body will store fat if you miss meals.

B：你说得很对,迈克尔。我必须加强锻炼了。不过我不喜欢跑步或去健身房,太枯燥了。我更喜欢球类运动。

A：Ball games? You know what，a few Chinese friends of mine and I are going to play baseball at the weekend. Would you like to join?

B：真的吗? 我非常愿意。我一直都想学习打棒球。听说棒球在美国很流行。

A：Right. Americans are crazy about baseball.

B：我对棒球了解不多。你能告诉我些基本知识吗?

A：With pleasure.

B：能不能简要介绍一下棒球场地的布局?

A：The field is divided into an infield and outfield. The infield square has the four bases at its corners and it is also called the diamond. The diamond is surrounded on two sides by the outfield which is fair territory, and on the other two sides by foul territory. To get a better idea of this, I'll show you to the field this afternoon.

B：太谢谢你了，迈克尔。投球手和击球手站在哪里？

A：On the pitcher's mound and at the home plate, respectively.

B：怎样才能跑垒得分呢？

A：A run is scored when a player makes his way round all of the bases and back to home without being put out.

B：想要击球成功，最重要的是哪些因素？

A：The batting stance, the backswing and stride, the swing and contact with the ball, and the follow-through—they are all very important. Tang, I didn't expect you can raise so many questions. The best way to find the answers is to play it personally.

B：千真万确。太感谢你了，迈克尔。我现在都等不及要去棒球场了。

对话口译

Dialogue B

词汇预习 *Vocabulary Work*

Study the following words and phrases and translate them into the target language.

决赛	削球、抽球、推挡、扣杀	无与伦比	the attacking style
synchronized diving	3 米跳板	10 米跳台	蛙泳动作
lead the way			

口译实践 *Text Interpreting*

Listen to the following dialogue and interpret it into the target language.

A：Hi, Wang. Did you watch the Olympics?

B：当然看了。中国队又赢了。太棒了！

A：Incredible! China has won all the gold medals and most of other medals of table tennis.

B：这一点也不奇怪。中国的乒乓球是世界上最棒的。有人说，在决赛中只有中国人才赢得了中国人。

A：That's true. In the final of men's team, Japan was defeated by China. And both the gold medals of women's single and team were swept by the Chinese players.

B：中国队还赢得了男子单打和女子单打的银牌。

A：Which team won the gold medal of men's single?

B：中国队。中国球员在削球、抽球、推挡、扣杀以及几乎所有的技术方面都是无与伦比的。

A：They are of the attacking style rather than defending.

B：我国是乒乓球的故乡。我想这可能是国人如此擅长乒乓球的原因吧。

A：But the other day I read that table tennis originated from Britain.

B：真的吗？不可能吧？

A：Yes. That article did say so, I'm sure.

B：坦率地说，看我国选手打乒乓球真是太精彩了。凡是有中国队参加的乒乓球比赛，我一场也没有错过。

A：China is also a dominant country in diving. How many medals have you won so far?

B：应该有七金二银了吧。

A：Synchronized events are amazing, aren't they?

B：是的。双人跳水的独特之处就在于运动员两人为一组参加比赛，无论是 3 米跳板还是 10 米跳台，同组运动员必须使用相同或相似的动作。

A：I have seen the performance of Wu, who impressed me most with her wonderful and perfect entry. How did she achieve it?

B：关键是她的刻苦训练再加上一些技巧。她手掌先入水，用手掌推压水面，而且在水下用手臂做蛙泳动作，使身体两侧形成气阱，这样一来水面只会产生泡沫却不会溅起水花。

A：Wow, that's something. I bet China will lead the way in table tennis and diving for long.

篇章口译(英译汉)

Passage A (E-C)

  Vocabulary Work

Study the following words and phrases and translate them into Chinese.

cricket	an international disaster	village green	batsman
onlooker	hit the ball a great distance	get excited enough to call out	

口译实践 Text Interpreting

Listen to the English passage and interpret it into Chinese at the end of each segment.

To most foreigners, cricket seems a dreadful boring game. // But English people think the sound of a wooden cricket ball striking against a wooden cricket bat is just about the most beautiful sound in the world. //

The All-England cricket team is the most important one. Its players, who may be either amateur or professional, are chosen from the country cricket teams. // The most important international matches are those played between England and Australia, and are held one year in one country, the next year in the other. // When these matches are being played, if an Englishman says, "The news is terrible", he does not mean that an international disaster has occurred—merely that England is not doing well at cricket. //

On Saturday and Sunday summer afternoons, on driving into any village, a visitor is certain to hear the crack of a bat hitting a ball. // Then presently he will come to a field and village green. // All around it, sitting on the ground, on benches, or in their cars, are the people of the neighborhood. They are not saying much, but their eyes are fixed on the cricket pitch. // When the batsman hits the ball a great distance, the onlookers get excited enough to call out. //

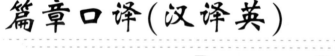

Passage B (C-E)

词汇预习 Vocabulary Work

Study the following words and phrases and translate them into English.

无与伦比	洛杉矶湖人队	名人堂	铭记
曼巴精神	天道酬勤	竞技精神	终极法则

口译实践 *Text Interpreting*

Listen to the Chinese passage and interpret it into English at the end of each segment.

尽管科比·布莱恩特离开了我们,但他在球场内外无可撼动的坚强意志永存。他强烈的进取心、职业道德以及干劲无与伦比。// 这些品质让科比带领洛杉矶湖人队获得了 5 次总冠军,并让他入选了名人堂,与入驻其中的最伟大的球员们一道被共同铭记。//

的确,科比无与伦比的坚持与投入令他从一众球员中脱颖而出。// 他拥有不超越对手绝不罢休的坚定信念。据《纽约客》杂志报道,科比将这一信念称为"曼巴精神","曼巴"一词取自世界上最致命的毒蛇之一"黑曼巴",以及 2003 年电影《杀死比尔》中的顶级杀手之名。//

"曼巴精神"大受欢迎,科比也在其所著的《曼巴精神:我是如何打球的》一书中详细讲述了自己的心路历程。// "曼巴精神就是关注过程,并在最关键的时刻相信天道酬勤,这是竞技精神的终极法则,"他在书中如此写道。//

尽管这位洛杉矶巨星在一场直升机事故中丧生的消息令无数人震惊悲痛,科比给人们留下的精神将影响一代又一代人。// 无论你是否是篮球运动员,你都无法否认科比的力量。它激励你成为最好的自己。//

口译讲评

Notes on the Text

Dialogue A

1. Hello, Tang. How is it going? 对于西方人来说,中国人的姓名既难发音又难记忆,所以他们往往只用姓氏称呼中国人。但回译成汉语时,应照顾到中国人的习惯,不宜只译姓氏一个字,否则有失礼貌。例如 Tang 可视不同对象和场合,译作"小唐""老唐""唐先生"等。

2. Ball games? You know what, a few Chinese friends of mine and I are going to play baseball at the weekend. You know what 是口语常用短语,用于提请听者注意,引出有趣的、重要的或出人意料的信息。可灵活译为"你知道吗""我告诉你""太巧了""真不可思议"等。

3. 能不能简要介绍一下棒球场地的布局。英语体育用语变化很多,不同运动场地各有各的名称。如棒球、足球场地应译作 field;篮球、排球、网球、羽毛球场地译作 court;乒乓球场地译作 arena;冰球场地译作 rink;高尔夫球场地译作 course;田赛场地译作 field;径赛场地译作 the tracks。而四周有看台的田径赛场,一般称体育场,译作 stadium。

4. A run is scored when a player makes his way round all of the bases and back to home

without being put out. 这个句子中的 run，base，home，put out 意义不同于日常生活用语。体育用语专业性强，术语多，而约定俗成的惯用法又颇为严格，因此翻译体育用语时要格外小心。

Dialogue B

1. 真的吗？不可能吧。"不可能吧？"采用反译法处理为 Is it possible? 所谓反译法，就是原文本来用肯定语气，而译文则用否定语气，反之亦然。例如 Leave me alone 译成"别烦我"；I couldn't agree more 译成"我完全同意"。

2. 凡是有中国队参加的乒乓球比赛，我一场也没有错过。这一句中的"比赛"是一般性的赛事，译为 tournament。各类体育赛事有不同的称呼。"锦标赛"称 championship；"大奖赛"称 grand prix；"邀请赛"称 invitational；"选拔赛"称 selective trials；"表演赛"可简称 exhibition；综合性运动会称 games。

3. 双人跳水的独特之处就在于运动员两人为一组参加比赛，无论是 3 米跳板还是 10 米跳台，同组运动员必须使用相同或相似的动作。这一句中的"运动员"最好具体译作 diver。athlete 是运动员的统称，但在分项体育中，却是特指"田径运动员"，其他如"体操运动员"译作 gymnast；"举重运动员"译作 weightlifter；"射击运动员"译作 shooter 或 marksmen/markswomen；"击剑运动员"译作 fencer；"滑冰运动员"译作 skater；只有少数球类和棋牌类项目的运动员才译作 player。

Passage A

1. But English people think the sound of a wooden cricket ball striking against a wooden cricket bat is just about the most beautiful sound in the world. 这个句子中的 English people 不宜译为"英国人"，而应译为"英格兰人"。英国全称为 the United Kingdom of Great Britain and Northern Ireland，包含四个组成部分，即 England，Scotland，Wales，and Northern Ireland，翻译时应注意区分。

2. The most important international matches are those played between England and Australia，and are held one year in one country，the next year in the other. 该句中的 one year in one country，the next year in the other 可简洁地处理为"每年一度轮流举办"。口译过程中应该充分利用汉语言简意赅的优势。

3. On Saturday and Sunday summer afternoons，on driving into any village，a visitor is certain to hear the crack of a bat hitting a ball. Then presently he will come to a field and village green. 英语的不定人称泛指可使用单数第三人称，而汉语则习惯只使用第二人称"你"和第一人称"我们"。因此这两句参考译作：在夏日周末的午后，驱车穿过任何一个小镇时，你都会听到棍棒击球的声音。映入眼帘的是一片绿地。

4. All around it，sitting on the ground，on benches，or in their cars，are the people of the neighborhood. They are not saying much，but their eyes are fixed on the cricket pitch. 前一句话是倒装句，主语是 the people of the neighborhood，正是后一句的主语。两句话关系密切，主语相同，又都比较短小，故可考虑采用合句法翻译。参考译作：从附近赶来的人们散坐在地面上、长椅上，或是车里，不动声色地关注着板球场上的一举一动。

Passage B

1. 尽管科比·布莱恩特离开了我们，但他在球场内外无可撼动的坚强意志永存。译为：Although Kobe Bryant is no longer with us, his unbreakable will on and off the basketball court lives on. 注意在英语表达习惯中，although 不能和 but 连用，这里 although 引导的是让步状语从句，表示"尽管……"，这句话的主句是 his unbreakable will on and off the basketball court lives on。其中，will 是名词作主语，表示"意志"。live on 意为"永存"，这里的 on 用作副词，表示"继续；向前"。例如：

Move on! 向前走！

Time marches on. 时光不停步。

Fight on to final victory. 战斗到最后的胜利

2. 这些品质让科比带领洛杉矶湖人队获得了 5 次总冠军，并让他入选了名人堂，与入驻其中的最伟大的球员们一道被共同铭记。译为：These qualities helped Bryant lead the Los Angles Lakes to five titles and have brought him to the Hall of Fame, where he will be enshrined with the greatest to have ever played the game.

名人堂 Hall of Fame 例如：

Former Houston Rockets center Yao Ming has been nominated for the Hall of Fame, in a move that could make him the first Chinese player to receive the honor. 前休斯敦火箭队中锋姚明被提名入选名人堂，此举或将使其成为首个获此殊荣的中国球员。

where he will be enshrined with the greatest to have ever played the game，这里 where 作为关系副词，引导的是个非限制性定语从句，对前文做进一步的修饰说明。

be enshrined 意为"被铭记；被珍藏"。例如：

These important rights are enshrined in the constitution. 这些重要的权利已庄严载入宪法之中。

3. 的确，科比无与伦比的坚持与投入令他从一众球员中脱颖而出。译为：Indeed, what elevated Bryant above his peers was his unmatchable commitment to be the best. 这句话的翻译我们用了 what 引导的强调句结构，强调科比无与伦比的坚持和投入，这样的译法重点突出。

4. 曼巴精神一般译为 Mamba Mentality. 科比曾在一个 Ted Talk 上以 Mamba Mentality 为主题分享了他心目中曼巴精神的意思，他认为曼巴精神的内涵是：恪守、虚心、专注、热爱、从不退却、永不放弃。

相关词语 *Relevant Words and Expressions*

爆冷门 produce an unexpected winner
壁球 squash
东道国 the host nation
腹部训练椅 abdominal bench

比赛地点 competition/sports venue
秋千 swing
发奖仪式 the prize-awarding ceremony
黑马 dark horse

火炬点燃仪式 the flame-lighting ceremony   健美 body-building

健骑机/健身车 cycling equipment   竞技性运动 competitive sport

竞技状态好 in good form   体格、体质 physique

耐力训练 endurance training   有氧操 aerobics

武术 martial arts   失常 to lose one's usual form

体育道德 sportsmanship

体育疗法 physical exercise therapy；sports therapy

全国运动会 National Games

世界大学生运动会 World University Games；Universiade

体育大国/强国 sporting/sports power

为祖国争光 to win honors for the motherland

乡间户外活动(如打猎，钓鱼，射击，赛马等) country sports

发展体育运动,增强人民体质 promote physical culture and build up the people's health

胜不骄,败不馁 Do not become cocky/be dizzy with success, nor downcast over/discouraged by defeat.

译技能 Interpreting Skills

跨文化意识(1)

　　跨文化意识是对文化差异的认识,口译员应培养对交际所涉及的两种文化的意识,不仅要熟悉了解本国文化,还应熟悉其他文化的风俗习惯以及与不同文化的人相处、工作的方法。在整个口译中,译员都应保持对文化差异的敏锐感,并应主动从讲话人和听众的角度去思考问题和采取行动,避免因文化差异而导致的沟通不畅和误会。

　　非语言交际包括身体语言、手势语以及面部表情等,是任何场合的交谈中不可缺少的组成部分。美国有研究表明,在表达感情和态度时,语言只占交际行为的7%,而声调和面部表情所传递的信息多达93%。由此可见,非语言交际的重要性。

　　和有声语言一样,非语言交际也是文化的载体,一样有强烈的民族性。很多事例表明他们随文化的改变而改变。由于不同民族的文化已经根深蒂固,不容易接受与自己的习惯相反的信号,所以我们不能忽视文化和环境差异所赋予非语言交际的不同含义。

　　对非语言交际的理解,不仅可以帮助译员更透彻地理解交际双方所想表达的内容,还可以促进译员与来自不同文化背景的客人之间的关系。下面列举一些口译过程中常见的非语言交际。

　　1. 身体接触

　　有些译员在陪同同性客人时,为了表示友好,常常和客人保持较近的身体距离,甚至在熟悉之后,会有轻抚客人等亲密动作。实际上,并不是每个国家的客人都认可这种表示友好的行为。

　　在中国,年轻的同性朋友之间,有身体接触如手牵手、手挽手等亲密动作,被视为正常;

而在美国,则有可能被误认为同性恋。意大利人、法国人、俄罗斯人和大部分亚洲人都像中国人一样,喜欢亲密的身体接触;而北欧人和美国人尊重个人空间,即使是朋友之间,也会保持一定距离,最多就是轻拍对方的后背(slap on the back),表示亲密。

2. 首语

点头表示肯定,摇头表示否定,人人皆知。但在伊朗、保加利亚、印度和土耳其,人们却用摇头(头部呈弧形,从一侧移到另一侧,类似摇头)表示肯定。埃塞俄比亚人用扭头,把头转向后,这半个摇头动作,表示肯定。

3. 手势

吃完饭后,中国人用手掌轻拍自己的肚子表示吃饱了,而美国人却用一只手放在自己的喉部,手心向下,表示 I am full to here,为"吃饱了"之意,这个手势在我国文化中表示杀头的意思;又如在表示叫某人过来这一含义时,中国人把手伸向被叫人,手心向下,手指同时弯曲几次;而美国人把手伸向被叫人,手心向上握拳,食指弯曲几次,这个手势在中国人看来是极其挑衅的;在中国,伸出食指往下弯,表示"九"这个数字,而在日本这个手势表示偷窃;在中国,人们伸出大拇指表示赞赏,而美国人除了可以表示赞赏外,在路边搭车时,也会伸出拇指,但同样的手势在澳大利亚人看来就非常粗鲁;中国人用手指点点自己的鼻子,表示"是我""我做的"等含义,而美国人则认为这一动作非常可笑,他们会用手指指自己的胸部表示本人。

在中国戏曲文化中,伸出两根竖起的食指从左右两边向中间慢慢靠近,表示男女相爱,匹配良缘。在中国,别人为自己倒茶或者斟酒时,伸出一只手,手指弯曲,在杯子边轻拍,表示感谢。这些手势都具有浓烈的东方色彩。

而在美国,用大拇指顶着鼻尖,其他手指弯曲一起动(thumb one's nose/make a long nose)表示挑战和蔑视;摇动食指(shake one's fingers at sb.)是在告诉别人不要做某事,示意对方做错了事;交叉食指和中指(cross one's fingers)意味着希望自己交好运,比如,美国人在参加比赛前会对家人朋友说:Keep you fingers crossed for me. 这些手势在中国也很少见。

遇到这些情况,为促进交流,避免误解,译员应该主动采取行动,做出解释说明,保证交际的顺畅。

4. 面部表情

东方人尽量掩饰自己的真实情感,而西方人倾向于表露自己的情感,面部表情非常丰富,比如他们常用耸肩(shrug)或者扬眉毛(raise one's eyebrows)表示惊讶、怀疑、不满等。所以美国人与中国人和日本人交往时,会常常抱怨对方面无表情,捉摸不透。而美国人对中国人的微笑常常不知所措,感到窘迫。有这样一个故事,有个美国人请一位中国朋友教他一些中文的日常用语,中国朋友一边教一边笑,那位美国人觉得受到了耻笑,非常生气。其实中国朋友并不是嘲笑他的发音奇怪,只是善意地表示友好,或是鼓励他。

为避免误会,译员作为双方的桥梁,不仅要注意自己使用的身体语言,不能误导客人,同时也应在必要情况下,对双方客人的身体语言做出解释说明。

口译练习 *Enhancement Practice*

第一项 Project 1
听力复述　Retelling

Listen to the following passages once and then reproduce them in the same language at the end of each segment.

English Passage：

The Olympic Games will be held in this country in four years' time. // As a great many people will be visiting the country, the government will be building new hotels, an immense stadium, and a fine new swimming pool. // They will also be building new roads and a special railway-line. The Games will be held just outside the capital and the whole area will be called "Olympic Park". // Workers will have completed the new roads by the end of this year. By the end of next year, they will have finished work on the new stadium. // The fine modern buildings have been designed by Kurt Gunter. Everybody will be watching anxiously as the new buildings go up. // We are all very excited and are looking forward to the Olympic Games because they have never been held before in this country. //

Chinese Passage：

　　运动减肥最健康,但不能马上见效,所以运动减肥必须持之以恒。// 走一小时的路或绕运动场慢跑十二圈(半小时)才能把脂肪烧完,这是运动减肥的难处。更何况运动后胃口大开,输入的食物热量一不小心就会超过辛苦运动时烧掉的热量。因此,很多人运动后体重不减反增。//

　　运动还必须配合节食才能有效燃烧体内多余的脂肪,减肥也才会有效。// 节食减肥的最初两周,体重下降得最快,但节食越久,减去的体重会越来越少。节食减肥满六个月后,人体的基础代谢率(指细胞的工作效率)会滑落四成,人体内脂肪烧得越来越慢,体重越来越难下降。// 人类到了中年开始老化后,也是由于基础代谢率变慢,才使脂肪在体内堆积而长胖;经常运动的人在停止运动后,也是基础代谢率变慢而积肥长胖。//

第二项 Project 2
主题讨论 Discussion
　　Hold a 5-minute discussion with your partners on the topic "Extreme Sports".

第三项 Project 3
听译练习 Listening and Interpreting

A. Sentence Interpreting

Listen to the sentences and interpret them into Chinese.

1. Walking up and down the stairs would beat any exercise machine.

2. Combining exercise with the diet may be the most effective way to lose weight.

3. I believe that the upcoming Paralympics will be the most dynamic and spectacular of its kind.

4. Bridge is not only an entertainment game，but a sports game；it is more instructive than interesting.

5. Extreme sports allow and encourage individual creativity in the innovation of new maneuvers and in the stylish execution of existing techniques.

B. Sentence Interpreting

Listen to the sentences and interpret them into English.

1. 日益流行的健身热潮正在风靡整个中国。

2. 准备活动有助于提高柔韧性，防止受伤。

3. 这座城市的体育设施远远不能满足人民日益增长的需要。

4. 极限运动要求参与者把高超的运动技巧与极大的冒险精神完美地结合起来。

5. 我们将突出"以人为本"的思想，以运动员为中心，提供优质服务，努力建设使奥运会参与者满意的自然和人文环境。

C. Dialogue Interpreting

Listen to the dialogue and interpret it into the target language.

A：欢迎光临银星体育中心。先生，下午好！

B：Good afternoon. Could you please tell me something about the facilities at your sports center?

A：好的。这里有健身房、游泳池、网球场、排球场和乒乓球房。

B：What should I do if I want to use the facilities regularly?

A：一般而言，最好成为我们俱乐部的会员，所以最好申请一张会员证。

B：How much is the membership fee?

A：每季 800 元。

B：No problem，but do I have to be a member?

A：不一定。但是会员比非会员价格优惠，而且可以优先使用各种器械。

B：I see. I also would like to find out fitness programs. What classes do you have?

A：我们开设了各种课程，比如太极拳、拳击等等。不知您有什么爱好？

B：I'd like to try boxing.

A：出于健康考虑，练习拳击的人在开始训练前要由主教练进行体检。您要预约吗？

B：Yes，please. Let me see. Could I make an appointment for Wednesday?

A：下午 3 点怎么样？

B：OK. That'd be great.

参考译文 Reference Version

对话口译 A：

A：你好，小唐。一切都好吗？

B：Hello, Michael. I'm fine. But actually I'm feeling a little tired these days. Well, I work so hard that I do not have the energy to exercise.

A：哎呀，那恐怕只是借口。锻炼的时间总是能找到的。

B：But I work hard all the time for long hours. Often I have no time for lunch. Yet I am still getting fatter.

A：小唐，你看，工作不同于锻炼，因为工作只能使你有压力而不能使你放松。而且不吃饭无助于减肥。实际上，如果你不吃饭，身体只会储存脂肪。

B：I know you are right, Michael. I have to get more exercise. But I do not care so much for jogging or working out in the gym. They seem boring to me. I prefer ball games.

A：球类运动？啊，太巧了，我正准备和一些中国朋友周末一起打棒球。你愿意来参加吗？

B：Really? Yes, I'd love to. I have always wanted to play baseball. It is very popular in the States, I hear.

A：是的，美国人对棒球很着迷。

B：I know little about baseball. Can you help me with some of the basic knowledge?

A：非常乐意。

B：Can you give me a brief introduction to the lay-out of a baseball field?

A：棒球场分为内场和外场。内场为正方形，四个角上各有一个垒位。内场也称"方场"，由界内地区和外场临界的两边与界外地区另外的两个边围绕而成。为了让你有更好的了解，我今天下午带你到棒球场去看一下。

B：It's so kind of you, Michael. Where do the pitcher and the hitter stand?

A：分别在投手区的平台上和本垒板旁边。

B：How is a run scored?

A：一名队员跑完全垒，送回本垒而未被判出局即得分。

B：What are the most important elements of successful batting?

A：站姿、向后引棒、伸踏、挥棒和后继动作，所有这些都很重要。小唐，没想到你能提出这么多问题。寻找这些答案的最好方法是亲自打棒球。

B：Exactly. Thank you ever so much, Michael. I cannot wait to go to the baseball field.

对话口译 B：

A：嗨，小王。看奥运比赛了吗？

B：Yes, certainly. China won again. It's fantastic.

A：真不可思议！乒乓球所有的金牌和其他的多数奖牌都被中国队夺走了。

B：It's nothing strange at all. As for table tennis, China is the best in the world. It's said only one Chinese player can defeat another Chinese in the final.

A：确实这样。在男子团体决赛中，日本队输给了中国队。女子单打和团体的金牌也被中国队夺得。

B：And they won the silver medals of both men's single and women's single.

A：那么男子单打哪个队摘得了金牌呢？

B：China. Chinese are unmatchable in chopping, driving, pushing shot, smashing and nearly in all techniques.

A：他们是进攻型的而不是防守型的。

B：China is the home of table tennis. I suppose that may be the reason why Chinese are so excellent at it.

A：但我几天前看的文章上说，乒乓球是起源于英国的。

B：Really? Is it possible?

A：是真的。那篇文章确实是这样说的。

B：Frankly speaking, to watch Chinese play table tennis is really thrilling. I've never missed a table tennis tournament involving China.

A：中国在跳水方面也是最强的。你们现在得了几枚奖牌了？

B：Seven golds and two silvers, I think.

A：双人跳水令人惊叹，是吧？

B：Yes. Synchronized diving is unique because it features two divers as a team. The two divers of a team perform either on the 3-meter springboard or 10-meter platform using the same, or similar dives.

A：我看过吴敏霞的比赛，给我印象最深的是她精彩、完美的入水动作。她是如何做到的呢？

B：The key was her painstaking practice coupled with some skills. She lands on the hands and opens the water with them. Also, she performs a breaststroke motion with her arms underwater, so creating pockets of air on either side of the body. This effect leaves foam on the surface of the water. There is no splash.

A：哇，真了不起！我敢肯定中国在乒乓球和跳水项目上的优势会保持很长时间的。

篇章口译 A：

　　对大多数外国人来说，板球运动似乎极其无聊。// 但英格兰人却认为板球与木棍之间的撞击声是世界上最动听的音乐。//

　　全英板球队是最重要的一支队伍，队员包括职业运动员和业余爱好者，都选拔自英格兰各地的球队。// 最有影响的板球国际赛事要算英格兰和澳大利亚之间的比赛了，两国每年一度轮流举办。// 赛事举行期间，如果一个英格兰人说"有坏消息了"，他并不是指世界上发生了什么灾难，而只是说英格兰板球队发挥得不够理想。//

　　在夏日周末的午后，驱车穿过任何一个小镇时，你都会听到棍棒击球的声音。// 映入眼帘的是一片绿地。// 从附近赶来的人们散坐在地面上、长椅上，或是车里，不动声色地关注着板球场上的一举一动。// 一旦击球手将球击出很远，观众们就会兴奋地欢呼起来。//

篇章口译 B：

Although Kobe Bryant is no longer with us, his unbreakable will on and off the basketball court lives on. His fierce competitiveness, work ethic and drive were unmatched. // These qualities helped Bryant lead the Los Angles Lakes to five titles and have brought him to the Hall of Fame, where he will be enshrined with the greatest to have ever played the game. //

Indeed, what elevated Bryant above his peers was his unmatchable commitment to be the best. // He was ruthless in his pursuit to dominate his opponents. He called it the "mamba mentality" after the black mamba, one of the world's deadliest snakes — and also after the top killer from the 2003 movie *Kill Bill*, according to *The New Yorker*. //

The mamba mentality became so popular that Bryant detailed his process in his book *The Mamba Mentality*: *How I Play*. // "Mamba mentality is all about focusing on the process and trusting in the hard work when it matters most. It's the ultimate mantra for the competitive spirit," he wrote in the book. //

Though many were shocked and sad when the Los Angles great died in a helicopter crash, Bryant's mentality will have an influence on generations to come. // Whether you're a basketball player or not, you can't deny Kobe's power to inspire you to be your best self. //

听译练习：

A：

1. 上下楼梯可比什么健身器都要好。

2. 运动与节食结合也许是减肥最有效的途径。

3. 我相信即将开幕的这一届残疾人奥运会将是最富动感、最为壮观的一次盛会。

4. 桥牌不仅是一项娱乐活动，也是一项竞技运动；不仅有趣，更富有教育意义。

5. 极限运动允许并鼓励个人在花样翻新和现有技巧上进行创新。

B：

1. A growing keep-fit fervor is sweeping over China.

2. Warm-up exercises are important for promoting flexibility and preventing injury.

3. The sports facilities in the city are far from enough to meet the growing demand.

4. Extreme sports require participants to well combine excellent athletic skill with pronounced risk.

5. In line with the "people-oriented" and "athletes-centered" ideas, we will spare no efforts to provide quality services and to build a natural and social environment that will satisfy all the Games' participants.

C：

A：Welcome to Sliver Star Sports Centre. Good afternoon, Sir.

B：你好！能请你介绍一下你们体育中心的设施情况吗？

A：Sure. We have a gymnasium, a swimming pool, a tennis court, a volleyball court as well as a table tennis room.

B：如果想经常使用这些设施，该怎么做呢？

A：Generally speaking，you have to become a member of our sports club，so you should apply for a membership.

B：会费多少钱？

A：It is 800 yuan for a season.

B：没问题。不过我必须成为会员吗？

A：No，but members pay less for using the facilities and they have preference over non-members，so they have more access to the facilities.

B：明白了。另外，我还想了解一下健身课程，你们有什么班？

A：We have all kinds of programs，ranging from Tai Chi to boxing. What is your particular interest？

B：我想练练拳击。

A：For health reasons，those who want to enroll must have a fitness check-up by our chief instructor before the start of the training. Would you like to make an appointment？

B：要预约。让我想想，可以约在周三吗？

A：How about 3 o'clock in the afternoon？

B：好啊。太棒了。

风俗节日

 Unit 13　Festivals

背景知识
Background Information

Festivals, of many types, serve to meet specific social needs and duties, as well as to provide entertainment. These times of celebration offer a sense of belonging for religious, social, or geographical groups. Modern festivals that focus on cultural or ethnic topics seek to inform members of their traditions. In past times, festivals were times when the elderly shared stories and transferred certain knowledge to the next generation. Historic feasts often provides a means for unity among families and for people to find mates. Select anniversaries have annual festivals to commemorate previous significant occurrences.

There are numerous types of festivals in the world. Though many have religious origins, others involve seasonal change or have some cultural significance. Also, certain institutions celebrate their own festivals to mark some significant occasions in their history. These occasions could be the day when these institutions were founded or any other event which they decide to commemorate periodically, usually annually.

Seasonal festivals are determined by the solar and the lunar calendars and by the cycle of the seasons. The changing of the season was celebrated because of its effect on food supply. Ancient Egyptians would celebrate the seasonal inundation caused by the Nile River, a form of irrigation, which provided fertile land for crops. A recognized winter festival, the Chinese New Year, is set by the lunar calendar, and celebrated from the day of the second new moon after the winter solstice.

Certain institutions decide to annually commemorate certain special events significant to their history. These institutions are usually educational institutes such as colleges and senior secondary, secondary, or high schools. Such festivals are usually called "fests".

对话口译

Dialogue A

 词汇预习 *Vocabulary Work*

Study the following words and phrases and translate them into the target language.

be enamored with	be addicted to	巧克力迷	indulgence
jovial	Halloween	Valentine's Day	营养价值
annual	gala	champagne	

 译实践 *Text Interpreting*

Listen to the following dialogue and interpret it into the target language.

A：你喜欢吃巧克力吗？

B：The word "like" is not adequate to describe my love for chocolate. I am absolutely, completely, enamored with and addicted to this food, like no other substance on earth.

A：哇。你真是个巧克力迷。我知道在西方文化中巧克力远不只是一种食品，对不对？

B：Yes. Chocolate not only fills belly but also makes people feel so good. Especially when holidays arrive, it always plays an important role in festive indulgences.

A：在哪些具体的节日里人们喜欢并珍爱巧克力呢？

B：At Christmas, people give chocolates as gifts. At Easter, chocolate eggs make a jovial spring. And at Halloween children don costumes and beg neighbors for candies, hoping most of all to get chocolate.

A：好像巧克力给这些节日增添了魅力。情人节呢？我知道巧克力是情侣们最喜欢的礼物。

B：You are right. Chocolate has long been associated with passion, romance and love. On Valentine's Day chocolate clearly says "I LOVE YOU!"

A：我还想知道为什么人们把巧克力当成爱情的象征，因为从营养价值来看，它不是健康食品。

B：Receiving a nicely wrapped box of chocolates on Valentine's Day is the dream of many lovers. The pleasure is kindled from unwrapping the box and from the sensual smell. When it finally passes your lips and starts to instantly melt, the taste and smell flood your senses with joy. Is there any better way to start off a journey of love?

A：你的描述让我想起一句老话，"玫瑰虽香，不及巧克力芬芳。"我听说在美国某些州有巧克力节，是这样吗？

B：Yes. For example，Virginia hosts the Chocolate Lovers Festival each year. The annual 2-day festival is held in early February.

A：对你这样的巧克力爱好者而言，这肯定有着莫大的吸引力了。这个传统是什么时候开始的呢？

B：The first festival was held in February 1992 and then continues an annual tradition with "love of chocolate" as a unifying theme. Now the event has grown each year in scale and scope.

A：你去过这种巧克力节吗？

B：Of course. It turns out to be the most jovial and romantic experience I have ever had. During the Gala there was cultural entertainment，chocolate body art，chocolate fountain，wine，champagne，and beer，and more chocolate than you can imagine. I shall definitely go there again.

对话口译

Dialogue B

 ### *Vocabulary Work* 词汇预习

Study the following words and phrases and translate them into the target language.

be ignorant of	connotation	丰富	虚构人物
长生不死药	immortally	太阳炙晒	施行暴政
auspicious	起义	纪念	

 ### *Text Interpreting* 口译实践

Listen to the following dialogue and interpret it into the target language.

A：I know "Zhong Qiu Jie"，or the Mid-Autumn Festival，is a traditional Chinese festival，but I am quite ignorant of the story behind such a typical Chinese holiday. Can you tell me the cultural connotations it carries?

B：好的。"中秋节"是农历的八月十五，在这天，家人和爱人团聚在一起，欣赏象征丰富、美满和好运的圆月。

A：The moon seems to be a special symbol for the Chinese. I once heard from one of my friends that the Chinese have a story about a lady living on the moon. Can you tell me the story?

B：住在月亮上的那个女子叫嫦娥。她是中国传说里的一个虚构人物。她喝下长生不死药，飞到了月亮上，一直孤零零地生活在那里。中秋时节，女孩子们会向她祈祷。

A：I don't quite understand. Is it a punishment? Because living alone plus immortally on the moon is not a happy ending, is it?

B：不，不是惩罚。嫦娥那样做是为了把她的人民从她的丈夫后羿手里解救出来。

A：Hou Yi was the one who shot 9 suns in one Chinese myth, right? How come he became the enemy of people?

B：后羿让大地免受太阳炙晒之苦，这之后他偷了长生不死药，当了首领。可是他对人民施行暴政。所以他的妻子嫦娥就偷了不死药，把它喝光，这样后羿就不会永生，人民就得到了解放。

A：So the festival started from the legend? But it seems that there is nothing to do with the auspicious connotations you mentioned just now.

B：不，不全是这样的。刚才那只是后来和月亮有关的一个故事。故事在中国流传很广，所以每当人们欣赏圆月，就总是想起它。至于中秋节的来历，并没有清晰的记载。但据说一开始它可能是一个收获节。

A：It sounds like Thanksgiving in China. You know, Thanksgiving in the US was originally celebrated for the good harvest. Then do you have some special customs, say, food or whatever, for that day?

B：有的。在那个特别的日子，月饼和灯笼是必不可少的。大人通常吃各种芳香的月饼，喝上一杯上好的中国茶，而孩子们就拎了明晃晃的灯笼四处跑。

A：I once saw the moon-cake on TV. Chinese people have moon-cakes at the Mid-Autumn because these cakes are as round as the moon, right?

B：是的。但这只是原因之一。14 世纪的时候，节日吃月饼有了新的含义。明朝的第一个皇帝朱元璋在推翻元朝的起义中把信息藏在中秋月饼里面。

A：This history gives a political color to the festival. Then Zhu won the war, and thus established the Ming dynasty, right? Of course, the moon-cakes played a significant role.

B：一点也没错。

篇章口译(英译汉)

Passage A (E-C)

词汇预习 *Vocabulary Work*

Study the following words and phrases and translate them into Chinese.

Easter Day	equinox	Resurrection	Jesus Christ
dye	penetrate	shell	pale brown
confectioner	sweet-shop		

口译实践 *Text Interpreting*

Listen to the English passage and interpret it into Chinese at the end of each segment.

Easter Day occurs on the first Sunday after the full moon following the spring equinox. // It is originally the day to commemorate the Resurrection of Jesus Christ. // But now for most people, Easter is a simple spring holiday, while for the children, it means, more than anything else, Easter eggs or chocolate eggs! //

On Easter Sunday morning, the breakfast eggs are boiled in several pans in some families. // Each contains a different vegetable dye, so that when they are served the shells are no longer white or pale brown in color, but yellow or pink, blue or green. The dyes do not penetrate the shell of course. //

Chocolate Easter eggs are displayed in confectioners' shops as soon as Christmas is over. // The smallest and simplest are inexpensive enough for children to buy with pocket money. //

As Easter approaches, more elaborate eggs than these fill the sweet-shop windows. // They are accompanied by all sorts of small presents designed to appeal to children. // Lucky children may receive several of these as presents from friends or relatives. //

Easter eggs are meant to give enjoyment—and they do! They are pretty and decorative. And they signal good wishes and shared happiness in the changing seasons. //

篇章口译(汉译英)

Passage B (C-E)

词汇预习 Vocabulary Work

Study the following words and phrases and translate them into English.

元宵节	猜灯谜	社会各阶层	狮子舞
秧歌舞	踩高跷	焰火	沉醉

口译实践 Text Interpreting

Listen to the Chinese passage and interpret it into English at the end of each segment.

在元宵节,街上挂着各式各样、大小不一的灯笼,吸引着无数游人。// 孩子们会拎着自制或是购买的灯笼,兴高采烈地在街上逛。//

猜灯谜是节日的主要活动。灯笼主们在纸上写下谜语,贴在灯笼上。// 如果游人知道谜底,就把纸条拿下,到灯笼主那里去看答案对不对。对的话,就会得到个小礼物。// 猜灯谜有趣多智,在社会各阶层中广受欢迎。//

节日的时候,会有很多节目上演,比如龙灯舞、狮子舞、秧歌舞、踩高跷和击鼓。// 晚上,除了壮丽的灯笼,焰火也是靓丽的风景。// 大多数人家都有一些春节剩下的焰火,到元宵节燃放。有的地方政府甚至会举办焰火晚会。// 在新年的第一个月圆之夜,焰火璀璨,明月当空,人们不由沉醉其间。//

口译讲评

Notes on the Text

Dialogue A

1. The word "like" is not adequate to describe my love for chocolate. I am absolutely, completely, enamored with and addicted to this food, like no other substance on earth.

这句话的用词程度甚深，强烈地表达了说话人对巧克力的喜爱之情，翻译时要注意保持同等的生动和力度。可译为："喜欢"这个词不足以形容我对巧克力的爱。我是百分之百地、完完全全地、喜欢它、迷恋它，世上再没有别的东西可比了。

2. Receiving a nicely wrapped box of chocolates on Valentine's Day is the dream of many lovers. The pleasure is kindled from unwrapping the box and from the sensual smell. When it finally passes your lips and starts to instantly melt，the taste and smell flood your senses with joy. Is there any better way to start off a journey of love? 这段话通过非常生动而细致的描写，讲述了在情人节收到巧克力，让它融在舌尖的快乐和喜悦。翻译时，要注意用词简洁、鲜明，让人有感同身受之效果。参考译文为：在情人节收到一盒精美包装的巧克力是许多爱侣的梦想。打开盒子，诱人的香味散出来，让人马上就快乐起来。最后巧克力滑入嘴唇，即刻融化，那种香和味蔓延过来，让人开心不止。还有别的更好的方法来开始一段爱的旅程吗？

3. 你的描述让我想起一句老话，"玫瑰虽香，不及巧克力芬芳"。遇到这类谚语的翻译要尤为用心，要译得同样文采出色。此处原文为押韵，译文恰好可套用英语中类似的谚语：Roses are fine，but chocolate is divine.

4. Now the event has grown each year in scale and scope。此句翻译要符合中文的习惯，可以将其具体化处理为：现在这个节日每年规模越来越大，人数越来越多。

Dialogue B

1. "中秋节"是农历的八月十五，在这天，家人和爱人团聚在一起，欣赏象征丰富、美满和好运的圆月。"农历的八月十五"译为 the 15th day of the 8th month of the lunar calendar，切不可用公历纪年的 August 来表示。

2. 故事在中国流传很广，所以每当人们欣赏圆月，就总是想起它。此句可用 so...that...进行连接，后半句中用 every time 连接。可译为：It is so popular in China that every time people enjoy the full moon，it conjures up.

3. 大人通常吃各种芳香的月饼，喝上一杯上好的中国茶，而孩子们就拎了明晃晃的灯笼四处跑。此句翻译并不难，但要注意选词须生动，表达人们过节的欢乐喜庆，可译为：Adults will usually indulge in fragrant moon-cakes of many varieties with a good cup of Chinese tea，while the little ones run around with their brightly lit lanterns.

4. 明朝的第一个皇帝朱元璋在推翻元朝的起义中把信息藏在中秋月饼里面。这是关于月饼的又一传说。据传中秋节吃月饼始于元代，当时，朱元璋领导人民反抗元朝暴政，约定在八月十五日这一天起义，以互赠月饼的办法把字条夹在月饼中传递消息。中秋节吃月饼的习俗便在民间传开来。原文此句的翻译要注意选择好恰当的词语作为句子的主要成分，本句可译为：Zhu Yuanzhang, the first emperor of Ming Dynasty, hid messages in Mid-Autumn moon-cakes in the revolt against the previous Yuan dynasty.

Passage A

1. Easter Day occurs on the first Sunday after the full moon following the spring equinox. 具体而言，每年在教堂庆祝的复活节指的是春分月圆后的第一个星期日，如果月圆那天

刚好是星期天,复活节则推迟一星期。日期年年不同,一般在 3 月 22 日至 4 月 25 日之间。

2. the Resurrection of Jesus Christ. 耶稣被钉死在十字架上,死后第三天复活。耶稣的复活是基督教信仰的核心,意味着复活的身体已脱离了必朽坏的状况,是上帝再创造的开始,复活节由此象征重生和希望,成为基督教纪念耶稣复活的一个重大节日。

3. Each contains a different vegetable dye, so that when they are served the shells are no longer white or pale brown in color, but yellow or pink, blue or green. 复活节彩蛋是西方国家在庆祝复活节时特别装饰性的蛋。传统上一般是使用经过染色的蛋类。现代的习惯通常是使用蛋状的巧克力代替。彩蛋一般事先藏好,然后由儿童来找寻。它是复活节的象征性物品,是表达友谊、关爱和祝愿的方式。正如这句话中所指,彩蛋五彩缤纷,寓指新生命的开始。

4. And they signal good wishes and shared happiness in the changing seasons. shared happiness 在此处翻译时可进行词性转化,处理为"与你分享季节更替的喜悦"。

Passage B

1. 在元宵节,街上挂着各式各样、大小不一的灯笼,吸引着无数游人。这句话在翻译时可用 lanterns 作主语,"各式各样、大小不一"按照英语习惯可以翻译为 lanterns of various shapes and sizes。

2. 猜灯谜有趣多智,在社会各阶层中广受欢迎。汉语的句子往往缺乏明确的逻辑连词,翻译时要按照英语的"形合"语言特征,适当添加,此句前后两句的关系为事实因果,可用 as 进行连接。

3. 节日的时候,会有很多节目上演,比如龙灯舞、狮子舞、秧歌舞、踩高跷和击鼓。"龙灯舞、狮子舞、秧歌舞、踩高跷和击鼓"是中国传统节日中常见的庆祝活动,可扼要译为:a dragon lantern dance, a lion dance, a yangge dance, walking on stilts and beating drums.

4. 在新年的第一个月圆之夜,焰火璀璨,明月当空,人们不由沉醉其间。此句结构较为松散,由三个独立分句构成,可选用"人们"一词作为主语构建全句,"焰火璀璨,明月当空"八字可以翻译为宾语 the imposing fireworks and bright moon in the sky,作为"沉醉其间"的原因跟上。

 相关词语 *Relevant Words and Expressions*

拜年 pay a New Year call
除夕 New Year's Eve
灯谜 lantern riddle
观灯 view the lanterns
龙灯舞 dragon lantern dance
年画 New Year picture

鞭炮 a string of small firecrackers
大扫除 year-end household cleaning
登高 hill climbing
贺岁片 New Year film
庙会 temple fair
扫墓 pay respect to the dead

狮子舞 lion dance　　　　　　　　　秧歌舞 yangge dance

粽子 a pyramid-shaped dumpling made of glutinous rice wrapped in reed leaves

春联 Spring Festival couplets (conveying best wishes for the year)

辞旧迎新 bid farewell to the old and usher in the new; ring out the old year and ring in the new

年夜饭 family reunion dinner on Lunar New Year's Eve

压岁钱 money given to children as a Lunar New Year gift

恭喜发财 May you be prosperous! / Wish you all the best!

跨文化意识（2）

很多人认为译员只是和语言打交道，实际上这种认识是片面的。译员在口译过程中，不仅需要考虑语言，也要考虑文化习俗等差异。译员是两种文化间的桥梁。如果口译只是寻求字词对等的话，那么机器就可以完成了。译员的工作是将一种文化传递到另一种文化，是在不同文化间寻求对等的表达。

动物在各个文化中都有其深刻的内涵，是人类感情表达的高级使者，但在不同文化中，动物所代表的民族内在心理特征是不同的。

中西文化中，有些动物具有相似的内涵。例如：狐狸（fox）象征着狡猾、精明、奸诈，狼（wolf）生性凶残贪婪，驴（ass）表示愚蠢、倔强，羊（sheep）表示温顺，天鹅（swan）表示圣洁，猪（pig）表示肥胖，猴子（monkey）表示顽皮，蜜蜂（bee）表示忙碌，骡子（mule）表示固执等。当遇到与这些动物有关的口译时，我们可以采取直译的办法：

a wolf in sheep's clothes 披着羊皮的狼

as busy as a bee 像蜜蜂一样忙

as stubborn as a mule 像骡子一样固执

但有些动物在中西方文化中有不同的内涵，如果译员不考虑这一点，统统采取直译的办法，将会闹出笑话。这里作简要概括：

1. 龙（dragon）

曾经有译员将"亚洲四小龙"直译为 Four Asian Dragons，让美国客人感到十分费解，而译员自己却没有意识到自己在跨文化意识上的不足。

在中国文化中龙是兽图腾的融合和化身，有着腾云驾雾、呼风唤雨、神通广大、威严无比的形象。历代帝王为"真龙天子"，世间有中国人是"龙的传人"一说。民间有"望子成龙""龙凤呈祥""龙腾虎跃"等说法。但在西方，dragon 是凶残恶魔般的怪物，《圣经》中把与上帝作对的恶魔撒旦称作 the great dragon。在现代英语中，dragon 仍然是"凶暴"的意思，常用来比喻对小孩严厉、凶暴的女人，类似汉语里的"母夜叉"。

了解了这些文化差异，我们可以看到 Four Asian Dragons 不但不能传递这四个地区"经济实力强，发展迅速，犹如腾飞的巨龙"这一信息，反而引起不必要的误解。这里译为 Four

Asian Tigers 更为符合西方人对于动物含义的理解。

2. 蝙蝠(bat)

蝙蝠的"蝠"和"福"谐音,而"蝠鹿"谐音"福禄";所以蝙蝠在汉语里表示"财富""地位""吉祥"。但在西方的民间传说中,蝙蝠却和罪恶、丑陋、吸血、黑暗势力联系在一起。人们甚至相信蝙蝠闯入私宅就是死亡的凶兆。对于一个不了解西方文化的人来说,下面的翻译就会令他摸不着头脑。

as blind as a bat 瞎得像蝙蝠

as crazy as a bat 疯得像蝙蝠

译员在遇到这样的情况时,不如不要将蝙蝠二字译出,以避免歧义,以上两句改为:

as blind as a bat 有眼无珠

as crazy as a bat 极度疯狂

3. 猫头鹰(owl)

和蝙蝠恰好相反,在中国,猫头鹰是厄运的凶兆。"夜猫子进宅"意味着厄运将至。但在西方,owl 却是"冷静""智慧"的象征。许多儿童读物和卡通片里,常常会出现猫头鹰的身影,它们通常严肃认真、机智果断,为百兽明断是非。He is as wise as an owl 这一句最好也不要译为"像猫头鹰一样聪明",反而是"他聪明机智"更容易让中国人理解。

4. 蟋蟀(cricket)

在传统的汉文化中,蟋蟀是忧伤、凄凉的象征。在《诗经》里蟋蟀的叫声就被作为农夫岁末困顿生活的映衬。但在英美文学中 crickets 大多给人带来安静、舒适甚至幸福之感。英语中有 as merry as crickets(像蟋蟀一样快乐)的说法,截然不同于汉语的联想。

5. 狗(dog)

狗在东西方文化中含义有很大的差异。在西方许多公司里,都有 anti-crime watchdog group 这一机构,如果译员把这里的 watchdog 译为"看门狗",中国人一定会觉得费解。因为中文常用狗形容不好的事物,有贬义。例如:"狗急跳墙"是指人无计可施,乱想办法;"狗拿耗子多管闲事"是指人好事;"狗嘴里吐不出象牙"指此人说不出好话来;"狗咬吕洞宾不识好人心"则是说猜忌别人的一片好心。

但在英语言民族中,宠物犬种类繁多。犬类集人们的需要与宠爱于一身,深受人们的喜爱。因此,dog 一词的比喻通常是褒义或中性的意义。例如用 Love me, love my dog 比喻"爱屋及乌";用 a top dog 比喻"身居高位的人";用 a lucky dog 比喻"幸运的人";用 Every dog has its day 比喻"人人皆有得意之日"。上面提到的 anti-crime watchdog group 实际上就是公司里的保安部门。

此外,各国不同的地理环境和文化风俗也影响到语言中提及动物的种类。

英国是一个海洋岛国,历史上航海业一度领先世界。因此,英语民族的生活与海洋、商业有着密切的关系,其习语文化具有典型的海洋商业文化特征。例如用 cold fish 比喻"冷冰冰的人";用 dull fish 比喻"枯燥无味的人";用 odd/queer fish 比喻"行为古怪的人";用 neither fish nor fowl 比喻"不伦不类",也就是汉语的"非驴非马"之意。译员不理解这些比喻意,直接译为"冰冷的鱼""枯燥的鱼"等,就会闹出笑话。

口译练习 *Enhancement Practice*

第一项 Project 1
听力复述　Retelling

Listen to the following passages once and then reproduce them in the same language at the end of each segment.

English Passage：

Labor Day was first celebrated on the first Monday in September，1882. On September 5th of that year the first Labor Day parade was held in New York City. // The occasion quickly gained support within the organized labor movement，and it was designated an official holiday by Congress in 1895 for the first Monday in September. // In September of 1882，the New York World reported that after a mass meeting in Union Square 20,000 cheering and singing workers marched up Broadway with banners that read: Eight hours for work；eight hours for rest；eight hours for recreation！Labor creates all wealth！//

Chinese Passage：

农历七月初七是中国人的情人节，这一天是女儿家们最为重视的日子。//七月初七之所以称为乞巧，是因为民间相信这天牛郎织女会天河，女儿家们就在晚上以瓜果朝天拜，向女神乞巧，希望能求得。//乞巧，她们除了乞求针织女红的技巧，同时也乞求婚姻上的巧配。所以，世间无数的有情男女都会在这个晚上夜深人静时刻，对着星空祈祷自己的姻缘美满。//

第二项 Project 2
主题讨论 Discussion

Hold a 5-minute discussion with your partners on the topic "Western Festivals in My Eye".

第三项 Project 3
听译练习 Listening and Interpreting

A. Sentence Interpreting

Listen to the sentences and interpret them into Chinese.

1. Christmas is typically the largest annual economic stimulus for many nations.

2. Labor Day is a "grass roots" holiday，which hails the dignity of working people and salute their individual efforts.

3. In many countries，businesses，schools and communities have Christmas parties and dances in the weeks before Christmas.

4. The average American today，when talking of Halloween，thinks of a children's holiday when all the children get dressed up and go door to door asking for candies.

5. While 75％ of chocolate purchases are made by women all year long，during the days before Valentine's Day，75％ of the chocolate purchases are made by men.

B. Sentence Interpreting

Listen to the sentences and interpret them into English.

1. 近年来，都市年轻人把七夕当作中国情人节来庆祝。

2. 在传统中式婚礼上，新娘常常戴着红盖头，遮住面孔。

3. 除了美丽的灯笼，元宵节另外一个重要的活动就是吃由糯米做成的小圆子。

4. 清明是放风筝的季节，那时许多地方举行风筝比赛，人们争着做出最漂亮、最别致的风筝。

5. 在新年，人们通常穿上红衣服，因为红色意味着驱除邪灵，而黑色和白色不能穿，因为它们意味着服丧。

C. Dialogue Interpreting

Listen to the dialogue and interpret it into the target language.

A：People told me Duan Wu Festival is around the corner. Is it a traditional Chinese festival like the Spring Festival?

B：是的。端午节是中国农历的五月初五。有人说它是纪念中国历史上最伟大的诗人之一屈原，有人说它是为祭祀龙王的仪式。但总体说来，这个节日主要就是吃粽子和赛龙舟。

A：That sounds interesting. If you don't mind，can you tell me more about the historical contexts of the festival? Let's start from the poet，OK?

B：好的。屈原是战国时期楚国的贵族。他被政敌暗箭所害，流放异乡 20 年。对国家前途失望之后，在农历五月初五那天他投汨罗自尽。之后人们就在每年的农历五月初五那天纪念他的爱国精神。

A：In summary，it is another sad story about rumors killing a man of integrity. But why do people eat Zongzi and race dragon boats to commemorate him?

B：赛龙舟应该是代表着当时楚国人民希望从汨罗江中找回屈原的尸体。粽子投入江中喂鱼是为了不让鱼靠近他的身体。

A：So Zongzi at that time was not for eating but for protecting his body. But the tradition must have changed with time because I see people nowadays eat Zongzi themselves.

B：是的。这是传统的演变，也是为了阻止浪费。此外，赛龙舟成了主要在中国南方流行的体育活动。每年在广州和香港都举行国际龙舟赛事。

A：Now，let's come to the second origin—the worship of Dragon King. I guess Zongzi and the dragon boats here were used as presents to him，right? What kind of a man was the king?

B：龙王不是一个人。他是中国古人在神话中创造出来的水神。在端午节，人们赛龙舟取悦他，献粽子给他作礼。这样做就是为了让他开心，保证一年风调雨顺。

A：But my impression on Zongzi is quite vague, though I saw people eating Zongzi once. Can you give me a specific description of it?

B：好的。北方的粽子常含有枣子，因为那里盛产枣子。在南方的广东省，人们在粽子里塞上肉、火腿、栗子等其他馅，口味非常丰富。在四川，粽子通常要拌上糖。

A：I didn't see there are so many variants of Zongzi according to the regional differences. Then, what about racing dragon boats?

B：龙舟外形很像龙，通常 20—40 米长，需要几十个人一起划。船夫随鼓声节拍划船，船长站在船头挥舞小旗帜指挥，比赛开始前，举行一个隆重的仪式祭祀龙王。

A：Dragon boat racing must be quite a spectacle, drums beating, colorful flags waving, thousands of people cheering on both sides of the river. I hope to see it with my own eyes here in China. Apart from Zongzi and racing boats, are there any other activities to commemorate the festival?

B：过去有一些有趣的习俗，不过现在不太流行了，虽然在农村的有些地方还有一些有趣的传统习俗。祛除疾病、驱赶邪恶是这些活动的主要目的。这是因为端午来的时候，仲夏将至，天气炎热，常伴有多种疾病。

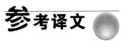 参考译文 **Reference Version**

对话口译 A：

A：Do you like eating chocolate?

B："喜欢"这个词不足以形容我对巧克力的爱。我是百分之百地、完完全全地喜欢它、迷恋它，世上再没有别的东西可比了。

A：Wow. You are a true chocoholic. I know in Western culture, chocolate is much more than food, isn't it?

B：对的。巧克力不仅填饱肚子，而且让人们感觉非常美妙。特别是节日来临时，它总是在节日狂欢中扮演了重要的角色。

A：On what specific holidays is chocolate being enjoyed and cherished?

B：在圣诞节，人们把巧克力当礼物送人。在复活节，巧克力蛋让春天充满欢乐。在万圣节，孩子们装扮自己，向邻居要糖果，他们最希望要的就是巧克力。

A：It seems chocolate really adds glamour to these festivals. How about Valentine's day? I know chocolate is a favorite gift for lovers.

B：没错。巧克力很久以来就和激情、浪漫和爱恋联系在一起。在情人节，巧克力明白地表示"我爱你"。

A：I still wonder why people take chocolate as a token of love for it is not considered a health food based on its nutritional value.

B：在情人节收到一盒精美包装的巧克力是许多爱侣的梦想。打开盒子，诱人的香味散出来，让人马上就快乐起来。最后巧克力滑入嘴唇，即刻融化，那种香和味蔓延过来，让人开心不已。还有别的更好的方法来开始一段爱的旅程吗？

A：Your description reminds me of an old saying, "Roses are fine, but chocolate is divine." I've heard in some US states, they have chocolate festivals. Is it true?

B：是的。比如,弗吉尼亚州每年举办巧克力爱好者节。这个每年为期两天的节日在二月初开始。

A：It must be a big draw with chocolate lovers as you. When did the tradition start?

B：第一届节日是 1992 年 2 月举办的,之后每年作为一种传统就一直延续下去,主题都是"热爱巧克力"。现在这个节日每年规模越来越大,人数越来越多。

A：Have you ever been to any chocolate festival of this kind?

B：当然去过。那是我经历过的最快乐、最浪漫的事情。在那个盛会上,有文化娱乐活动、巧克力人体艺术、巧克力喷泉、美酒、香槟、啤酒,还有你都想象不到的各种巧克力。我肯定还要再去的。

对话口译 B：

A：我知道"中秋节"是传统的中国节日,但是我不知道这个典型中国节日背后的故事。你能和我说说它所具有的文化含义吗?

B：Well, "Zhong Qiu Jie" is celebrated on the 15th day of the 8th month of the lunar calendar for family members and loved ones to congregate and enjoy the full moon, which is an auspicious symbol of abundance, harmony and luck.

A：月亮对中国人而言似乎是特殊的标志。一个朋友曾在信里告诉我,中国有个故事说有个女子住在月亮上。你能把这个故事告诉我吗?

B：The lady living on the moon is named Chang-E. She is an imaginary figure derived from a Chinese legend. She drank the elixir of life and ascent to the moon, living there all alone. Young girls would pray to her at the Mid-Autumn Festival.

A：我不太明白。这是惩罚吗? 一个人孤零零地在月亮上生活,而且永远死不了,很凄惨啊,是不是呢?

B：No, it's not. Chang-E did that to save her people from Hou Yi, her husband.

A：后羿是中国神话里射下九个太阳的人,对吗? 他怎么会成为人民的敌人?

B：After he saved the earth from the scorching suns, he stole the elixir of life and became the leader. But he tyrannized them. His wife, Chang-E, therefore stole the elixir and drank it to deprive him of immortality and free the people.

A：节日就这样从这个传说开始了吗? 可是你刚才提到节日有好运的含义,这好像并没有什么联系啊。

B：No, not exactly. That is just a story later dedicated to the moon. It is so popular in China that every time people enjoy the full moon, it conjures up. As to the origin of the Mid-Autumn Festival there is no clear record. But it is said that it probably began as a harvest festival.

A：听起来很像中国的感恩节。你知道吗,美国的感恩节最初是为了庆祝大丰收的。你们的中秋节有什么特殊的习俗吗? 比如,有什么吃的或其他什么吗?

B：Yes, moon-cakes and lanterns are a must on that particular day. Adults will usually indulge in fragrant moon-cakes of many varieties with a good cup of Chinese tea, while the little ones run around with their brightly lit lanterns.

A：有一次我在电视上看到过月饼。中国人在中秋节吃月饼是因为这些饼像月亮一样圆，对吗？

B：Yes. But this is just one reason. In the 14th century, the eating of moon-cakes at the festival was given a new significance. Zhu Yuanzhang, the first emperor of Ming Dynasty, hid messages in Mid-Autumn moon-cakes in the revolt against the previous Yuan dynasty.

A：这段历史给了这个节日一抹政治色彩。接着朱打了胜仗，建立了明朝，对吗？当然，月饼扮演了重要的角色。

B：Exactly.

篇章口译 A：

　　复活节在过了春分月圆后的第一个星期日来临。// 它原是纪念耶稣复活的日子。// 而现在对大多数人来说，复活节只是一个春天的普通节日。对于孩子们来说，没有比复活节彩蛋或巧克力蛋更重要的了。//

　　复活节早上，有的家里把早餐用的蛋分放在几个锅里煮。// 每个锅里都盛有不同颜色的植物染料，这样端上来的蛋不再是白色或浅棕色的，而是黄色或粉红色，蓝色或绿色的。当然，染料是不会渗透到蛋壳里去的。//

　　圣诞节一过，复活节巧克力蛋便在糖果店里摆出来了。// 那些最小和花样最简单的很便宜，孩子们用自己的零花钱就可以买下来。//

　　复活节临近时，糖果店的橱窗里会摆满比这些更精美的彩蛋。// 同时还有各种各样吸引孩子们的小礼物出售。// 幸运的孩子可能从亲友那儿得到好几种这样的礼物。//

　　复活节彩蛋是为了给人们带来快乐——确实如此！这些彩蛋精美漂亮且富有装饰性，它们代表着人们的美好心愿，并与你分享季节更替的喜悦。//

篇章口译 B：

On Lantern festival, lanterns of various shapes and sizes are hung in the streets, attracting countless visitors. // Children will hold self-made or bought lanterns to stroll with on the streets, extremely excited. //

"Guessing lantern riddles" is an essential part of the Festival. Lantern owners write riddles on a piece of paper and post them on the lanterns. // If visitors have solutions to the riddles, they can pull the paper out and go to the lantern owners to check their answer. If they are right, they will get a little gift. // As riddle guessing is interesting and full of wisdom, it has become popular among all social strata. //

In the daytime of the Festival, performances such as a dragon lantern dance, a lion dance, a yangge dance, walking on stilts and beating drums while dancing will be staged. // On the night, except for magnificent lanterns, fireworks form a beautiful scene. // Most families spare some fireworks from the Spring Festival and let them off in the Lantern

Festival. // Some local governments will even organize a fireworks party. On the night when the first full moon enters the New Year, people cannot help but become really intoxicated by the imposing fireworks and bright moon in the sky. //

听译练习：

A:

1. 对许多国家而言,圣诞节正是一年一度最大的经济刺激点。
2. 劳动节是"老百姓"的节日。它庆祝人的尊严得到尊重,欢呼靠自我奋斗取得胜利。
3. 在许多国家,公司、学校和团体纷纷在圣诞之前的几周内举办圣诞晚会和舞会。
4. 现在一般美国人谈到万圣节,就想到是孩子的节日,那天孩子们装扮好自己,挨家挨户地要糖果。
5. 虽然一年里四分之三的巧克力都是女人们购买的,但是在情人节来临前的那些天,四分之三的巧克力都是男人们购买的。

B:

1. In recent years urban youths have celebrated the Double Seventh Festival as Valentine's Day in China.
2. At a traditional Chinese wedding, the bride is often seen with a red veil on her head, which covers the bride's face.
3. Besides beautiful lanterns, another important part of the Lantern Festival is eating small dumpling balls made of glutinous rice flour.
4. Qing Ming is a kite-flying season, and in many places the festival is used to hold kite competitions, with people vying to create the most stunning and imaginative kite.
5. On the New Year's day people usually wear something red as this color is meant to ward off evil spirits—but black and white are out, as these are suggestive of mourning.

C:

A：人们告诉我端午节就快来了。它是不是像春节一样的传统中国节日呢?

B：Yes. The Duanwu Festival falls on the fifth day of the fifth month of the Chinese lunar calendar. Some say it is observed to commemorate Qu Yuan, one of the greatest poets in Chinese history. Others say it is for a ceremony to worship the Dragon King. But generally, this festival is marked by eating Zongzi and racing dragon boats.

A：听起来很有趣。如果你不介意的话,能否多说说这个节日的历史背景? 就从那个诗人开始,好吗?

B：All right. Qu Yuan was a noble of Chu during the Warring States Period. He was stabbed in the back by his political enemies and sent into exile for 20 years. On the fifth day of the fifth lunar month, he drowned himself in the Miluo River, because he was hopeless about his country's future. People later commemorate him on that day for his patriotism.

A：简而言之,这又是一个谗言杀死忠良的悲惨故事。但是人们为什么要吃粽子、赛龙舟来纪念他呢?

B：Racing boats is believed to be representative of how the people of Chu tried at the time to recover Qu Yuan's body from the Miluo River. Zongzi were thrown in the river to feed the fish, so they would stay away from Qu Yuan's body.

A：所以那时候的粽子不是为了吃而是为了保护他的身体。但是随着时间流逝，传统一定变了，因为我看到现在人们自己吃粽子。

B：Yes. This is a development of tradition as well as prevention of waste. Besides, racing dragon boats becomes a popular sporting activity mainly in southern China. International dragon boat races are held in Guangzhou and Hong Kong every year.

A：现在谈谈另一个来由——祭祀龙王吧。我猜粽子和龙舟在这里是用作给龙王的礼物，对不对？龙王是个什么样的人？

B：Dragon King wasn't a man. He was created by ancient Chinese people as a mythical god in charge of water. On the day of Duanwu, people raced dragon boats to entertain him and offered him Zongzi as a treat. The sole purpose was to please the god to ensure a year of favorable weather.

A：但是我对粽子的印象很模糊，虽说我有次见过有人吃粽子。你能详细描述一下吗？

B：OK. Zongzi is often made of rice mixed with dates in Northern China, because dates are abundant in the area. In the southern province of Guangdong, people stuff Zongzi with pork, ham, chestnuts and other ingredients, making them very rich in flavor. In Sichuan Province Zongzi is usually served with a sugar dressing.

A：以前我不知道地方不同，粽子也有这么多的不同。那么，赛龙舟呢？

B：A dragon boat, shaped like a dragon, is usually 20 to 40 meters long, and needs several dozen people to row it. Boatmen row the boat in cadence with the drumbeats, as the captain standing in the bow of the boat waves a small flag to help coordinate the rowing. Before the race gets underway, a solemn ceremony is held to worship the Dragon King.

A：龙舟赛一定很壮观，鼓声激昂、彩旗挥舞、成千上万的人们站在两岸欢呼。我希望在这里亲眼看看。除了粽子和龙舟赛，还有什么活动纪念这一节日吗？

B：It used to have other interesting customs that are no longer commonly observed, though you may still find them practiced in some rural area. Mostly, dispelling disease and driving out evil were the main purposes of those practices. This is because midsummer is around corner when the Duanwu comes and hot weather used to bring various diseases.

文化风情 第14单元

Unit 14

National Cultures

背景知识

Background Information

In some contexts, a frequent usage of the term culture is to indicate artifacts in music, literature, painting and sculpture, theater and film. Anthropologists understand "culture" not only refer to consumption goods, but also to the general processes which produce such goods and give them meanings, and to the social relationships and practices in which such objects and processes become embedded. As a result, culture thus includes technology, art, science, as well as moral systems.

Most nations are partly defined by a shared culture. Unlike a language, a national culture is usually unique to the nation, although it may include many elements shared with other nations. Additionally, the national culture is assumed to be shared with previous generations, and includes a cultural heritage from these generations, as if it were an inheritance. As with the common ancestry, this identification of past culture with present culture may be largely symbolic.

Since the Old Stone Age, the ancient Chinese people have had its own continuous social development and cultural traditions. Ancient China had its unique artistic styles and a tradition of independent technological development, from the painted-pottery culture of the late New Stone Age to the embroidery culture of Qing dynasty.

Cultures can be different between continents or nations, because the perception is different and often selective. People would feel surprised, disorientated or confused when they have to operate within an entirely different cultural environment, such as a foreign country. When trying to assimilate the new culture, people will encounter difficulties in knowing what is appropriate and what is not.

对话口译

Dialogue A

 Vocabulary Work

Study the following words and phrases and translate them into the target language.

大开眼界	virtually	大熔炉	evolve
包办婚礼	time-consuming	a wedding planner	the thousand-and-one details
文化障碍	婚礼誓言		

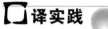  **Text Interpreting**

Listen to the following dialogue and interpret it into the target language.

A：几天前有人请我去参加了一个美式婚礼。真是大开眼界。不仅气氛其乐融融,而且感觉和中国的婚礼大不相同。你们美国人的婚礼习俗真的很独特。

B：Well，a wedding ceremony will surely give you good and romantic memories about the United States. But we have few wedding traditions that are totally unique to the US.

A：真的吗? 那么所有这些传统和习俗都是从哪里来的呢?

B：Virtually all of our wedding traditions and customs have either been taken directly from a wide range of other countries and cultures—primarily European—or they have evolved from the traditions in other nations.

A：明白了。我知道美国很久以来被称为"大熔炉"。就婚礼来说,它把其他许多地方不同的传统融入了自己的熔炉。对吗?

B：You can say that again. The United States was originally populated by immigrants from many lands，primarily Europe. These immigrants brought in their own wedding traditions with them，and these traditions，stirred in this melting pot，have slowly evolved into the traditional "American" wedding ceremony.

A：很有趣。不同种族的婚礼传统依旧保存下来,它折射了美国的社会现实,是不是呢?

B：Yes，this has become part and parcel of the "American" wedding ceremony. In the US we are very comfortable with a wide diversity of traditions and ceremonies.

A：我知道美国人一直很重视爱情。你们会接受"包办"婚礼来增进家族事业或是影响力吗?

B：No，I don't think so. I think most marriages in the States are based on love. Most people will not go into marriage that are arranged.

A：在中国,筹办一次婚礼花一年以上的时间一点也不稀奇。在美国怎么样呢?

B：Almost the same. Wedding planning can be time-consuming and many brides today opt to have a professional wedding planner take care of the thousand-and-one details of the wedding day.

A：婚礼真是庞大而复杂的一件事。还有,你能和我说说婚礼誓言吗?

B：Sure. Wedding vows are written by the bride and the groom, in which they speak of their love and their desire to make their partner happy and secure, and to be faithful to their partner and their partner alone for the rest of their lives.

A：每次我听到结婚誓言,都会很感动。受邀参加婚礼的客人给新人送礼物是不是一种习俗?

B：Yeah. Gifts are an important part of the American wedding tradition. Gifts are given to help the new couple establish a new home together; often gifts of cash are given.

对话口译

Dialogue B

词汇预习 *Vocabulary Work*

Study the following words and phrases and translate them into the target language.

handicraft	实用性	礼仪性	折扇
souvenir	steep	扇骨	象牙
calligraphy	Lady Windermere's Fan	桃花扇	withdraw

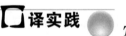译实践 *Text Interpreting*

Listen to the following dialogue and interpret it into the target language.

A：In China fans appear to be more than a cooling device. They seem to have evolved into a fine handicraft. Could you tell me more about fans in China?

B：当然可以。3000 年前,中国人就开始使用扇子了。从古时候起,扇子就一直被视为一种很有魅力的艺术形式,将实用性、礼仪性和装饰性融为一体。

A：As far as I know, fans in China are made from various materials, like paper, silk, feathers. Did they appear at the same time or one after another?

B：它们是依次出现的。首先是羽毛扇。圆形的丝绸扇在唐朝很流行。折扇首先出现在 2 世纪初期，但直到 14 世纪的明朝才风行起来。

A：Once when I was in Hangzhou, I saw different kinds of folding fans in a souvenir shop, some of which were gorgeous but expensive. Why are they priced so steep?

B：折扇的扇骨通常都是竹子做的，但也有一些由珍稀材料制成，比如象牙。杭州产的折扇用了珍贵的材料作为扇骨，所以就比较贵了。

A：Some fans have Chinese calligraphy and paintings on them. Is it a tradition to write or paint on a fan? Is that for decoration or other purposes?

B：扇子上有书法或绘画，很有观赏性。许多著名的书法家，尤其是画家都喜欢在扇子上留下墨宝。

A：In this sense, fans are de-materialized, carrying artistic features. Does the fan have special symbolic significance?

B：是的。在古代，许多戏剧和小说都用扇子作为题材。它代表了爱情、象征了地位或是用来表达人们的心情和情感。

A：Western literature has a famous play called "Lady Windermere's Fan". Is there any Chinese masterpiece on the fan?

B：中国有关扇子的最著名戏剧应该就是《桃花扇》了。以一把溅血绘就的桃花扇为线索，讲述了爱国歌女李香君和文人侯方域在朝代更迭时的动人故事。

A：Now advances in science and technology have forced fans to withdraw from people's daily life. It would be a great pity if the Chinese culture of fans disappears in the future.

B：这个很难说。在舞台上，扇子依然必不可少，人们频繁地用扇子，在传统戏剧中尤其如此。

A：Well, the stage use could be counted as its sustainable cultural value. But the daily use of fans could no longer be as frequent as before. After all, fans are disappearing from households.

B：是的。现在扇子通常是艺术品。虽然扇子在日常生活中用得越来越少，它们却越来越受到收藏家们的青睐。

篇章口译（英译汉）

Passage A (E-C)

  Vocabulary Work

Study the following words and phrases and translate them into Chinese.

yellow ribbon	folklore	inspiration	oak
pull over	ballad	customarily	adverse

  Text Interpreting

Listen to the English passage and interpret it into Chinese at the end of each segment.

Where did the Yellow Ribbon Tradition come from? // Most music historians trace the custom to a 19th century Civil War song. // And folklore has it that the inspiration for the song came from a true incident that occurred on a bus bound for Miami, Florida. // It seems that one of the passengers had just been released from prison and he was bound for home. // He had written to his wife and let her know he still loved her and wanted to be with her. // He asked her to tie a yellow ribbon around the lone oak tree in the Town Square, if she still had feelings for him and wanted him to be with her. // Everyone in the bus asked the driver to slow down as they approached, there it was! // The driver pulled over and phoned the wire services to share the story. It quickly spread throughout the country. Then two songwriters wrote the ballad from the news story. //

Display of a Yellow Ribbon is a sign of loyalty to family, friends or loved ones who are welcome home. // Customarily it is used to welcome home men and women who have been away for a long time under adverse or particularly difficult circumstances such as war or prison. //

篇章口译(汉译英)

Passage B (C-E)

 词汇预习 Vocabulary Work

Study the following words and phrases and translate them into English.

不可或缺	挑剔	海拔	泉水
雨季	水质	上茶	关爱

 口译实践 Text Interpreting

Listen to the Chinese passage and interpret it into English at the end of each segment.

茶是中国人日常生活中不可或缺的饮料。街上茶馆随处可见,就像咖啡馆在西方一样普遍。//

中国人对饮茶非常挑剔。通常,最好的茶生长于海拔 910 米到 2124 米之间。// 人们常用泉水、雨水和雪水来制茶。其中泉水和秋天的雨水最好,雨季的雨水也最合适不过。// 水质和味道最为重要。好的水必须是纯净,凉爽,清澈流动的。//

茶在中国人的情感生活中扮演了重要的角色。到中国人家里做客,主人家总是立刻就敬上一杯茶。// 上茶不只是礼貌,它象征着团聚,代表着尊重,主人与访客共享美好时光。// 主人沏茶只倒七分满,此外杯中三分装的是友情和关爱。// 对访客而言,一杯茶须三饮而尽。在有些地方,一口茶都不喝被视为是十分无礼的。//

口译讲评

Notes on the Text

Dialogue A

1. These immigrants brought in their own wedding traditions with them, and these traditions, stirred in this melting pot, have slowly evolved into the traditional

"American" wedding ceremony. 这句话中的 stir 一词运用得非常形象,它呼应 melting pot 的比喻,生动地体现了各自习俗在美国大环境中的消化吸收过程,口译时可以略微虚化处理,直接译为"融入"即可。

2. This has become part and parcel of the "American" wedding ceremony. part and parcel of 这是英语中的固定搭配,意思是"……不可缺少的一部分"。

3. In the US we are very comfortable with a wide diversity of traditions and ceremonies. comfortable 一词在此处若是直译,会显得十分生硬,可以按照中国人的表达习惯,翻译为动词,即"美国人很喜欢这样"。

4. 你们会接受"包办"婚礼来增进家族事业或是影响力吗?"包办"是中国旧传统中的一种婚姻现象,翻译时应先理解包办的性质为何,即并非自主的自由婚姻,而是在他人安排下进行的婚姻,因此可以翻译为 arranged。

5. Wedding vows are written by the bride and the groom, in which they speak of their love and their desire to make their partner happy and secure, and to be faithful to their partner and their partner alone for the rest of their lives. 这句话的翻译要注意简洁有力,尤其是后半句中的 to be faithful to their partner and their partner alone for the rest of their lives 可以翻译为"终其一生只爱对方一个",以保证句子所传递的情感和力量。

Dialogue B

1. 从古时候起,扇子就一直被视为一种很有魅力的艺术形式,将实用性、礼仪性和装饰性优雅地融为一体。汉英翻译时要注意分清主次。因为汉语句子往往呈流水式,信息依次渐进,而英语则不同,一句之中主次分明,结构严谨。这句话的后半部分"将实用性、礼仪性和装饰性优雅地融为一体",可以用-ing 分词结构和前面的主句部分跟上,译为:Since ancient times, fans have been considered a charming form of art, combining functional, ceremonial and decorative uses.

2. 许多著名的书法家,尤其是画家都喜欢在扇子上留下墨宝。"墨宝"一词可以简单处理为 masterpiece,比较符合英语的表达习惯。

3. In this sense, fans are de-materialized, carrying artistic features. de-materialize 的字典含义为去物质化,若直译,则与对话文风格格不入,翻译时应尽量选择贴近生活的词语,此处可以使用反译法,译为"扇子已经不单单是一件物品"。

4. 以一把溅血绘就的桃花扇为线索,讲述了爱国歌女李香君和文人侯方域在朝代更迭时的动人故事。这句话的翻译处理比较难。可以选择"动人故事"为句子主语,串联起句子的各个成分,整句可翻译为:Through a fan, with a blood drawing of peach blossoms, a moving story is told about a patriotic singer, Li Xiangjun, and a scholar, Hou Fangyu, during the period of dynasty transition.

Passage A

1. 黄丝带:本篇章简述了黄丝带这一习俗的由来。如今黄丝带在美国已经成为牵系亲人,并等待其归来的象征。1980 年,美国各地大街小巷也曾到处悬挂黄丝带,用以提醒政府及大众,美国驻伊朗大使馆数十名工作人员被挟持为人质。波斯湾战争结束,美军正分批返国,迎接他们的除了欢迎仪式、庆功宴会之外,就是各小城小镇悬系的黄丝带。

2. And folklore has it that the inspiration for the song came from a true incident that occurred on a bus bound for Miami, Florida. Folklore has it... 为固定句型,意思是"据民间流传"。这句话在翻译时宜拆分为多个独立短句,原句中的地点状语前可适当添加动词。

3. The driver pulled over and phoned the wire services to share the story. pull over 为固定词组,意思是"把车驶向路边",wire service 指向报社、电台、电视台等提供新闻的电讯社。

4. Customarily it is used to welcome home men and women who have been away for a long time under adverse or particularly difficult circumstances such as war or prison. 此句较长,其中的关系从句须处理成为用字精简、句意凝练的前置定语"的"字结构,可译为:按照习俗,黄丝带用来欢迎那些因战争或牢狱等艰难困境而睽别故里的人回家。

Passage B

1. 街上茶馆随处可见,就像咖啡馆在西方一样普遍。You can see teahouses scattered on the streets similar to the way coffee-houses are often seen in the West.

2. 到中国人家里做客,主人家总是立刻就敬上一杯茶。在诸如此句的汉英翻译中,译者要注意识别句中的重心所在。例如此处全句核心为"一杯茶",所以不妨选用被动语态进行翻译,使句意更为清晰,可翻译为:A cup of tea is always offered immediately to a guest in Chinese home.

3. 上茶不只是礼貌,它象征着团聚,代表着尊重,主人与访客共享美好时光。此句较长,翻译时可注意信息的切分和断句,可译为 Serving a cup of tea is more than a matter of mere politeness; it is a symbol of togetherness. It signifies respect and the sharing of something enjoyable with visitors.

4. 主人沏茶只倒七分满,此外杯中三分装的是友情和关爱。此句中的"七分"与"三分"可译为 seven tenths 和 three tenths。

5. 对访客而言,一杯茶须三饮而尽。在有些地方,一口茶都不喝被视为是十分无礼的。"三饮而尽"可用 gulp 的概念来表达,在后半句"一口茶都不喝被视为是十分无礼的"之中,可以用 might be considered rude,使句意更为充分。

 相关词语 *Relevant Words and Expressions*

版画 engraving	彩塑 painted sculpture
瓷器 porcelain; china	刺绣 embroidery
雕刻 carving	国画 Chinese painting
剪纸 paper-cut	景泰蓝 cloisonné enamel
蜡染 batik	木/石/竹刻 wood/stone/bamboo carving
木刻画 wood engraving	泥人儿 clay figure
皮影 shadow puppet	水墨画 Chinese brush drawing; ink and wash painting

檀香扇 sandalwood fan　　　唐三彩 Tang tri-colored pottery
图章 seal　　　　　　　　　微雕 miniature engraving
象牙雕刻 ivory carving　　　篆刻 seal-cutting

 译技能　*Interpreting Skills*

称谓的口译

　　某译员在一次外事会谈时，发现中方代表中有三位"主任"，分别是外经贸委主任、大学管理系主任和后勤服务中心主任。她凭借自己对中方机构和头衔的了解，将三位主任分别译作 commissioner，chairman 和 director，使外方代表清楚地知晓了中方代表各自的职位。

　　在联络陪同口译中，译员经常需要翻译各种职位、职衔或学衔，这统称作称谓。在各国文化中，称谓都体现出一个人的资历和地位。错译称谓是对有关人员的不尊重，也会造成不必要的麻烦和误解。因此，议员必须对各种组织机构的职位、职衔或学衔准确理解，切忌望文生义。

　　同时，称谓的翻译也是有一定规律可循的。掌握了规律，许多常见的称谓便可在口译时不假思索脱口而出。下面让我们对这些规律作一初步分析和归纳。

　　1. 各类机构或组织首长

　　介绍中国各类机构或组织的首长时，不一定千篇一律地将他们的头衔译作 head，而应该使用特定的、规范的称谓语：minister，president，principal/headmaster，dean，chairman，director 等等。例如：

　　部长（国务院各部） Minister of Foreign Affairs

　　校长或院长（大学） President of Pujiang University

　　校长（中小学） Principal/Headmaster of Pujiang Middle School

　　院长（大学下属） Dean of the Graduate School

　　系主任（大学学院下属） Chairman/Chair of the English Department

　　主任（中心） Director of the Business Center

　　主任（行政） Director of the Teaching Affairs Office

　　会长/主席（学会/协会） President of the Student Union

　　厂长（企业） Director of Pujiang No. 1 Machine Tools Enterprise

　　院长（医院） President of Pujiang Hospital

　　董事长（企业） President/Chairman of the Board of Directors

　　董事长（学校） President/Chairman of the Board of Trustees

　　2. 带"总"字的首席长官

　　汉语中带"总"字的首席长官称谓很多。译成英语时，"总"常用 chief，head，general，managing 等词来表示。但具体到某一特定称谓的翻译时，"总"字却需遵循英语头衔的表达习惯。例如：

　　总经理 general manager；managing director

总裁判 chief arbiter

总教练 head coach

总书记 general secretary

总督 governor-general；governor；viceroy

总监 inspector-general；chief-inspector

总指挥 commander-in-chief

总领事 consular-general

总工程师 chief engineer

总厨/厨师长 chief/head cook

总编 chief editor；editor-in-chief

3. 部门或下属机构负责人

有些部门机构的领导或主管的英译,可用一些通用的头衔词表示。下列部门或机构的负责人可以用 director,head 或 chief 来表示:

司(部属)department

厅(省属)department

局 bureau

所 institute

处 division

科 section

室 office

教研室 program/section

区 district

镇 town

居委会 neighborhood committee

村 village

例如"局长"可以译为 director of the bureau,head of the bureau 或 bureau chief。但在正式场合,director 相比之下用得更广泛些。譬如某直辖市政府网站上,城建局局长、公园管理处处长、林业局局长就分别译为 Director of Municipal Construction Bureau,Director of Administrative Department of Parks 和 Director of Forestry Bureau。一般来说,像区长、镇长、居委会主任、村长这类基层领导头衔英译时,用 head 一词居多,译为 the head of a district，town head,the head of the neighborhood committee 和 village head 等。

4. 副职的头衔

汉语中表示副职的头衔一般都冠以"副"字,英译时"副"字可选择 vice,associate,assistant,deputy,second,under,adjutant 等词来表示,其中 vice 使用得相对较广泛些。虽然以上表示"副"字的词少数情况下同一头衔可替换使用,如副市长可译为 vice mayor 或 deputy mayor,但多数需视词语的固定搭配或表达习惯等而定。例如:

副总统(或大学副校长等) vice president

副总理 vice premier

副部长 vice minister

副省长 vice governor
副领事 vice consul
副校长(中小学)vice principal
副驾驶员(航空)second pilot
二秘(外交)second secretary
二副(航海)second mate; second officer
副官长 adjutant general
副部长/次长 undersecretary
表示副职的学术头衔或职称，多用 associate 表示，例如：
副教授 associate professor
副研究员 associate research fellow
副主编 associate managing editor
以 manager 或 headmaster 表示职位的副职可冠以 assistant 一词，例如：
副总经理 assistant general manager (或 assistant /deputy managing director)
大堂副经理(宾馆) assistant manager
副校长(中小学) assistant headmaster

以 director 表示职位的副职常冠以 deputy 一词，如国家统计局副局长译作 Deputy Director of the State Statistics Bureau。此外，secretary，mayor，dean 等头衔的副职也可以冠以 deputy 一词，例如：

副秘书长 deputy secretary-general
副书记 deputy secretary
副院长 deputy dean

5. 职位头衔中"助理""代理""常务""执行"等称谓语

联络陪同口译时，常遇到"助理……""代理……""常务……""执行……""责任……"以及"襄理""协理"这一类头衔或职位。"助理"常用 assistant 表示，而"代理""常务""执行"及"责任"则可分别译作 acting，managing 和 executive，"代理"有时也译为 agent。例如：

助理教授 assistant professor
助理研究员 assistant research fellow
助理工程师 assistant engineer
助理秘书长 assistant secretary-general
代理市长 acting mayor
代总理 acting premier
代理主任 acting director
代理领事 consular agent
襄理、协理 assistant manager
常务副校长 managing vice president
常务董事 managing director
执行主席 executive chairman
执行主任 executive director

执行秘书 executive secretary

责任编辑 executive editor

以上列举的只是工作、生活中常遇到的称谓及其一般翻译规律。对于那些某一具体领域的称谓,译员则必须时时留心,加以积累,方可做到口译时不至于为职位、头衔的错译而影响"尽情尽意"的效果。因为很难想象,一个不知如何翻译出纳员(teller)、收账员(runner)、审计员(auditor)、信贷记账员(loan record keeper)、信用调查员(credit verification officer)的译员,在为银行经理做现场口译时不会遇到麻烦。

译练习　*Enhancement Practice*

第一项 Project 1

听力复述　Retelling

Listen to the following passages once and then reproduce them in the same language at the end of each segment.

English Passage:

A window candle has been a traditional practice in many cultures. // We love to watch the dancing flames as the fire's warmth flows into the deepest and coldest parts of our bodies. // Sitting in front of the hearth on a cold wintry day gives us a feeling of warmth and security. It makes us feel like all is right with the world. // In most cultures a candle in the window was used to signal a family's loyalty to a loved one who was away traveling. // It let that person know the family awaited their return and the hearth was warm and waiting for them. //

Chinese Passage:

中国古典戏曲是中华民族文化的一个重要组成部分,她以富于艺术魅力的表演形式,为历代人民群众所喜闻乐见。//而且,在世界剧坛上也占有独特的位置,与古希腊悲喜剧、印度梵剧并称为世界三大古剧。//中国古典戏曲从萌芽到形成、发展、终结,经历了一个漫长的历史时期,在朝代的交替中,曾先后出现了宋元南戏、元代杂剧、明清传奇、清代花部等四种基本形式。//

第二项 Project 2

主题讨论　Discussion

Hold a 5-minute discussion with your partners on the topic "The Present Days of Chinese Traditional Culture".

第三项 **Project 3**

听译练习 **Listening and Interpreting**

A. Sentence Interpreting

Listen to the sentences and interpret them into Chinese.

1. Singaporean cuisine is a prime example of diversity and cultural diffusion in Singapore.

2. Film production and film-going are social habits and important aspects of twenty-first century life in the US.

3. Britain's cultural and artistic scene reflects the nation's superb blend of established traditions and new influences.

4. Nowadays, changes in social customs and working hours mean that most Britons only take afternoon tea on special or formal occasions.

5. Canadian culture has historically been heavily influenced by British and French cultures and traditions, and over time has been greatly influenced by American culture.

B. Sentence Interpreting

Listen to the sentences and interpret them into English.

1. 中国的戏剧艺术历史悠久,历经了 800 年的演变。

2. 古时候,帝王们用的扇子都有很长的手柄,它象征着高贵的地位。

3. 虽然中国茶有数百种之多,但仍可主要分为五大类:绿茶、红茶、砖茶、香茶和乌龙茶。

4. 书法自古被视为中国视觉艺术的最高形式,甚而至于人的性格也可以从书法中加以甄别。

5. 对孩子而言,糖人是有趣的玩具,但是对大人来说,它们是可以吃的艺术品,装载着童年的记忆。

C. Dialogue Interpreting

Listen to the dialogue and interpret it into the target language.

A：I am really curious about Qipao, or cheongsam, the traditional costume for women in China. Can you tell me more about this kind of beautiful dress?

B：好的。旗袍有着非凡魅力,是中国绚丽时尚风景中的美丽花朵。今天你看到的旗袍源自于清朝的皇室和贵族服饰。

A：Do you mean the history of Qipao began from the Qing Dynasty? But the name of Qipao sounds to have nothing to do with that particular dynasty. Why don't you just call it "Qing Dress"?

B：从字面上看,旗袍是指旗的袍。旗指的是清朝的八旗制度,皇室和贵族按此归分为八部。所以,在那时,旗袍是贵族的服饰。

A：I see. So Qi is the collective name for those noblemen. By the way, what did the Qipao at that time look like? Was it the same as we see today?

B：不完全一样。旗袍最初是一种无领桶形,宽松,长至足背的长衫。后来,加入了贴身的高领以求保暖。

A：It's hard to imagine a baggy Qipao. In my mind, it represents the feminine curve in the best way. It must have undergone a dramatic development.

B：是的。不管怎么变，中心肯定是对优雅或美丽的渴望。毕竟，展示人体优雅性的唯一方法就是一件优雅的衣服。

A：I agree with you. As you mentioned before, the collar on Qipao is high and tight-fitting. But undoubtedly, it looks gorgeous, and so is the button at the collar. They must be delicately made, right?

B：是的。旗袍的领子通常是半圆形，左右两边对称，贴合女性柔软纤细的颈部。旗袍的领子做得很细致，特别是扣圈，是锦上添花。

A：Apart from the collar, the designers' artistic originality is shown in other parts, like the slits. Can you tell me why there are two slits on each side?

B：好的。为了活动方便，也为了展示女性纤细的腿部，旗袍在两边下摆处都有两个大开衩。不像短裙，旗袍的开衩，使女性在走动时腿部若隐若现，就像"雾里看花"一样有着朦胧的吸引力。

A：I think it is just like the Chinese women, modest, gentle and elegant. Today, designs or styles of fashions are so dazzling that the eye cannot take them all in. As a traditional costume, do you think Qipao still has a niche?

B：我认为旗袍那经久不衰的优雅和宁静是当今的各种时尚所无法比拟的。此外，旗袍也给设计师们提供了宽广的创作空间：有低领、高领，甚至无领的长短各款。

A：Lastly, if a lady is going to wear a Qipao for some big occasion, do you have any advice or suggestion?

B：穿旗袍的时候，女性一定要注意整体的搭配，中老年女性尤其要注意，发型、首饰、袜子和鞋子要在颜色和款式上和旗袍相得益彰。

参考译文　*Reference Version*

对话口译 A：

A：I was invited to an American wedding ceremony days ago. It was a real eye-opener for me, not only because it was beaming with joy and harmony, but because I found it was a far cry from that of a Chinese wedding. You Americans have truly unique wedding traditions.

B：嗯。婚礼肯定能让你对美国留下美好而浪漫的回忆。但是我们的婚礼习俗大多都不是美国所独有的。

A：Really? Then where do all the wedding traditions and customs come from?

B：几乎所有的婚礼传统和习俗要么直接取自其他国家和文化，主要是取自欧洲，要么就是从其他国家的传统演变而来。

A：I see. I know the United States has been called as "a melting pot". And as far as wedding is concerned, it has melted many different traditions from other places into one big pot of its own. It is right?

B：对。美国最初是由来自许多国家，尤其是来自欧洲的移民组成。这些移民带来了自己独特的婚礼传统，之后融入美国的大熔炉，慢慢地演变成为传统的"美国"婚礼。

A：It is very interesting. A diversity of ethnic wedding traditions are still retained. It mirrors the social reality in the US, doesn't it?

B：是的。这已经成为"美国"婚礼的必要部分了。在美国，各种不同的传统和婚礼并存，美国人很喜欢这样。

A：I know Americans always value love. Will you accept "arranged" marriages to strengthen family business or influence?

B：不，不会。我认为在美国，大多数婚姻是建立在爱情的基础上。如果包办的话，多数美国人是不会结婚的。

A：In China, it is nothing unusual that a wedding can be planned for more than a year. What about in the US?

B：几乎一样。筹划婚礼很费时，现在许多新娘选择找个专业的婚礼策划人打点那个好日子的千头万绪。

A：A wedding is a fairly large and elaborate affair. By the way, can you tell me more about the wedding vows?

B：当然可以。新娘和新郎撰写结婚誓言，表达对彼此的爱，发誓要让对方平安、快乐，并且终其一生只爱对方一个。

A：Each time I hear wedding vows, I would be moved. As for a guest invited to the ceremony, is it customary to present a gift to the newly wed?

B：是的。礼物是美国婚礼传统中的重要部分。送礼物是为了帮助新人一起建立自己的家庭，通常给的是现金。

对话口译 B：

A：在中国，扇子好像不只是纳凉的工具。它们似乎已经发展成为一项精美的艺术品。你能和我多介绍一些中国扇子的情况吗？

B：Sure. The use of fan in China can date back to 3,000 years ago. Since ancient times, fans have been considered a charming form of art, combining functional, ceremonial and decorative uses.

A：据我所知，中国的扇子由各种材料制成，比如纸张、丝绸、羽毛。这些材料制成的扇子是一起出现的，还是先后面世的呢？

B：They appeared by sequence. Fans were first made of feathers. Round silk fans were popular during the Tang dynasty. Folding fans first appeared in early 2nd century, but did not come into vogue until the Ming dynasty in 14th century.

A：我去过杭州，在一家纪念品商店看到了几乎各种式样的折扇，有些极其精美，也贵得惊人。它们为什么会那么贵呢？

B：The ribs of folding fans are generally made from bamboo, but some are made from rare materials such as ivory. Folding fans produced in Hangzhou use valuable materials for the fans' ribs. Therefore, they are comparatively expensive.

A：有些扇子上有中国字和中国画。在扇子上写字、画画是不是一种传统？是为了美观还是出于其他目的呢？

B：Fans with calligraphy or painting on them are highly decorative. Many famous Chinese calligraphers and painters in particular liked to leave their masterpieces on fans.

A：这样说来，带有艺术色彩的扇子已经不单单是一件物品。那么，扇子是不是有特殊象征含义呢？

B：Yes. In ancient times, fans became subjects in many ancient dramas and novels. In them, the fan is a token of love, a symbol of status or a tool for expressing people's moods and emotions.

A：西方文学中有一部著名的戏剧叫《温德密尔夫人的扇子》。中国有什么关于扇子的名作吗？

B：In China the most famous play on the fan should be *The Peach Blossom Fan*. Through a fan, with a blood drawing of peach blossoms, a moving story is told about a patriotic singer, Li Xiangjun, and a scholar, Hou Fangyu, during the period of dynasty transition.

A：现在科技的发展已经迫使扇子退出人们的日常生活了。如果中国的扇子文化未来消亡了，那就太遗憾了。

B：It's really hard to tell. But on stage, fans are still indispensable and they are frequently used, especially in traditional operas.

A：对。扇子在舞台上的应用可以看作是扇子的一种可持续性艺术价值。但是在日常生活中，扇子不可能和以前一样应用频繁。毕竟，扇子正在从家庭中消失。

B：You are right. Nowadays, fans, more often than not, are artifacts. Though fans are used less in daily lives, they become more desirable as collectors' items.

篇章口译 A：

　　黄丝带的传统从何而来呢？// 多数音乐历史学家将这一习俗追溯到 19 世纪南北战争时期的一首歌曲。// 民间流传这首歌的灵感来自于一桩真实事件。据说，在一辆去佛罗里达州迈阿密市的汽车上，有一位乘客刚从监狱释放出来，踏上回家的路。// 之前他写信给妻子，告诉她他还爱着她，希望能和她在一起。// 如果妻子仍然对他有感情，希望和他在一起的话，他请她在小镇广场的那棵大橡树上系上一条黄丝带。// 车越开越近，车上的每一个人都请司机开慢点。那里果然系着黄丝带！// 司机把车开到路边，打电话给电讯社，把这个故事告诉了大家。故事很快传遍全国，之后两位词曲家把这则新闻故事谱成民谣。//

　　挂上黄丝带标志着对家人、朋友或爱人忠诚，欢迎他们回家。// 按照习俗，黄丝带用来欢迎那些因战争或牢狱等艰难困境而暌别故里的人回家。//

篇章口译 B：

　　Tea is an indispensable beverage in daily lives of Chinese people. You can see tea-houses scattering on the streets similar to the way coffee-houses are often seen in the

West. //

Chinese people are very critical about tea. Normally, the finest tea is grown at altitudes from 910 m to 2,124 m. // People often use spring water as well as rain and snow water to make tea. Among the three, spring and rain water in autumn are considered to be the best; besides, rain water in rainy seasons is also perfect. // The emphasis is on water quality and taste. Fine water must be pure, cool, and clean flowing. //

Tea plays an important role in Chinese emotional life. It is always offered immediately to a guest in Chinese home. // Serving a cup of tea is more than a matter of mere politeness; it is a symbol of togetherness. It signifies respect and the sharing of something enjoyable with visitors. // A host will pour tea into a teacup only seven tenths, and the other three tenths will be filled with friendship and affection. // As for the guest, the teacup should be empty in three gulps. Not to take at least a sip might be considered rude in some areas. //

听译练习：

A：

1. 新加坡饮食是新加坡多姿多彩和文化传播的主要例证。

2. 拍电影和看电影是 21 世纪美国人生活中的大众习惯和重要方面。

3. 英国的文化和艺术体现出国家把现有的传统和新兴的影响极好地融合在一起。

4. 如今社会习俗和工作时间的变化意味着多数英国人只在特殊的场合或正式的场合喝下午茶。

5. 加拿大文化在历史上深受英国和法国的文化和传统的影响，随着时间推移，现在颇受美国文化的影响。

B：

1. China has a time-honored tradition of dramatic art, which has undergone about 800 years of evolution.

2. In ancient times, emperors had fans with long handles, which symbolized their notable status.

3. Although there are hundreds of varieties of Chinese tea, they can be mainly classified into five categories, which are, green tea, black tea, brick tea, scented tea, and Oolong tea.

4. Calligraphy has traditionally been regarded as China's highest form of visual art—to the point that a person's character can be judged by the elegance of their handwriting.

5. For kids, sugar figures make attractive toys, but for adults, they are pieces of edible artwork that carry memories of childhood.

C：

A：我对旗袍这种中国女性传统的服装非常好奇。你能和我多说说这种美丽的衣服吗？

B：OK. Qipao is a wonderful flower in the Chinese colorful fashion scene because of its particular charm. The Qipao you see nowadays is derived from the dress in royal palace and the nobility in the Qing Dynasty.

A：你是说旗袍的历史是从清朝开始的吗？但听起来旗袍这个名字和这个朝代没有什么联系。为什么你们不叫它"清装"呢？

B：Qipao literally means the gown of the banner. The banner stands for the Eight Banner System set up in Qing dynasty，by which the royalties and nobilities are classified into eight parties. So at that time，Qipao was the dress for the noble.

A：我明白了。所以旗是那些贵族的统称。那么，那时候的旗袍是什么样子的呢？和我们今天看到的一样吗？

B：Not exactly. The embryo of the Qipao was a collarless tube-shaped gown，loosely fitted and long enough to reach the insteps. Later，high and tight-fitting collar was incorporated to keep warm.

A：很难想象旗袍是宽松的。旗袍在我看来最好地呈现了女性曲线。它一定经历了巨大的发展过程。

B：Yes. Whatever the changes were，the core must have been the thirst for elegance or beauty. After all，the only way to display the elegance of a human body is an elegant costume.

A：你说得对。正如你刚才说起的，旗袍的领子很高也很贴身。但是毫无疑问，它看起来很华丽，领子上的扣子也是如此。它们一定制作得很精致，对不对？

B：Yes. The collar of Qipao generally takes the shape of a semi-circle，its right and left sides being symmetrical，flattering the soft and slender neck of a woman. The collar of Qipao is nicely made，especially the buttonhole loop on the collar，which serves as the finishing touch.

A：除了领子，其他地方，比如开衩，也显示了设计师的艺术独创性。你能告诉我为什么两边都有两个开衩吗？

B：Well，Qipao generally has two big slits at each side of the hem for convenient movement and display of the slender legs of women. Unlike a short-length skirt，the slits of Qipao expose a woman's legs indistinctly when she walks，as if there was a blurred emotional appeal of "enjoying flowers in mist".

A：我想这正是中国女性，她们内敛、温柔、优雅。如今时尚的设计和风格绚丽得令人目不暇接。你认为旗袍作为传统服饰还有一席之地吗？

B：I think Qipao's long-standing elegance and serenity are beyond comparison with the fashions nowadays. And in addition，Qipao provides designers with vast，creative space：some short，some long，with low，high，or even no collars at all.

A：最后，如果一位女士要穿旗袍去参加某大场合，你有什么建议吗？

B：When wearing Qipao，women should pay attention to the match as a whole；particularly middle-aged or elderly women should do so. Hairstyles，jewelry，socks and shoes should match Qipao properly in color and design.

第 15 单元

艺术风潮

Unit 15

Art and Fashion

背景知识
Background Information

Throughout the Chinese history, every scholar learns and strives to excel in four art forms: music, board game, calligraphy and painting. Fine points of these arts are taught as part of one's formal education; and skills in these arts are diligently honed and improved upon all one's life. We often see these arts illustrated and mentioned in paintings and poems.

The music instrument which one learns to play is a 5 or 7-string musical instrument called Guqin, which is played by plucking and pressing the strings with the right hand and left hand respectively, producing rich and colorful quiet sound. In the past, it was frequently used for accompaniment. With a long history of development, the playing of this instrument has become a distinctive performing art. Wei Qi (chess), commonly referred to in the Western literature by its Japanese name of Go, is the ultimate two-person board game. And then calligraphy and painting are very much shown in today's art world.

As for the western art form, here we specifically talk about literature, music, fashion and some culture-related art forms.

对话口译

Dialogue A

 Vocabulary Work

Study the following words and phrases and translate them into the target language.

Thomas Jefferson	Hawthorne	Walt Whitman	Ernest Hemingway
四行诗	佛家思想	沉思	polymath
encyclopedic	draft	Declaration of Independence	古民歌行体
emblem	ambiguity	dilemma	The Scarlet Letter
讽刺诗	moment of truth	preoccupation	

 Text Interpreting

Listen to the following dialogue and interpret it into the target language.

A：I just finished an essay about the overview of American literature.

B：太好了。我对世界文学也很感兴趣,特别是美国文学与中国唐诗。

A：Among those big names in the history of American literature，I do have some of my personal favorites like Jefferson，Hawthorne，Whitman and Hemingway.

B：我也是。我所钟爱的几位诗人都生于唐代。按时间顺序,依次是王维、李白和白居易。他们的写作风格各不相同。比如王维写的是四行诗,大多描写自然风光。他的作品受到佛家思想的熏陶,讲求静寂与沉思。

A：I admire Thomas Jefferson the most. In the eighteenth century，he has been called the polymath，a man of encyclopedic knowledge and accomplishment.

B：我知道他同时也是政治家、艺术家、发明家、教育学家,并且是创新流派的文学家。

A：And above all，because of his wide knowledge of political philosophy，Jefferson was chosen to draft *the Declaration of Independence*. His famous saying "We hold these truths to be self-evident，that all men are created equal" comes from it.

B：我还很喜欢另外一位唐代的诗人,李白。他写的是富于想象力的诗篇。题材多为他的梦境、幻想和其对酒的爱好。与同时代大多数诗人所不同的是,他的诗歌多为古民歌行体。

A：He reminds me of another great American writer whose major themes were the effects of hidden sin and guilt and the destructive impulses of the human mind. He used masks，veils，shadows，emblems，ironies and ambiguities to give dramatic form to the universal dilemmas of man. His masterpiece was *The Scarlet Letter*.

B：我知道他是谁了,霍桑。他让我想起了另一位唐代诗人,白居易。他的创作多为乐府讽刺诗,表现了其对当时统治者政策的不满。真是个伟大的诗人啊!

A：Of course. America also has some famous poets. One of them is Walt Whitman. Emerson once wrote to Walt Whitman，"I find your poems the most extraordinary piece of wit and wisdom that America has yet contributed."

B：如此的互相分享真是有意思。

A：The last but not least writer I'd like to tell you also plays an important role in my life. His work *The Old Man and the Sea* inspired me a lot as a young man.

B：我也读过这本书。是海明威写的吧?

A：Yes. Hemmingway's primary concern was an individual's "moment of truth"，and his fascination with the threat of physical，emotional，or psychic death is reflected in his lifelong preoccupation with stories of war. He even accomplished a revolution in literary style and language.

B：我想你的论文一定很有意思,希望能够早日拜读。

对话口译

Dialogue B

 词汇预习 **Vocabulary Work**

Study the following words and phrases and translate them into the target language.

rock	jazz	folk	soul
rap	music for easy listening	新奥尔良	节奏
切分乐	布鲁斯	improvisation	indispensable
variation	Swing era	impromptu rendition	top-notch
instrumentalist	流行巨星	叛逆	公民权
核辐射	困惑	发人深省的	

译实践 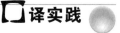 *Text Interpreting*

Listen to the following dialogue and interpret it into the target language.

A：These days I've been showing great interest in western pop music. Of all the varieties of music which fill the concert halls, theaters, and nightclubs, which type is your favorite?

B：西方流行音乐到底有哪些门类？

A：There are so many like rock, jazz, country, folk, soul, rap and music for easy listening.

B：我最喜欢爵士。在如今喧嚣的现代都市中，爵士乐可以真正让我心平气和一些。据我了解，爵士乐起源于新奥尔良，黑人的后代。它结合了非洲黑人音乐的节奏以及情感，并且转变到了后来的切分乐和布鲁斯。

A：Exactly. In Jazz, there's a special term called Improvisation, which is an indispensable element in Jazz.

B：你说的"即兴创作"是什么意思？

A：In solo performance, musicians were permitted plenty of freedom to play in whatever variations as their creative mood happened to lead them along. But during the Swing era(1930s—1950s), impromptu renditions gave way to arrangement. It was a period when jazz had its widest popular appeal with the big bands that boasted of such outstanding bandleaders as Duke Ellington, Glenn Miller and a whole galaxy of top-notch instrumentalists.

B：我最喜欢的爵士歌手是路易斯·阿姆斯特朗，他是新奥尔良爵士乐的代表人物。他的成名曲"一个美妙的世界"曾出现在多个广告和影视作品中。

A：Do you like rock music? Actually, I've been studying it these days.

B：是的，有时我也喜欢听听摇滚，但绝不是那种很吵的。

A：Rock music in the 1960's is a sociological expression rather than a musical force. And the rock arena was seen as a sort of debating forum, a place where ideas clash and crash, where youngsters struggle to define and redefine their feelings and beliefs.

B：在众多摇滚歌星中，我最喜欢猫王(Elvis Presley)。他是一代流行巨星。也许是因为他体现了现代年轻人那种儿时最疯狂的想法，鼓励他们不拘泥于传统。从这个层面上来说，摇滚乐是一种青年叛逆的音乐表达。

A：I can't agree with you more. Feelings, always a part of any musical expression, were a major subject of rock.

B：我还很喜欢另一位摇滚歌手，名叫鲍勃·迪伦。他的歌反映了一系列的题材比如公民权、核辐射、寂寞感、时代的变迁以及对过去的困惑。他的歌总是那样发人深省。

A：It's really nice talking to you. Maybe we can appreciate those songs and music together some day.

B：当然可以。

篇章口译（英译汉）
Passage A (E-C)

 词汇预习 *Vocabulary Work*

Study the following words and phrases and translate them into Chinese.

mercilessly	put aside	wardrobe	alter
neckline	durability	outward appearance	put up with
discomfort			

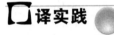 **口译实践** *Text Interpreting*

Listen to the English passage and interpret it into Chinese at the end of each segment.

London itself is a living museum, with more than 2,000 years of history and culture. It also boasts one of the greatest concentrations of significant museums of any city in the world. // The jewel in this cultural crown is the British Museum, with 4 kilometers of galleries and more than 4 million exhibits. The Victoria and Albert Museum displays an important and varied collection of applied arts. Across the street are the National History Museum with its dinosaurs, and the Science Museum, which includes a renowned section on the history of medicine. // The Museum of London effectively introduces visitors to London's history by walking them through successive eras chronologically. //

London is a major repository of the greatest Western art and a creative center for contemporary artists. // The National Gallery on Trafalgar Square contains Britain's premier art collection, with holdings from every major European art school. Next door is the National Portrait Gallery, with thousands of striking portraits of Britons. The Tate Gallery contains the principal collection of British art and modern international art. //

篇章口译（汉译英）

Passage B (C-E)

 词汇预习 *Vocabulary Work*

Study the following words and phrases and translate them into English.

剪纸	流派	高雅精致	点染
色彩斑斓	丰收	饲养牲口	长寿
刺绣图案	岩画	恒久	

 译实践 *Text Interpreting*

Listen to the Chinese passage and interpret it into English at the end of each segment.

　　中国剪纸流派众多,各有特色。北方剪纸简洁粗犷,沿海地区的剪纸高雅精致,蔚县剪纸经过点染后,色彩斑斓。// 春节期间,点染的剪纸花样繁多,主题有关于丰收的,有表示饲养牲口的,还有祝愿幸福长寿的。// 贵州省的苗族剪纸主要参考刺绣图案,描绘神话故事和当地的习俗。//

　　剪纸图样取材于古代陶器和岩画中的人物形象,有的像青蛙、蛇、鱼、鸟、龙,还有古代神仙。// 剪纸通常具有象征性,老虎图案的剪纸含中国文化中长寿的意义;// 树和鹿头代表恒久;鱼、荷花、葫芦、龙凤等图案的剪纸常用作对孩子的美好祝愿。//

　　在农村的许多地方,女孩子从小就学剪纸了。有人说女孩子剪纸的水平就是智慧的体现。// 日常生活中,少女们通过剪纸表达自己的情感和想象力。//

口译讲评

Notes on the Text

Dialogue A

1. 按时间顺序,依次是……。可以译成 They were, in the order of birth, ...

2. He has been called the polymath, a man of encyclopedic knowledge and accom-

plishment. 这句话的谓语虽然是被动,但为了更加符合中文表达习惯,我们可以加上一个主语,译成:人们称他为一个真正的博学者,也就是一个具有百科全书般知识和成就的人。

3. He used masks, veils, shadows, emblems, ironies and ambiguities to give dramatic form to the universal dilemmas of man. 这句话初看很复杂,但只要把主干内容抽出,自然可以表达流畅。因此译成:他习惯运用面具、面纱、阴影、寓意、讽刺和歧义来展现人类思想的进退两难。

4. 表现了其对当时统治者政策的不满。这里不需把"表现"译出,可直接译成:He protested against various government policies of his day.

Dialogue B

1. 在如今喧嚣的现代都市中。这里"喧嚣"可以用英语习语 hustle and bustle 更加地道。

2. 据我了解,爵士乐起源于新奥尔良,黑人的后代。它结合了非洲黑人音乐的节奏以及情感,并且转变到了后来的切分乐和布鲁斯。可以译成:It drew on the rhythms as well as the emotionalism of the African music of the Black ancestors, which had been transformed into ragtime and the blues.

3. But during the Swing era (1930s—1950s), impromptu renditions gave way to arrangement. 这句中的词组 give way to 表示替代,例如 A gave way to B 相当于 B 替代了 A,所以可译成:20 世纪 30 年代到 50 年代,也就是摇摆乐时期,既定演奏代替了即兴表演。

4. It was a period when jazz had its widest popular appeal with the big bands that boasted of such outstanding bandleaders as Duke Ellington, Glenn Miller and a whole galaxy of top-notch instrumentalists. 这句话比较长,要分意群断开,译成:那是一个爵士乐大放光彩的年代,并出现了许多一流的乐器演奏家,比如艾林顿公爵和戈兰·米勒。

5. Rock music in the 1960's is a sociological expression rather than a musical force. 这里的 rather than 可以翻成"与其说……不如说……"。

6. a place where ideas clash and crash. 这里的 clash and crash 是习惯用语,表示"碰撞"的意思。

Passage A

1. It also boasts one of the greatest concentrations of significant museums of any city in the world. 译为:它集中了一个庞大的博物馆群,为世界其他城市所少见。这里的 boast 意为"拥有;以……为荣",是褒义,不宜翻译成"自夸;吹嘘"。

2. London is a major repository of the greatest Western art and a creative center for contemporary artists. 译为:伦敦是西方艺术精华的一个主要陈列馆,也是当代画家的创作中心。repository 意为"博物馆;陈列馆"例如:
The internet is the largest repository of information which can provide huge network resources. 因特网是最大的信息宝库,它可以提供巨大的网络资源。
the greatest Western art 译作"西方艺术精华"更加准确精炼。

3. The National Gallery on Trafalgar Square contains Britain's premier art collection, with holdings from every major European art school. 译为:坐落在特拉法尔加广场上的国家美术馆收藏了英国最重要的美术作品,作品代表着欧洲的每个主要流派。这里的

holdings 是指博物馆、图书馆等的馆藏，school 是指"流派；学派"，在翻译的时候，我们要根据上下文判断其合适的意思。例如：

the historical school 历史学派

Venetian school 威尼斯画派（意大利文艺复兴时期的主要画派之一）

The Prague School has three important points. 布拉格学派有三个至为重要的观点。

Passage B

1. 中国剪纸流派众多，各有特色。这里的"各有特色"可以作为伴随状态，跟在后面用 with 连接。译成：There are many schools of papercut in China，each with its own unique characteristics.

2. 春节期间，点染的剪纸花样繁多，主题有关于丰收的，有表示饲养牲口的，还有祝愿幸福长寿的。这里"主题有……"可以用 feature themes of，所以全句可译成：Dyed papercuts，always abundant during Spring Festival，feature themes of harvesting，animal raising，happiness and longevity.

3. 剪纸图样取材于古代陶器和岩画中的人物形象。这句中"取材于……"可用 be derived from 所以全句译成：Papercut designs are often derived from figures found on ancient pottery and rock paintings.

4. 有人说女孩子剪纸的水平就是智慧的体现。此句中"……是……的体现"可译成 ... is a yardstick for...，所以全句可译成：Some say that a girl's papercutting ability is a yardstick for her intelligence.

相关词语 *Relevant Words and Expressions*

书法艺术 calligraphy	文艺复兴 Renaissance
新浪潮 new wave	视幻艺术 op art
拼贴艺术 collage	先锋派 Avant-garde
拜占庭式 Byzantine	罗马式 Romanesaue
哥特式 Gothic	巴洛克式 Baroque
新古典主义 neoclassicism	浪漫主义 romanticism
印象主义 impressionism	超现实主义 surrealism
自然主义 naturalism	未来主义 futurism
轻歌剧 light opera	清唱剧 oratorio
即兴曲 impromptu	进行曲 march
狂想曲 rhapsody	变奏曲式 variation form
小步舞曲 minuet	奏鸣曲式 sonata form
赞美诗 hymn	圆舞曲 waltz
小夜曲 serenade	咏叹调 aria
赞美歌 anthem	

口译技能 *Interpreting Skills*

中国菜名的口译

中国饮食文化源远流长。中国菜以其流派纷呈和深邃的历史文化内涵而闻名于世。在国际交往中,以宴会友是一种最常见的交往形式,是表示友谊,营造良好合作气氛的方式,同时也是弘扬文明和宣传民族饮食文化的机会。中国菜不仅色、香、味俱全,而且大多有一个动听的名字。如何在宴会上将中国菜尽可能按"信、达、雅"的原则译出来,这个问题就突出摆在译员面前。

谈到中国菜的口译问题,就要涉及一些专门描述如何做菜的动词,掌握这些动词对译员会有很大的帮助。

"炒"(stir fry 或者简述为 fry),如"清炒虾仁"stir fried shrimps,"炒豌豆苗"fried pea shoots;"炸"(deep fry)与"煎"(pan-fry 或者说 fry in shallow oil)的区别在于油放得多与少,用于菜名时,经常简述为 fried,如"炸童子鸡"deep fried spring chicken,"炸肉茄夹"fried eggplant with meat stuffing,"蛋笋煎蟹肉"fried crab with eggs and bamboo shoots;"烤"是 roast,如"北京烤鸭" roast Beijing duck,"烤乳猪" roast suckling pig;"炖"为 stew,如"腐乳炖肉" stewed pork with preserved bean curd;"焖"译成 braise,如"黄焖鸭片" braised duck with brown sauce;"红烧"即 braise in soy sauce 或者 braise with brown sauce,如"红烧羊肉"mutton braised in brown sauce;"蒸"是 steam,如"清蒸鳊鱼"steamed bream。

除了以上动词以外,还有"煮"boil,"焙"broil,"煨"simmer,"烘"bake,"熏"smoke,"铁扒"grill,"涮"rinse,"煸"saute,"卤"spice,"腌制"stuff,"白灼"scald,"回锅"twice cooked 等等,使用时应理解原意,灵活掌握,切忌生搬硬套。譬如"烤"面包时就应用 toast,而不能用 roast,"煮"荷包蛋应用 poach,而不用 boil。

下面介绍以下中国菜口译时的几种方法和技巧:

一、直译法

1. 烹饪法动词（ed)＋主要原料

卤鸭 Spiced duck

油焖鲜菇 Braised fresh mushroom

煨牛肉 Simmered beef

盐水虾 Salted water shrimps

铁扒鸡 Grilled chicken

冬瓜盅 Stuffed white gourd

白灼海螺片 Scalded sliced conch

油爆蛤蜊 Fried clams

2. 原料＋介词＋配料

葱油块鸭 Duck pieces with onion sauce

芙蓉蹄筋 Pig's tendons with egg white

青鱼划水 Braised herring tail in brown sauce

京烧羊肉 Mutton with soy sauce

醋溜黄鱼 Fried yellow fish with vinegar

香糟鸡片 Sliced flavored chicken in wine sauce

白煨肉圆 Stewed pork balls with white sauce

3. 原料＋器具/外包装

涮羊肉 Mutton slices quick-boiled in hot pot

什锦火锅 Mixed meat in hot pot

砂锅鸡 Stewed chicken in casserole

透明鸡 Chicken slices in cellophane

网包鸡 Chicken in net

小笼粉蒸牛肉 Beef with rice flour cooked in small bamboo steamer

铁板牛肉 Beef cooked in iron pan

荷叶饭 Fried rice wrapped in lotus leaves

香芋蕉叶鸡 Steamed sliced chicken and taro wrapped in banana leaves

其实直译法远不止以上所举的三种结构。有的菜名与中草药有关(五味子猪肝 Braised pork livers with herbs),有的与地名有关(黄河鲤鱼 Yellow River carp),还有的在菜名后加 style(成都童子鸡 Stir fried spring chicken,Chengdu Style)等等。这类菜名与英语菜名的构成基本相同,译员在翻译这类菜名时只要多加留心,总结常见的结构,熟记相应的英语烹调和原料用词,即兴口译并不困难。

二、意译法为主,直译法为辅

中国名菜往往利用菜肴原料的色、香、味、形的特点、烹调方法的特点及造型上的特点,为迎合食客的心理,赋予菜肴悦耳动听(象征着吉祥如意)的名字。与直译的菜名相反,这类菜名在菜谱上往往不出现原料及烹调方法。菜谱的印制、设计及装帧十分考究,一般没有太多的空间去容纳冗长累赘的英译文。但口译菜名时就可以灵活地利用时间,给国际友人说明菜肴所用的原料或烹饪方法,这样既活跃了餐桌气氛又传播了中国的饮食文化。如"贵妃鸡"这个菜名,在菜单里只写着 Highest-ranking imperial concubine chicken,外国客人看后可能会一头雾水。译员这时应通过"望""问""听""尝"等途径去弄清做这道菜所用的原料或烹饪方法,简单明了地用英语表达出来。译员可稍加注释:Stewed chicken, invented in the Qing Dynasty and named after Lady Yang who was highest ranking imperial concubine in the Tang Dynasty。

口译最主要的特点就是临场性,译员没有足够的时间对译文精雕细琢。虽然口译人员不可能像笔译者那样讲究"信、达、雅",却可以按"准、顺、快"的要求翻译菜名。在口译实践中,译员可事先向有关部门询问,收集有关资料和普及读物,熟知饭店的特色菜、名菜大体的烹饪方法及使用原料,同时推想该菜可能涉及的范围和深度。比如在口译福建名菜"佛跳墙"(Buddha jumping over the wall)时,外国客人也许会问它是由什么菜做成的,甚至会问它的典故之类的问题。这时事先做好充分准备的译员就会解释道:The well-known "Buddha jumping over the wall" is the chief traditional dish in "Ju Chun Yuan Restaurant". It is stewed with more than twenty materials including shark's fin, sea cucumber，scallop，abalone，fish maw，etc.

以下列举几种中国名菜，括号里是主要原料或典故。

桃园三结义 The three sworn brothers at Taoyuan（mashed dates，lotus，and green peas）

狮子头 Lion's head（pork meatballs）

全家福 Happy family（stewed assorted meat）

龙虎凤大会 Stewed dragon，tiger and phoenix（snake，cat and chicken shreds）

玉凤还朝 Phoenix returning to its nest（stewed duck，Shanghai specialty）

掌上明珠 A pearl in the palm（duck webs with eggs）

叫花鸡 Beggar's chicken（chicken toasted in lotus leaf and earth mud，invented by two beggars in the Qing Dynasty）

东坡肉 Braised pork（invented by Su Dongpo who was a famous poet in the Song Dynasty）

母子大全 Mother and son reunion（stewed quail and eggs）

蚂蚁上树 Ants climbing the tree（stir-fried vermicelli with minced pork）

三、音译法＋意译法

有些中国菜具有明显的民族文化色彩，在翻译时很难找到一个对等词，这时就要采用音译法并用意译法加以补充说明。饺子和馄饨是中华民族的传统美食，汉英词典及其他一些资料把两者都译成 dumpling，或略加上一些解释。外国人看到 dumpling 会误以为两者是一样的。其实 dumpling 这个词的意义与我们的饺子或馄饨相距甚远，根据最新的 *Collins Cobuild* 英语词典，dumpling 要么是一种与肉和菜一起煮的面疙瘩，要么是一种把苹果或其他水果放在甜面粉里做成的布丁蛋糕，可见它与饺子或馄饨风马牛不相及。外国人看到 dumpling 一定以为我们吃的是和他们吃的一样的、至少是相似的食品。所以译员可用拼音分别将其译为 jiaozi 和 huntun，必要时再加些注释。译员通过这种方法可使外国人慢慢熟悉这些名字，达到向国外介绍中国食品的目的。外国人大都通过在中式餐馆就餐，熟悉诸如 chow mein（中式炒面）、chop suey（用绿豆芽炒的杂碎）等原译自广东方言的中国食品。例如：

麻婆豆腐 Mapo's bean curd（stir-fried bean curd in hot sauce）

云吞汤 Wonton soup（meat dumplings）

鱼排 Fish pie（fish fillet）

它似蜜 Tasimi（stir-fried mutton fillet in sweet sauce）

值得注意的是，同一种中菜名可以有不同的英语表达方式。像麻婆豆腐既可译成 bean curd with minced pork in chili sauce，又可译成 Mapo's bean curd；宫保鸡丁既可译成 Sauted chicken with chili pepper，也可译成 Diced chicken with peanuts in hot sauce。所以口译时，译员就不要局限于一种表达法。

观察上面的几种技巧，我们也可知道，菜名的口译往往将几种技巧糅合在一起。这就需要译员熟练并灵活掌握口译菜名的技巧，在实践中不断总结经验，不断学习，提高知识面。总之，口译的性质、特点以及中西饮食文化的差异，决定了"准、顺、快"是口译中菜名的理想标准。口译前应尽量弄清宴席的重头菜，熟知它大体烹调方法及原料，然后用外国人可接受的方式加以传译。

译练习 Enhancement Practice

第一项 Project 1
听力复述 Retelling

Listen to the following passages once and then reproduce them in the same language at the end of each segment.

English Passage：

In the eyes of many people，Africa is a continent subject to terribly hot climate. This is really the case，yet on the other hand，Africa is a diversified continent regarded as a paradise of adventures，strange customs and peculiar lifestyle. // Music and dance in Africa show the musical cultures of African people that have aroused people's interest and curiosity. So many people fall in love with the culture there and they really want to go there one day. //

Chinese Passage：

迪士尼的第 36 部动画长片《花木兰》中的主人公是个独立果敢、足智多谋的年轻女子。// 为了保护自己年迈的父亲,她做出了很大的牺牲,替父从军。木兰剪短头发,穿上男装,但她意识到自己体力上的弱点,于是她依靠足智多谋和顽强的意志弥补了不足,赢得了大伙的信任和尊敬。// 影片结尾时,木兰发现了自己:她成了一个自信成熟的女人,很显然,迪士尼在与木兰一同成长。迪士尼终于明白,在这个世界上,女性不只需要王子,各色人物,哪怕是动画人物都是丰富多样的。//

第二项 Project 2
主题讨论 Discussion

Hold a 5-minute discussion with your partners on the topic "Fashion contributes anything or nothing to our modern society".

第三项 Project 3
听译练习 Listening and Interpreting

A. Sentence Interpreting

Listen to the sentences and interpret them into Chinese.

1. The words of this Eskimo song，so full of meaning，came to us over great distances like some small shining treasure brought by Marco Polo from ancient China.

2. Polish culture is the product of one thousand years of tradition，the country's geographical position and its turbulent，often tragic，history.

3. The growth of mass and popular culture has increased the potential audience for a wide

range of cultural activities, and the availability and scope of the arts has spread to greater numbers of people.

4. The pub, as an institution, has changed somewhat over the years, but still caters for a wide range of different groups and tastes.

5. People expect a great deal from Italy. That's a golden rule because there is no other country in Europe with as much to give as Italy.

B. Sentence Interpreting

Listen to the sentences and interpret them into English.

1. 电影业的命运在波兰，正如在其他国家一样，经历了不同的盛衰时期。

2. 由于缺乏历史资料，任何再现非洲音乐历史的努力都是没有成功把握的。

3. 假面舞者其实是一位演员，他必须表演出其假面具所代表的人物特征。

4. 事实上，不了解这个国家传统习俗的这些独特方面，就无法真正了解阿根廷这个国家。

5. 盆栽是一种在浅花盆中种植小型树木的艺术，许多西方国家都已经模仿借鉴了日本的盆栽艺术和折纸术。

C. Dialogue Interpreting

Listen to the dialogue and interpret it into the target language.

A：I like the pattern on your T-shirt, Lily. It's so cool. Is it a dragon or something?

B：是的。我上周在市中心的一家店里买的。龙可是象征中国人的一种吉祥动物。

A：Do you know in the folklore of many European and Asian cultures, dragon is a legendary beast?

B：各种传说把龙描写成蜥蜴般的巨兽，能喷火，长长的尾巴上还有鳞片。

A：But in Europe, dragons are traditionally portrayed as ferocious beasts that represent the evils fought by human beings.

B：龙在不同的文化中蕴含着不同的意义。

A：And according to some medieval legends, dragons lived in wild, remote regions of the world. The dragons guarded treasures in their dens, and a person who killed one supposedly gained its wealth. The English epic hero Beowulf died in a fight with a treasure-guarding dragon.

B：龙在我们这里却有着完全不同的含义。在亚洲，特别是中国和日本文化中，龙是一种与人类为善的动物，可以带来好运和财富。

A：I heard about it. It's very strange many European legends tell how a hero slew a dragon.

B：说来听听。我对中西方文化的差异相当感兴趣。

A：Sure. For example, Apollo, a god of the ancient Greeks and Romans, once killed a dragon called Python. Saint George, the patron saint of England, rescued a princess from a dragon by slaying the beast with a lance.

B：真的吗？但在中国，龙和新年节日也有很大的联系。传统的中国春节街头庆贺游行会有舞龙表演。

A：I read from a book that dragon in China symbolizes the upright spirit fighting against the evil ones. Is it true?

B：是的。在古代中国人的观念中,龙能阻止邪恶的幽灵破坏新年的气氛。另外还有一个中国传统信仰,人们还相信龙能够呼风唤雨,负责掌握每年收成所需的降雨。

A：My thanks to your T-shirt. I really learned a lot about a different culture today.

B：我也学到了许多。

参考译文 *Reference Version*

对话口译 A：

A：我刚刚完成了一篇关于美国文学纵览的论文。

B：Great. I'm also very interested in literature around the world, especially American literature and Chinese Tang poetry.

A：在这么多伟大的美国文学家中,有几位是我个人非常钟爱的。比如杰斐逊、霍桑、惠特曼、海明威。

B：Me too. My favorite Chinese poets all lived in the Tang Dynasty. They were, in the order of birth, Wang Wei, Li Bai, and Bai Juyi. They were different types in writing. For example, Wang Wei wrote four-line poems that describe scenes from nature. His works, which emphasize quietness and contemplation, show the influence of Buddhism.

A：我最崇拜托马斯·杰斐逊。在 18 世纪,人们称他为一个真正的博学者,也就是一个具有百科全书般知识和成就的人。

B：I know he was a statesman, artist, inventor, patron of education and a literary stylist.

A：但最重要的是,由于他在政治哲学方面的非凡造诣,由他起草的《独立宣言》从此提出了"人人生来平等"的伟大真理。

B：Another poet from the Tang Dynasty I'm interested in is Li Bai, who wrote imaginative poems about his dreams and fantasies and his love of wine. Unlike most poets of his time, he wrote in the style of old Chinese ballads.

A：这让我想起了另一位伟大的美国作家。他通常选用的主题是一些隐藏的罪恶和人类思想的冲动与毁灭。他习惯运用面具、面纱、阴影、寓意、讽刺和歧义来展现人类思想的进退两难。他的代表作是《红字》。

B：I know who he is. He is Hawthorne, who reminds me of another Tang poet. Do you know Bai Juyi? He wrote satiric poems in the ballad style. He protested against various government policies of his day. What a great poet!

A：当然,美国也有许多有名的诗人。其中一位就是沃尔特·惠特曼。爱默生曾经写信告诉他说:"我认为你的诗充满了睿智与智慧,可以代表美国有史以来最好的作品之一。"

B：What an interesting sharing of knowledge.

A：我想和你分享的最后一位作家对我的人生起了很大的作用。他的作品《老人与海》给予青年时代的我无比的激励和启发。

B：I've read that. Is it Ernest Hemingway?

A：是的。海明威所关注的往往是那些个人的"重要时刻"，他迷恋于描写人类面临的身体、精神以及情感方面的死亡威胁，他一生对于战争故事乐此不疲的描写充分体现了这一思想。他一生成就了对于文学风格以及语言的一场革命。

B：Your essay must be very instructive. I Hope to read it soon.

对话口译 B：

A：最近，我对西方流行音乐越来越感兴趣。在所有那些充斥于音乐厅、戏院以及酒吧的流行音乐中，你最喜欢哪一类呢？

B：How many types of pop music are there?

A：很多，比如摇滚乐、爵士乐、乡村音乐、民谣、灵魂乐、说唱乐以及轻音乐。

B：I love Jazz the most. In the hustle and bustle of modern society, Jazz music can really calm me down. Actually, I know Jazz was born in New Orleans, the child of the Blacks. It drew on the rhythms as well as the emotionalism of the African music of the Black ancestors, which had been transformed into ragtime and the blues.

A：是的，在众多爵士术语中有一个叫作"即兴创作"，这可是爵士乐中不可或缺的一部分。

B：What do you mean by improvisation?

A：在独奏中，音乐家可以有充分的自由空间，随着他们的创造力而随时变化曲调。20世纪30年代到50年代，也就是摇摆乐时期，既定演奏代替了即兴表演。那是一个爵士乐大放光彩的年代，并出现了许多一流的乐器演奏家，比如艾林顿公爵和戈兰·米勒。

B：My favorite Jazz singer is Louis Armstrong, who is the representative figure of New Orleans Jazz. His jazz song "What a Wonderful World" has been used in a lot of advertisements and movies.

A：你喜欢摇滚乐吗？事实上，最近我在研习这个音乐门类。

B：Yes, sometimes I do like to listen to some rock music, but not those noisy ones.

A：20世纪60年代的摇滚乐，与其说是一种音乐形式，倒不如说是一种社会形态的表达。很多时候，摇滚乐变成了辩论的平台，许多思想在这里碰撞。年轻人努力地去一而再再而三地表达了他们的感受和信念。

B：Among those rock singers, my favorite one is Elvis Presley, who later became the pop icon. Maybe it's just because he acted out youngsters' wildest teenage spirit, encouraged the young to protest against traditional values. In this sense, rock is the music of teenage rebellion.

A：我非常同意。情感，作为音乐表达的主要目的，从来就是摇滚的创作体裁。

B：Another rock singer I like is Bob Dylan. He spoke of civil rights, nuclear fallout, and loneliness. He spoke of change and of the bewilderment of an older generation. His songs are very enlightening.

A：真高兴和你聊天。也许以后我们俩可以一起欣赏这些音乐。

B：Absolutely.

篇章口译 A：

伦敦自身就是一座活生生的博物馆,有着 2000 年的历史和文化。它集中了一个庞大的博物馆群,为世界其他城市所少见。// 大英博物馆是镶刻在这顶文化皇冠上的一颗宝石,拥有四公里长的展廊和 400 万余件展品。维多利亚及艾伯特博物馆展出的是各种重要的不同类型的应用艺术品。街对面是有着恐龙展品的自然博物馆,以及有着闻名遐迩的医药发展使馆的科学博物馆。// 进入伦敦博物馆的参观者可以通过伦敦各个发展阶段的演变来了解这座城市的历史。//

伦敦是西方艺术精华的一个主要陈列馆,也是当代画家的创作中心。// 坐落在特拉法尔加广场上的国家美术馆收藏了英国最重要的美术作品,作品代表着欧洲的每个主要流派。与国家美术馆为邻的国家肖像陈列馆里陈列着数以千计的不列颠人逼真的肖像。泰特美术馆除了拥有一大批国内美术作品外,还收藏了许多现代国际美术作品。//

篇章口译 B：

There are many schools of papercut in China, each with its own unique characteristics. In north China, papercuts are simple yet bold. Along coastal areas papercuts tend to be more exquisite and fine. Weixian County papercuts are dyed and therefore more colorful. // Dyed papercuts, always abundant during Spring Festival, feature themes of harvesting, animal raising, happiness and longevity. // Miao papercuts from Guizhou Province feature embroidery patterns depicting fairy tales and local customs. //

Papercut designs are often derived from figures found on ancient pottery and rock paintings. Papercuts often resemble frogs, snakes, fish, birds, dragons, and gods of the ancients. // Papercuts tend to be very symbolic. Papercut tigers implicate longevity in Chinese culture. // Trees and deer heads symbolize continuity. To express wishes for children, papercuts are made to resemble fish, lotus flowers, gourds, dragons, and phoenixes. //

In many Chinese rural villages, girls have to learn papercutting at a young age. Some say that a girl's papercutting ability is a yardstick for her intelligence. // In daily life, the girls express their sentiments and imaginations through their papercuts. //

听译练习：

A：

1. 这首爱斯基摩民歌的歌词寓意丰富,它就像是马可•波罗从古代中国带来的一些小巧的珍宝,长途跋涉来到了我们身边。

2. 波兰文化是该国的千年传统、地理位置和动荡的常常带有悲剧色彩的历史产物。

3. 大众文化和流行文化的发展已使得更多的人想要参加更为广泛的文化活动,并使众多的人可以接触到更多形式的艺术活动。

4. 作为一种娱乐机构,酒吧近些年来或多或少地发生了一些变化,但仍然能够迎合许多不同的品味并满足不同人群的需要。

5. 人们对意大利往往有很多期望。这是一条金科玉律,因为在欧洲的所有国家中,意大利可以向人们展示的东西最多。

B：

1. The fate of Polish films have waxed and waned as in other countries.

2. Attempts to reconstructure African musical history are highly speculative without the evidence of historical sources.

3. A masked dancer is an actor who has to play out the character his mask represents.

4. Indeed，it's impossible to understand Argentina without understanding these peculiar aspects of the country's traditions.

5. Bonsai，the art of growing miniature trees in shallow pots，and paper-folding have also been borrowed from Japan by the nations of the west.

C：

A：我非常喜欢你 T 恤衫上的图案，莉莉。好酷啊！是龙的图形吗？

B：Yes，exactly. I picked it up from one of the stores in the downtown area last week. Dragon is the symbol of all the Chinese people.

A：你知道在很多欧洲以及亚洲文化中，龙是一种传说中的动物。

B：Of course. Legends describe dragons as large，lizard-like creatures that breathe fire and have a long，scaly tail.

A：但是在欧洲，龙一直被描绘成凶猛危险的野兽，代表邪恶，人类与之进行搏斗。

B：Due to different cultures，dragon does embody various meanings.

A：根据中世纪的传说，龙生活在地球的蛮荒、偏远之地。他们守护藏在洞穴中的珍宝。杀死龙的人据说可以掠得龙的财宝。英国史诗中的英雄贝奥武甫在与一条守护珍宝的龙争斗中牺牲了。

B：You know we have completely different implication about dragon here. In Asia，especially in China and Japan，they are generally considered friendly creatures that ensure good luck and wealth.

A：我有所耳闻。很奇怪的是在很多欧洲神话中都有英雄屠龙的传说。

B：Could you tell me some of those tales? I'm really interested in different cultures of the east and the west.

A：好啊！比如古希腊罗马神话中的阿波罗神曾杀死了一条叫帕森的龙。英格兰的守护人圣乔治用长矛刺杀了巨龙，并救了一位公主的性命。

B：Really? But in China，dragon even has something to do the New Year Festival. The traditional Chinese New Year's Day parade includes a group of people who wind through the street wearing a large dragon costume.

A：我读到过龙在中国象征着正义的力量，并且能驱赶邪恶。是这样吗？

B：Yes. The dragon's image，according to an ancient Chinese belief，prevents evil spirits from spoiling the coming new year. Another traditional Chinese belief is that certain dragons have the power to control the rainfall needed for each year's harvest.

A：多亏了你的 T 恤衫，我今天从不同的文化中了解了很多。

B：Me too.

生态环境

Unit 16

Ecology and Environment

背景知识

Background Information

In recent years scientists have begun to study the environment and what man is doing to it. Any closed world in which life exists is called an ecosystem. The world, too, is a large ecosystem in which plants, animals, insects and humans all depend on one another in some way.

The word ecology was coined in the late 1860s. It is derived from two ancient Greek words meaning "study of the home". The science of ecology is the study of the relationships among plants, animals, and their homes, or environment. Ecologists use information from many branches of science: biology, chemistry, the earth sciences, and so on. They must deal with all this information because the life of every plant and animal depends upon complex interaction of its internal environment, its physiology, and its external environment, its habitat.

Environmental protection, therefore, has been drawing more and more attention globally. It is generally believed that environmental pollution has adverse effects on human health. And many people are worried about it. When industrialization was in its infancy, the impact of pollution was localized and minimal. With rapid worldwide modernization, however, as petrochemicals are used as an energy base, toxic pollution has increased to global proportions. The stress placed on our planet by pollution has far-reaching effects and constitutes a grave crisis.

All of us hope that in the world of tomorrow man will learn to take care of the environment and achieve the goal of sustainable development.

对话口译

Dialogue A

词汇预习 *Vocabulary Work*

Study the following words and phrases and translate them into the target language.

呼吸道疾病	迎面扑来	由……所造成的	流动性
水污染	消化道疾病	致命的	get ahead
后果			

译实践 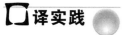 *Text Interpreting*

Listen to the following dialogue and interpret it into the target language.

A：How do you feel about living in New Delhi，Mr. Xia?

B：一切都还可以，除了一件事。我的喉咙总是不舒服。我的新德里朋友告诉我说这叫作"新德里咳嗽"，我不太理解这是什么意思。

A："New Delhi Cough" is just one example of the respiratory problems that almost anyone who visits，and certainly everyone who lives in New Delhi，suffers from. The pollution problems in India hit you in the face the moment you step off the airplane，and you can't escape them in any major city in India.

B：马丁教授,这种情况只有新德里才有吗？还是印度的其他城市也是如此？

A：Well，it's the case in many large cities and increasingly in smaller cities as well. It's estimated that in recent years 25% of all deaths in India have resulted from some kind of respiratory distress.

B：那么水污染问题,您是怎么看的？

A：Water pollution is a little bit harder to see because you don't necessarily come face to face with polluted water when you are asked to drink. Certainly as a tourist you stay in hotels where the water is drinkable. But，in many villages，the water supplies are contaminated，and people are at a constant risk of quite serious digestive diseases，some of which can even be fatal.

B：马丁教授，您刚刚提到了较为严重的空气污染和水污染问题,人们死于呼吸系统疾病,污水不断让人们的健康受到威胁。中国的环境污染问题以前也很严重。近年来,中国坚决完成《巴黎气候协定》中承诺的气候变化国家自主贡献目标。2019 年单位国内生产总值二氧化碳排放同比下降 4.1%，完成年度预期目标。我国空气质量持续改善，全国 337 个地级及以上城市优良天数平均达到 82%。

A：China has done a great job. I've heard a lot about China's endeavor to launch a popular environmental education campaign in favor of long-term benefits.

对话口译
Dialogue B

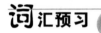 **Vocabulary Work**

Study the following words and phrases and translate them into the target language.

乳腺癌	污染物	荷尔蒙系统	synthetic chemical
estrogen	基因	devastating	neon sign
pesticide	wastewater		

 Text Interpreting

Listen to the following dialogue and interpret it into the target language.

A：随着乳腺癌发病率的上升，有关专家们正在研究如何降低乳腺癌发病的危险。他们表示污染物对于人体荷尔蒙系统的影响有待进一步探究。

B：Now as we learn more about how synthetic chemicals can act like estrogen, it makes a lot of sense to give priority to finding out whether these synthetic chemicals also increase breast cancer risk.

A：但是环境似乎与很多疾病都有关系。也许问题在人们的基因里。因此，有人正采取新的方式去发现真相。

B：If we really know the bad factors, based on the genetics of our population, then we could focus on those that cause the devastating diseases and clean those up first.

A：近年来，对于预防女性乳腺癌，有人提出了很多方法，比如不吸烟，少饮酒，吃低脂食品，加强锻炼等。除此以外，有没有一些其他的发病诱因呢？

B：There are a couple of different types of evidence that I think are like a neon sign that says the environment is a place we should look. When women live in one region and then move to another, their breast cancer rates change and so do their daughters' and their granddaughters'.

A：如今乳腺癌研究又有什么新的发现吗？

B：We're looking at pesticides. And earlier research suggests that pesticides may be related to breast cancer risks. But some studies haven't found this association，so it's still a question that we need to pursue. The second thing we're looking at is pollution from wastewater.

A：您刚刚提到了杀虫剂和污水。有没有其他与乳腺癌相关的污染源呢？

B：Well，we haven't really made the link to humans yet，but we do see a lot of indicators from wildlife. The Environmental Protection Agency recently released a report which made us see effects on wildlife reproduction at very low levels because of contamination.

A：乳腺癌与污染问题的讨论已经进行了很多年，并且还在继续。但是许多科学家仍然认为要去证明它们之间的联系相当困难。您同意这种说法吗？

B：That is so true. It is a very hard area of research. One thing that's making it harder now is that we're learning things that suggest it may make a difference when in a woman's life she's exposed to pollutants. We face a tremendous challenge in trying to go back in history to find out what kinds of pollutants may have been in the environment some time in the past.

A：那么，针对你们对于乳腺癌与环境污染的研究，我们的政府需要采取什么行动吗？

B：Yes，I think we are ready to act in some ways，even though we don't know yet everything we want to know about breast cancer and the environment.

A：非常感谢您接受我们的采访。

B：Thank you. It was a pleasure to be here.

篇章口译（英译汉）

Passage A (E-C)

  Vocabulary Work

Study the following words and phrases and translate them into Chinese.

ecosystem	food chain	morsel	alga
tadpole	devour	water snake	hawk
grasshopper	robin	food pyramid	transformation

Listen to the English passage and interpret it into Chinese at the end of each segment.

The paths of food materials through the ecosystem are many and complex. A food chain describes how one morsel of food might "travel" through the system. // A typical food chain begins with a one-celled green alga that produces food. The alga is eaten by a tadpole. The tadpole in turn is eaten by a fish, which later may be devoured by a water snake. A hawk may then swallow the snake. Indirectly, then, the hawk has eaten the green alga. //

How much food and energy pass along a food chain? How many kilograms of grass are needed to produce one kilogram of grasshoppers? // How many kilograms of grasshoppers are consumed to form one kilogram of robins? Ecologists use the term food pyramid to describe the quantities of materials that pass from one kind of eater to another. //

The word "pyramid" is used because the amount of energy associated with the food material becomes smaller at every link, or upward step. // More than one kilogram of grass is needed to create one kilogram of grasshoppers. More than one kilogram of grasshoppers goes into making one kilogram of robin flesh. // The net losses in weight are due to the fact that part of the material is converted into energy to power the transformations of grass into grasshoppers and grasshoppers into robins. //

篇章口译（汉译英）

Passage B (C-E)

Study the following words and phrases and translate them into English.

生态学家	自然学家	意义	翻倍
排放到	有毒的	废气	依赖性
生存			

口译实践 *Text Interpreting*

Listen to the Chinese passage and interpret it into English at the end of each segment.

　　人类是自然界的一个组成部分。// 多年来虽然生态学家和自然学家都清楚这一点，但是大多数人还是近年来才意识到其重要性和意义。//

　　我们突然发现地球上的人变得十分拥挤。// 随着每一代人的出生（即 25—30 年），世界人口成倍增长的周期越来越短了。// 人口在 1850 年到 1950 年间增长了一倍，而 1990 到 2000 年这短短的时间内也翻了一番。//

　　越来越多的人们开始认识到绝对不能将有毒废气排放到空气、水和土壤中。// 总之，人类越来越清楚地意识到自身对其他生物的依赖性，只有保证这些生物的存在，人类自己才能生存。//

口译讲评

Notes on the Text

Dialogue A

1. hit you in the face the moment you step off the airplane. 翻译此句型 the moment... 可译成：可能当你一下飞机，这种感受就会向你迎面扑来。

2. Certainly as a tourist you stay in hotels where the water is drinkable. But，in many villages, the water supplies are contaminated，and people are at a constant risk of quite serious digestive tract disease, some of which can even be fatal. 这句话比较长，所以在翻译时应注意按照意群适当断句，所以译成：作为游客，你所下榻的酒店自然会提供安全的饮用水，但是在很多村子里，水源受到了污染，人们随时有感染消化道疾病的危险，有的疾病甚至是致命的。

3. 国家自主贡献（nationally determined contributions）指根据《联合国气候变化框架公约》(the United Nations Framework Convention on Climate Change)缔约方会议相关决定，提出的中国应对气候变化的强化行动和措施（enhanced actions and measures on climate change）。

Dialogue B

1. 因此，有人正采取新的方式去发现真相。在这里不一定要用"有人"做主语，可以把"新的方式"作为主语，译成：A new effort is underway to find out the truth. 使译文更加地道。

2. 有人提出了很多方法，比如不吸烟，少饮酒，吃低脂食品，加强锻炼等。译成：There are many ways recommended... Don't smoke, don't drink too much, eat a low-fat diet,

more exercise，and so on. 比较符合英语口语的表达习惯。

3. contamination：contamination 与 pollution 虽然都是污染的意思，但也有细微的差别。contamination 通常表示通过两种物质的混合，把原先干净的东西弄脏了。所以将水污染翻译成 water contamination 较妥。

Passage A

1. A food chain describes how one morsel of food might "travel" through the system. 食物链描述了一小块食物是如何在生态系统中"运行"的。one morsel of food 一小块食物或一小口食物。

2. The word "pyramid" is used because the amount of energy associated with the food material becomes smaller at every link，or upward step. at every 后面加上 link，upward step，表示"每一个环节"或"每上升一级"。

3. The net losses in weight are due to the fact that part of the material is converted into energy to power the transformations of grass into grasshoppers and grasshoppers into robins. 这句话比较长，在翻译时，特别是口译的表达中，经常要采用断句的方式，所以译成：重量的净消耗是由于部分物质已转化为能量，能量在由青草变为蝗虫，又由蝗虫变为知更鸟的转化过程中起着推动的作用。

Passage B

1. 大多数人还是近年来才意识到其重要性和意义。这里的"意义"虽然可以翻成 meaning，但是译成 implications 更符合原意。

2. 随着每一代人的出生（即 25—30 年），世界人口成倍增长的周期越来越短了。这里的主语可以用 the time。句子的主要结构就是 With...，time to do sth. is shortened，所以译成：With every generation—that is，every 25 or 30 years—the time it takes to double the world's human population is shortened.

3. 人类越来越清楚地意识到自身对其他生物的依赖性。此句可翻成 man is becoming aware of his dependency on other living things.

 相关词语 *Relevant Words and Expressions*

环境恶化 environmental degradation	致癌的 carcinogenic
农药残留 pesticide residue	有机污染物 organic pollutants
食物过敏 food allergy	臭氧层 ozone layer
温室效应 greenhouse effect	水土流失 water and soil erosion
水土保持 conservation of water and soil	生态农业 environment-friendly
水资源保护区 water resource conservation zone	agriculture；eco-agriculture
造林工程 afforestation project	自然保护区 nature reserve
森林砍伐率 rate of deforestation	绿化面积 afforested areas；greening space

矿物燃料 fossil fuel　　　　　　　　森林覆盖率 forest coverage
濒临灭绝的鸟类 endangered bird species　　垃圾处理站 rubbish disposal station
开发可再生资源 develop renewable resources　天然气汽车 gas-fueled vehicles
生态示范区 eco-demonstration region　　　环保产品 environment-friendly products
推行可持续发展战略 pursue the strategy of sustainable development

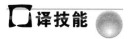

口译技能 *Interpreting Skills*

学习资源

　　本教材在这里为联络陪同口译的学习者提供一些相关的口译学习资源。学习者可以通过登陆所列举的一些国际翻译组织、翻译协会了解口译理论的最新发展动态以及口译技能、标准和职业准则。另外还提供部分中外口译研究机构和培训机构,供有志于在口译领域深造的学习者参考。

国外部分翻译组织、翻译协会网址:

American Translators Association (ATA):www. atanet. org

Association Internationale des Interprètes de Conférence (AIIC):www. aiic. net

Australian Institute of Interpreters and Translators Inc. (AUSIT):www. ausit. org

California Healthcare Interpreters Association (CHIA):www. interpreterschia. org

Conference of Interpreter Trainers (CIT):www. cit-asl. org

European Forum of Sign Language Interpreters (EFSLI):http://www. efsli. org/

Institute of Linguists (IoL):www. iol. org. uk

Institute of Translation and Interpreting (ITI):www. iti. org. uk

International Federation of Translators (FIT):www. fit-ift. org

Massachusetts Medical Interpreters Association (MMIA):www. mmia. org

National Accreditation Authority for Translators and Interpreters (NAATI):www. naati. com. au

National Association of Judiciary Interpreters and Translators (NAJIT):www. najit. org

National Council on Interpretation in Health Care (NCIHC):www. ncihc. org

Registry of Interpreters for the Deaf Inc. (RID):www. rid. org

Society of Federal Linguists,Inc. (SFL,):www. federal-linguists. org

The American Association of Language Specialists (TAALS):www. taals. net

国内外部分口译研究、培训机构网址:

北京外国语大学高级翻译学院

http://www. bfsu. edu. cn/old/chinese/dxgk/yxsz/gjfyxy. htm♯1

上海外国语大学高级翻译学院

http://giit. shisu. edu. cn/

香港城市大学中文、翻译及语言学系
http://ctl.cityu.edu.hk/index.asp
香港中文大学翻译系
http://traserver.tra.cuhk.edu.hk//
香港理工大学中文及双语学系
http://www.cbs.polyu.edu.hk/
美国蒙特瑞国际研究学院
http://www.miis.edu
英国巴斯大学翻译研究所
http://www.bath.ac.uk/esml//int-trans/index.htm
英国新堡大学
http://www.ncl.ac.uk/postgraduate/taught/subjects/modernlanguages/cou-rses/82
澳大利亚马奎理大学
http://www.ling.mq.edu.au/translation/index.htm
澳大利亚西雪梨大学
http://handbook.uws.edu.au/hbook/course.asp? course＝0a74
加拿大赛门费雪大学
http://www.sfu.ca/cstudies/lang/aip/

 口译练习 **_Enhancement Practice_**

第一项 Project 1

听力复述　Retelling

Listen to the following passages once and then reproduce them in the same language at the end of each segment.

English Passage：

In the past，man did not have to think about the protection of his environment. There were few people on the earth，and natural resources seemed to be unlimited. // Today，things are different. The world has become too crowded. // We are using up our natural resources too quickly，and at the same time we are polluting our environment with dangerous chemicals. If we continue to do this，human life on earth will not survive. //

Chinese Passage：

唐朝诗人李白曾赞誉过黄河的流水。他看到黄河之水天上来,奔流到海不复回。// 然而在今天,每年有超过 300 天,黄河没有一滴水流入大海。// 干旱不是大自然唯一的惩罚。有关专家调查后称,如果人类任由这种情况持续下去,黄河也许就会改变流向。//由于没有足够的水量冲走下游的泥沙,河床每年都在不断升高。// 我们人类向自然索取得太多,回

报得太少。如果黄河中游、上游的植被得到好好保护的话,我们也就能亲眼看到李白所描述的景观了。//

第二项 Project 2
主题讨论　Discussion

Hold a 5-minute discussion with your partners on the topic "Man and Nature".

第三项 Project 3
听译练习 Listening and Interpreting

A. Sentence Interpreting

Listen to the sentences and interpret them into Chinese.

1. The whole earth is an ecosystem, a system of give-and-take among plants, animals and their surroundings.
2. The sun's energy is not the only essential element to life. Green plants are also essential to our planet's ecosystem.
3. Medical researchers have always been eager to study technological advances in their search for ways to apply these advances to their specialties.
4. Black holes are the most fascinating and mysterious objects in the heavens.
5. The great whales are among the most fascinating creatures that have ever lived on earth, and one of them, the blue whale, is the largest.

B. Sentence Interpreting

Listen to the sentences and interpret them into English.

1. 生态系统运转所需的能量来自太阳。
2. 荒野指的是所有人类未涉足的地区,远离拥挤不堪的都市、污染的工业中心和拥挤的交通。
3. 地球生物最显著的特征之一是对其周围环境的节奏变化具有极强的适应性。
4. 若在外层空间探测到黑洞——据悉已发现了一个——不仅对天文学家而且对物理学家也具有非常重要的意义。
5. 食物中所含的碳和其他元素在动植物的作用下,通过循环回到土壤、水和空气时,所有能量都被耗散掉了。

C. Dialogue Interpreting

Listen to the dialogue and interpret it into the target language.

A:美国三大汽车巨头掀起了一阵未来绿色汽车热,并承诺甚至是比赛型用车也将更加环保。

B:All the technology it takes to do that exists now. Whoever does it first is going to own the market.

A:为什么这些汽车制造商要在现在推出这些更环保、更节能的车呢?

B：In a word，competition.

A：能为我们具体讲一讲吗？

B：Toyota has just started marketing a double-efficiency hybrid electric car in Japan. Together with Honda，Toyota has made it clear that they intend to do to Detroit all over again what they did in the 70s. Only this time，Detroit woke up a lot faster.

A：说到市场，如今的市场可以说是无处不在。有关人士指出，如果美国汽车业想拓展到全世界，他们必须认识到这样一个事实，那就是其他许多地方的油价要比美国的高。

B：I think the difference this time is that efficiency will not depend on how high the gasoline price is. In America it's cheaper than bottled water，but that's no obstacle to engineering the car because it's actually a better car.

A：你认为《京都议定书》对那些想进一步提高汽车性能的生产商们会造成一定压力吗？

B：It's very clear that the automakers，having initially hoped there would not be an agreement in Kyoto，now realize the trading framework that will reward people for reducing CO_2 emissions changes the economics quite a lot，because it means you can make money off carbon savings. And that，I think，changes the whole tone of how the business community looks at global warming. They're starting to see it now as a major business opportunity.

A：你刚刚提到在美国汽油价格像水一样便宜。你认为这会影响到节能汽车的潜在市场占有率吗？

B：I don't think the cheap gasoline in the US is going to matter at all to the efficiency of the car.

A：你提到现在技术都已经到位。我想知道为什么过去不具备这些技术呢？

B：Green cars are not a new idea. Porsche invented those in 1900，but the equipment he had were not a tenth as good as we have now.

A：感谢你接受我们的采访。

B：Thank you. It was a pleasure to be here.

参考译文 Reference Version

对话口译 A：

A：夏先生，住在新德里感觉如何？

B：Everything is good except one thing. My throat is always uncomfortable. My Indian friends tell me maybe it's "New Delhi Cough". I just don't understand what it is.

A：对于来新德里旅游的人或是住在新德里的居民来说，"新德里咳嗽"只是呼吸道疾病中的一种。印度的环境污染问题在很多大城市都存在，可能当你一下飞机，这种感觉就会向你迎面扑来。

B：Is that just in New Delhi，Professor Martin，or is that the case of other parts of India？

A：其实，这个问题不仅在印度的大城市比较显著，如今在很多小城市里也越来越普遍。据估计,近年来 25% 的人口死亡是由与呼吸系统相关的疾病所造成的。

B：What about the water pollution?

A：水污染其实很难用眼睛去看。通常当你需要喝水的时候,你不太可能和污水面对面地接触。作为游客,你所下榻的酒店自然会提供安全的饮用水,但是在很多村子里,水源受到了污染,人们随时有感染消化道疾病的危险,有的疾病甚至是致命的。

B：Professor Martin, you mentioned serious air pollution and water contamination, people dying of respiratory diseases, dirty water making people sick constantly, etc. Pollution problems used to be serious in China. In recent years, China has fully implemented its commitment to nationally determined contributions on climate change under the Paris climate agreement. Carbon dioxide emissions per unit of GDP fell 4.1% in 2019 from the previous year, meeting the country's annual target. Air quality continued to improve, with 337 cities at and above prefecture-level recording good air quality on an average of 82 percent days last year.

A：中国做得太棒了。我常常听说中国在努力开展普遍的环境教育,这是一种着眼于长远利益的好做法。

对话口译 B：

A：With breast cancer rising, researchers are exploring ways of cutting breast cancer risk. And they say pollutants that affect the body's hormonal system need closer examination.

B：现在我们已经了解到,有许多合成化学制品与雌激素有同等的功能。所以首先去了解化学制品对乳腺癌发病率的影响就显得相当必要了。

A：But the environment links to other diseases. The problem may lie in our genes. Therefore, a new effort is underway to find out the truth.

B：如果我们真的了解这些基于人类基因的根本原因,我们就可以专门去研究,从而尽快扫除这些致病的原因。

A：In recent years, there are many ways recommended to reduce women's risk of getting breast cancer. Don't smoke, don't drink too much, eat a low-fat diet, more exercise; and so on. Is there any other possible cause of it?

B：有相当多的证据表明,就好像有个霓虹灯广告牌在提示说,环境问题值得探究。我们发现当女性从一个地方搬移到另一个地方后,她们乳腺癌的发病率会发生明显的变化,包括她们的女儿们以及孙女们也有相同的变化。

A：What about the findings of the breast cancer research nowadays?

B：我们现在正关注杀虫剂。之前的研究表明杀虫剂与乳腺癌有很密切的联系。但是许多研究却很难证明其中的联系。所以,这是我们一直在探究的问题。其次就是污水问题。

A：You mentioned wastewater and also pesticides. What other types of pollution are we talking about that may possibly be linked to breast cancer?

B：现在我们并没有发现其与人类自身的联系。但我们从野生生物那里看到了一些蛛丝马迹。环保局最近发布了一则报告,让我们看到了污染所造成的野生动物生育率下降的问题。

A：This link between breast cancer and pollution has been discussed and studied for many years, and study is still ongoing. But some scientists say it's just very, very hard to prove. Do you agree?

B：这种说法非常正确,这确实很难证明。现在放在我们面前的问题是接触污染物的女性确实更加容易患上这种疾病。我们面临着很大的挑战,试图从过去发现曾经存在的一些污染物。

A：Well, should our government take any action based on the concerns that you and others have about breast cancer and pollution?

B：是的,我想我们已经做好了行动的准备,哪怕我们并没有完全掌握乳腺癌与环境的联系。

A：Well, thank you very much for joining us.

B：我也很荣幸,谢谢。

篇章口译 A：

食物在整个生态系统中的循环具有各种途径,而且十分复杂。// 食物链描述了一小块食物是如何在生态系统中"运行"的。// 普通的食物链始于能产生营养物的单细胞绿藻。绿藻被蝌蚪吃了,鱼又吃了蝌蚪,水蛇吞掉了鱼,鹰又吞掉那条蛇,那么可以说鹰间接吃掉了绿藻。//

有多少食物和能量通过食物链呢? 要多少公斤草才能产生一公斤蝗虫? // 消耗多少蝗虫才能喂成一公斤的知更鸟? 生态学家用"食物金字塔"来描述物质从一种食者到另一种食者所消耗的量。//

使用"金字塔"一词是因为与能量相关的食物在每一个环节或每向上升一级就会减少一部分。// 要一公斤以上的草才能生成一公斤蝗虫,而一公斤以上的蝗虫才能产生一公斤的知更鸟肉。// 重量的净消耗是由于部分物质已转化为能量,能量在由青草变为蝗虫,又由蝗虫变为知更鸟的转化过程中起着推动的作用。//

篇章口译 B：

Man is part of nature. // Although ecologists and naturalists have known this for many years, the majority of people have only recently become aware of the importance, and implications, of this fact. //

Suddenly we notice that the earth is becoming crowded with people. // With every generation—that is, every 25 or 30 years—the time it takes to double the world's human population is shortened. This population doubled between 1850 and 1950; from 1990 to 2000 it doubled again. //

More and more people are beginning to realize that wastes must not be dumped into the air, water, and soil if they are known to be toxic. // In short, man is becoming aware of his dependency on other living things and then he can survive only as long as he ensures their survival. //

听译练习：

A：

1. 整个地球是一个互相制约的生态系统。该系统内，动植物及其环境之间相互协调并相互创造生存条件。

2. 对生命来说太阳能不是唯一必要的条件，绿色植物对地球生态系统也极为重要。

3. 医学研究者总是在如饥似渴地研究高新技术，并不断地探索如何将这些先进技术应用到医学领域中。

4. 黑洞是天体中最神奇，最引人入胜的物体。

5. 巨鲸是生活在地球上最迷人的生物之一，最大的鲸为蓝鲸。

B：

1. The energy that operates the ecosystem originates in the sun.

2. Wilderness is all that land which remains untouched by man, free of overcrowded cities, polluted industrial centers, and traffic jams.

3. One of the most notable aspects of life on earth is its remarkable adaptation to the rhythmic characteristics of its environment.

4. If a black hole is detected in outer space and one is believed to have been discovered, the event will be significant for physics as well as for astronomy.

5. By the time the carbon and other elements found in food are cycled through the plants and animals and back into the soil, water, and air, all of the energy has been dissipated.

C：

A：The big three US automakers unveil a green fleet for the future, and promise that even sport utility vehicles will run cleaner.

B：现在我们所需要的技术都有了，谁第一个去做就等于占领了市场。

A：Why are the US automakers coming out with all these cleaner, more efficient cars now?

B：一个词概括，那就是竞争。

A：Can you tell us about it specifically?

B：日本丰田汽车已经开始在日本市场推广高效节能电力汽车。与日本本田一道，这两家汽车公司准备再一次进军底特律，就好像把 70 年代的一幕重新上演。但是这一次，底特律的反应要快得多。

A：And speaking of markets, markets are worldwide now. And some have pointed out that if US industry wants to expand worldwide it has to acknowledge the reality that the gas is a lot more expensive in many other countries.

B：我认为这一次并不取决于油价的高低。在美国，油价也许低于矿泉水的价格。但是这并不影响人们去发动一辆车，如果这辆车的性能更加好的话。

A：Do you think the global warming agreement reached in Kyoto put pressure on the automakers to increase the development of these more efficient cars?

B：很明显，起先汽车生产商们并不想看到议定书的达成。但如今他们意识到新的贸易框架将使他们通过降低二氧化碳的排放量而赢利。这一形势大大地改变了传统的经营模式，因为这意味着节能就等于赢利。我认为,这改变了整个汽车制造业对全球变暖的看法。他们都开始意识到这一重要的商机。

A：You mentioned that in America gasoline is as cheap as mineral water. Do you think that will hurt the potential demand for fuel-efficient vehicles?

B：我想美国的油价根本不会影响到汽车的性能。

A：So the technology exists now. It makes me wonder why this hasn't happened in the past.

B：绿色汽车并不是一个新的概念。保时捷在 1900 年就已经发明了,只是当时的设备性能还比不上现在的十分之一。

A：Thank you for being here with us.

B：我也很荣幸,谢谢。